STUDIES IN ENGLISH LITERATURE

Volume XCVII

THE THRONE
AND
THE CHARIOT

STUDIES IN MILTON'S HEBRAISM

by

KITTY COHEN

1975
MOUTON
THE HAGUE · PARIS

© Copyright 1975
Mouton & Co. B.V., Publishers, The Hague

BPR '77 p. 742

This book was intended to appear in 1974, the
three-hundredth anniversary of Milton's death
and the publication of *Paradise Lost* in twelve
books, and we regret that its publication was
delayed

ISBN 90 279 3293 X

Photoset in Malta by St. Paul's Press Ltd.
Printed in The Netherlands by Intercontinental Graphics

To the Memory of My Mother

TABLE OF CONTENTS

PREFACE

The meeting of cultures is a subject which has surrounded me most of my life as a wandering Jew without my having been fully conscious of what my own culture really represented. There was no need to define it for I lived it. It was only when I came to Yale University as a graduate student of English literature that I found myself confronted with the need to define what Judaism and Hebraism meant. The main ideas expressed in the essays included in this book took shape when I participated in a most enlightening and stimulating Milton seminar given by the late Professor Davis Harding. His lectures, discussions and books on Milton encouraged me to reconsider various facets of hebraism and examine their relevance to the understanding of both *Paradise Lost* and the main issues of recent Milton scholarship.

In writing and revising these essays I have been greatly helped by the criticisms of Professors Davis Harding and Dwight Culler of Yale University and Professor Miriam Starkman of the City University of New York as well as by the advice of Professors Harold Fisch and Murray Roston of Bar-Ilan University. To Professor Louis Martz of Yale University, a master of English literature, and to my father-in-law, Justice Haim Cohn, a great hebraic scholar, I am thankful for their generous appraisal of my manuscript. I am indebted more than I can acknowledge to the writings of many scholars without which we would not have witnessed the great revival of interest in Milton in the past decades.

I would also like to thank James D. Simmonds, editor of *Milton Studies*, and the University of Pittsburgh Press, for permission to reprint chapter IV in this book.

To my friend, Mrs. Valerie Arnon, I am grateful for her intelligent help in preparing the manuscript for publication. To my husband, Eliahu, who has given above all Time and Patience, I owe the greatest debt of all.

Tel-Aviv, 1974.   Kitty Cohen

LIST OF ABBREVIATIONS

AJSL	*American Journal of Semitic Languages and Literatures*
AL	*Archivum Linguisticum*
Bib.	*Biblica*, Roma
CBD	*Chamber's Biographical Dictionary*
DNB	*Dictionary of National Biography*
ELN	*English Language Notes*
E&S	*Essays and Studies*
ETL	*Ephemerides Theologicae Lovanienses*
HLQ	*Huntington Library Quarterly*
HTR	*Harvard Theological Review*
HUCA	*Hebrew Union College Annual*
IDB	*Interpreter's Dictionary of the Bible*
JBL	*Journal of Biblical Literature*
JCS	*Journal of Cuneiform Studies*
JEGP	*Journal of English and Germanic Philology*
JHI	*Journal of the History of Ideas*
JSS	*Journal of Semitic Studies*
JWCI	*Journal of the Warburg and Courtauld Institute*
MLN	*Modern Language Notes*
MLR	*Modern Language Review*
MP	*Modern Philology*
MQ	*Milton Quarterly*
NAR	*North American Review*
N&Q	*Notes and Queries*
PMLA	*Publications of the Modern Language Association of America*

I

INTRODUCTION

Like many *isms*, the word *hebraism* – rarely used in the Renaissance – was recoined in the nineteenth century as a term of dispraise. Influenced by Heine and Ludwig Börne, Matthew Arnold applied the word in its abstract sense to the moral as opposed to the intellectual mode of human thought and action. His distinction between Hellenic spontaneity of consciousness and hebraic strictness of conscience, between the unfettered quest for knowledge and the preference of doing to thinking, has become a *locus classicus*.[1] It need not have concerned us here had it not resulted in the disparaging association of hebraism with an unbending and restrictive mode of life and culture, as exemplified in Puritan Christianity.

Today, though often met in the Arnoldian sense, the word no longer has its derogatory connotations. Berenson, discussing Raphael's classical humanism, calls "the Hebraic element" that which "has come to us from the Old and New Testaments". Compared to the Hellenic element, it is "much less important in our conscious intellectual life, and of much less interest to the pictorial imagination" but, nevertheless, it is "morally superior and poetically grander".[2]

Among Jewish scholars hebraism and Judaism are sometimes used synonymously.[3] With the revival of interest in the Old Testa-

---

[1] *Culture and Anarchy* (Cambridge, 1932), chapter IV.
[2] Bernhard Berenson, *The Italian Painters of the Renaissance* (1930, 1960), p. 160.
[3] See, for example, Erwin I. J. Rosenthal, "Torah and *Nomos* in Medieval Jewish Philosophy", *Studies in Rationalism, Judaism and Universalism*, ed. by Raphael Loewe (London, 1966), p. 215.

ment and Biblical theology, a new meaning is now attached to the
word dissociating it from traditional Judaism and associating it
with the existential trends of thought expressed in the works of
Hermann Cohen, Martin Buber, and Franz Rosenzweig. It is
doubtful, however, whether seventeenth-century Christians would
have appreciated the suggestion that they shared Cohen's ethic
universalism or Buber's existentialism. For them a *hebraism* was
a phrase or idiom characteristic of the Hebrew language, and the
word *hebrician*, or the later *hebraist*, of earlier origin than *hebraism*,
signified "hebrew scholar" just as the term *humanist* which pre-
ceded the term *humanism* by some 250 years referred to a classical
scholar. These semantic developments have resulted in a confusion
in basic definition to which many Milton scholars have fallen
victim. The numerous studies on Semitic, Biblical, Rabbinic,
Kabbalistic and hebraic influences on Milton bear ample witness
to the challenge the poet's "hebraism" has always presented to
Milton scholars. It is worth looking into some of these.

The first attempt at a survey of Milton's Semitic studies was
made by Harris Fletcher. Though by the term *Semitic* Fletcher
refers to the group of kindred languages including Arabic, Hebrew,
Phoenician and Aramaic, he deals primarily with Milton's knowledge of Hebrew.[4] Today, more than forty years after the publication of *Milton's Semitic Studies and Some Manifestations of them in
His Poetry* and *Milton's Rabbinical Readings*, the question of
Milton's knowledge of Hebrew and usage of Buxtorf's Rabbinical
Bible is no longer controversial. While Fletcher's basic findings
have been accepted and he deserves the credit for having been the
first to acknowledge fully the extent of Milton's learning and his
training at St. Paul's School and in Cambridge, some of his conclusions have been refuted. Whiting did not deny the fact that
Milton was familiar with Rashi and other Rabbinical commentaries, but he condemned "claims of influence based upon somewhat
slender evidence and made plausible only by some little distortion

---

[4] Fletcher admits that it is necessary for him to use the term 'Hebrew studies'
indiscriminately with 'Semitic studies'. *The Intellectual Development of John
Milton*, 2 vols. (Urbana, 1956), Vol. II, p. 291.

of the poet's meaning".[5] Conklin was even harsher to Fletcher
than Whiting and, in his *Biblical Criticism and Heresy in Milton*,
he emphasized Milton's individuality of thought and argued that
there was a profound dichotomy "between the competent reader
of Biblical Hebrew and the learned scholar of Hebraica ... in
terms of training and erudition".[6]

That Milton knew Hebrew well enough to read the Old Testament and its commentators in the original is now beyond dispute.[7]
His knowledge of Hebrew is felt on every page of his writings and
pervades the style of his prose as well as his poetry. He certainly
was a hebraist in the old sense, that is, a Hebrew scholar. If it is
generally accepted that he had the use of a Rabbinical Bible, his
indebtedness to other Hebrew sources has been seriously ques-
tioned. He probably had no access to early Midrashic and Tal-
mudic literature[8] and he did not read the *Zohar*. Denis Saurat was
the first to claim that Milton was influenced by the *Zohar*, but his
findings have been refuted by Maurice Kelley and R. J. Zwi
Werblowsky. Saurat's thesis with regard to *Paradise Lost* is that
Milton, like Blake, was a Kabbalist and that this is the explanation
for his originality of thought.[9] In the *Zohar*, Saurat finds the source
of Eve's jealousy, Satan's incest with his daughter Sin, Milton's
conception of Chaos, Creation through the retraction of God
(the passage in which Saurat sees the core of Milton's thought is
Paradise Lost VII.170–173), God's infinity, Milton's concept of
Urania, of woman, and he believes that such parallels "could be
carried on *ad infinitum*".[10] Maurice Kelley was the first to refute
Saurat's contentions that Milton conceived of creation as a result
of the sex life of God. Kelley also found Saurat's alleged influences

---

[5] George W. Whiting, "Notes on 'Milton's Rabbinical Readings'", *N & Q*, CLXII
(1932), pp. 344–347.
[6] *Biblical Criticism and Heresy in Milton* (New York, 1949), p. 45. See also my "Note
on Milton's Semitic Studies", *MQ*, IV, 1970, pp. 7–10, and note 7 below.
[7] See Harold Fisch, "Hebraic Style and Motifs in *Paradise Lost*", *Language and
Style in Milton*, ed. by R. D. Emma and J. T. Shawcross (New York, 1967),
pp. 33–36.
[8] Fisch, p. 34.
[9] Denis Saurat, *Milton. Man and Thinker* (New York, 1925), p. v.
[10] Saurat, pp. 289–291, 297.

of the *Zohar* on the invocation to Urania unconvincing.[11] R. J. Zwi
Werblowsky refutes all the supposed correspondences proving
Milton to have been a Kabbalist from a Kabbalistic point of view.
He distinguishes between Jewish and Christian Kabbalah and
proves that the correspondences are Neoplatonic or Christian
commonplaces, or, at best, Kabbalistic concepts that Milton
learned not from the *Zohar* and the Jewish Kabbalah but through
Renaissance and seventeenth-century Kabbalah as expressed in
the writings of Pico, Reuchlin, Fludd and Henry More.[12] The issue
is dead now.

Most recent source studies and scholarly works dealing with
conjectured "hebraic" influences on *Paradise Lost* have been
placed in perspective within the exegetical and literary tradition
on Genesis by Maurice Evans in his recent *Paradise Lost and the
Genesis Tradition*. Evans reviews the exegetical problems inherent
in the Genesis text and the reshaping of the Genesis story. He
shows how Christianity reinterpreted the first chapters of Genesis,
developing Near Eastern legendary elements contained in the
apocalyptic narratives. He then surveys Rabbinic and Patristic
commentaries on Genesis and brings the literary versions and
variations of the story up to Milton's *Paradise Lost*, which he
rightly considers the climax of the tradition. This approach is helpful to the present study for several reasons. First, in surveying the
exegetical treatment of the Genesis story, Evans wisely warns
that similarity does not always prove dependence. His chapter on
the Jewish interpretations corrects the incomplete and often mis-
leading picture projected by some of the recent source studies
dealing with "hebraic" influences on Milton's poem. Second,
while his work traces Milton's indebtedness to exegetical and
literary traditions on Genesis, it stresses the poet's profound
originality. But the application of modern research techniques to
the seventeenth-century understanding of Biblical exegesis creates
its own problems. One of these is how to reconcile "the characters

[11] Maurice Kelley, "*Paradise Lost* VII. 8–12 and the 'Zohar'", *MLR*,XXIX (1934),
pp. 322–324.
[12] R. J. Zwi Werblowsky, "Milton and the Conjectura Cabbalistica", *JWCI*, XVIII
(1955), pp. 90–113.

of God and Man as they were portrayed in P with their behaviour as it was related in J".[13] This problem, of course, never existed for a poet in Milton's day for the simple reason that whereas modern criticism looks for psychological consistency in characterization, Milton's age made no such demands. The application of modern psychological criteria to the analysis of the narrative and characters of *Paradise Lost* has led critics such as Tillyard and Waldock to charge Milton with not having written the poem he intended to write, and others such as Empson to think that Milton's poem is so good because his God is so bad, a view fundamentally shared with Evans.[14] But Milton did not attempt to provide "possible motives" in order to make his Eden or his God acceptable to twentieth-century readers. Nor did he aim at a realistic or naturalistic representation of Genesis. If Adam and Eve, God as well as Satan, come alive in the poem, it is because Milton's genius transcends time and place. The greatness of the poem does not lie in the psychological consistency of its characters; it lies in the description of the moral forces underlying man's soul. The characters as well as the scenery in which they move are portrayed in an essentially ethic way. They exist in terms of the moral order Milton believed in.

Biblical scholarship in the seventeenth century was not what it is today. But even without the benefit of modern linguistic studies and archeological discoveries, Milton and his contemporaries could and did sense the different stylistic and narrative streams in the Biblical text.[15] They were, however, primarily concerned with textual problems of interpretation and with issues of a spiritual and moral order rather than with questions of authorship and intention. To suggest, then, that Milton "solved" the problems of the P and J texts with "such delicacy that we are scarcely aware of them as we read their solutions"[16] is to miss the unquestionable authority the Bible had for seventeenth-century readers like Milton. True, Milton incorporated the "allegorical and typo-

---

[13] J. M. Evans, *Paradise Lost and the Genesis Tradition* (Oxford, 1968), p. 23.
[14] Evans, pp. 223–241. These issues are discussed in chapters III and IV below.
[15] See chapter III.
[16] *Paradise Lost and the Genesis Tradition*, p. 221.

logical as well as the literal patristic interpretations", and with them "he blended notions derived, directly or indirectly, from rabbinic commentaries, apocryphal documents, Christian–Latin Biblical epics, medieval legends, and recent plays, poems, and tracts on the same subject".[17] True also that "the principle which determined his selection from and manipulation of the mass of extra-Biblical amplification at his disposal was essentially literary".[18] However, one major source is omitted from the list and that is the Bible. For his own part, claims Milton

> I adhere to the Holy Scriptures alone – I follow no other heresy or sect. I had not even read any of the works of heretics, so called, when the mistakes of those who are reckoned for ortho-dox, and their incautious handling of Scripture, first taught me to agree with their opponents whenever those opponents agreed with Scripture. If this be heresy, I confess with St. Paul, Acts xxiv. 14. *that after the way which they call heresy, so worship I the God of my fathers, believing all things which are written in the law and the prophets* – to which I add, whatever is written in the New Testament. Any other judges or chief interpreters of the Christian belief, together with all implicit faith, as it is called, I, in common with the whole Protestant Church, refuse to re-cognize.[19]

This passage speaks for itself. To suggest, therefore, that Milton was influenced rather by Biblical exegesis than, in the first place, by the Bible itself is to overlook the Protestant zeal for indepen-dent Biblical reading. Milton's editors and critics have been unanimous in recognizing that Milton is as indebted to the Bible as he is to the classics. Where Evans has classified the variants of the Genesis story, James Sims has recently brought together the Biblical allusions in Milton's epics and shown to what extent the Old and New Testaments permeate the music and imagery and influence the characterization and thematic content of Milton's poem.[20]

---

[17] Evans, p. 219.
[18] Evans, p. 221.
[19] *The Christian Doctrine*, Dedication.
[20] James H. Sims, *The Bible in Milton's Epics* (Gainesville, Florida, 1962).

These studies all reflect modern interest in Milton's Biblical and hebraic sources and in their influence on his poetry. The view that has gained most ground in our century is the one which conceives of Milton as a Christian humanist. This historical approach, though valid, has tended to ignore other factors that influenced the poet and modified his Christian humanism. It is only natural that distinguished Miltonists like Grierson, Tillyard, C. S. Lewis and Bush, who are trained in the Christian humanist tradition, should place Milton in that milieu; not being hebraists themselves, it is not surprising that they should have overlooked somewhat the hebraic element in Milton. That is why the recent source studies dealing with hebraic influences on Milton have contributed a point of view that was lacking. Yet they did more than stimulate interest in Milton's Hebrew learning. Saurat concluded that Milton was not a seventeenth-century Protestant at all but a profound original thinker indebted to complex mystical traditions such as the *Zohar*; Fletcher detected Semitic influences on Milton's conceptions of the Holy Spirit, the Muse and others. At the same time, Fletcher was aware of the danger of unduly emphasizing rabbinic influences on Milton. He recognized it was an important factor but "in no way superseding, for instance, his use of classical material, of orthodox or heterodox Christian theological ideas." He believed that "when the time comes for a final accounting of the many influences at work upon him, his rabbinical readings will take their place, perhaps a lowly one, among the whole mass of his various studies, which are so interrelated and connected that to invoke one is to invoke them all".[21] While the purpose of Sims is to make modern readers aware of Milton's artistic use of Biblical allusions, he also tries to make them more "receptive to the Christian tradition which is firmly based on the Bible".[22] All these detailed studies have been extraordinarily suggestive, yet none of them has attempted to define and assess the literary and intellectual influence of hebraic materials in the broader context of Milton's thought. It is perhaps natural that source studies came first. They

---

[21] *Milton's Rabbinical Readings* (Urbana, 1930), p. 310.
[22] This is what Sims tells about his own background and interests. *The Bible in Milton's Epics*, p. v.

were now to be followed by historical theories concerning the nature of hebraism.

The first serious attempt to define hebraism as a theological and poetic influence was made by Harold Fisch in his *Jerusalem and Albion*. The chief merit of this book is that its author drew a clear distinction between the Puritan ethic and that of Moses and the prophets. In so doing he freed the term hebraism from its Arnoldian overtones. Furthermore, in his assessment of the "tremendous impact of Scripture as a first-hand imaginative experience and as a spiritual illumination for seventeenth-century writers",[23] he has indeed opened new paths in literary criticism. For by thus explaining hebraism, Fisch has provided a comprehensive definition designating a style and trend of thought in European culture that is a pervading influence and not merely a period concept. He goes on to claim that among the writers he discusses

> the Jewish factor, or to take a word of more universal significance – the factor of Jerusalem – is pre-eminent. It was for them the solvent, the catalyst, which promised to make possible a new and more dynamic order in place of the old philosophies. It represented a new unitary principle which could be invoked instead of the old inadequate unity of the *logos*.[24]

He believes that

> the Covenant-idea in its authentic form brought together the spheres of Man, God and Nature, severed by the anarchy of the Counter-Renaissance revolt against order, and bestowed upon them a common purpose jointly undertaken. Thus the possibility of a new unity was held out to men. The Covenant could come to replace the *logos*, to offer a hope of spiritual integration on new lines significantly different from those of traditional Christian humanism.[25]

Fisch is well aware of the danger of an "importation into seven-

---

[23] *Jerusalem and Albion. The Hebraic Factor in Seventeenth-Century Literature* (New York, 1964), p. 3.
[24] Fisch, p. 114.
[25] Fisch, p. 111.

teenth-century fields of a modern reading of Old Testament theology",[26] yet he believes that a "new pattern may be glimpsed with
significant iteration":

> As a corrective to the Counter-Renaissance Natural philosophy,
> we glimpse the Hebrew doctrine of Creation; as a corrective to
> the new Anthropology, we find the Hebrew doctrine of Salva-
> tion, and as a corrective to the narrower forms of evangelical
> piety, we discern the Hebrew doctrine of Revelation. The syntax
> by which these three, Revelation, Salvation, and Creation are
> bound together is that of the *Brith* or Covenant.[27]

If the chief merit of this book is its assessment of the inspiring
influence of Old Testament themes and style on specific authors
and periods in English literature, its weakness is that by applying
modern terminology to, and projecting existential views of Judaism
into seventeenth-century Christian-hebraic concepts, it blurs the
distinction between hebraism and Judaism. True, many things
overlap in hebraism and Judaism, so much so that the terms are
nowadays often interchanged. Judaism is, after all, rooted in the
hebraic culture. The difference between the two is mainly one of
emphasis. In hebraism the emphasis is on the cultural values per-
taining to the Hebrew language and the Old Testament from which
Judaism as well as the two other great monotheistic religions
sprang. In Judaism, whether the emphasis is seen to be on faith
in and obedience to the 613 commandments of the Pentateuch or
whether it is on the idea of a national identity, the basic creed is
that of a religio-national entity. According to this very broad
definition, a man may be a Jew and a classical humanist; he may
also be a Christian and a hebraist, but he may not be a Jew and
a Christian (although this is not always as obvious as it sounds).
To define the hebraic element in Milton's poetry, some aspects of

---

[26] Fisch, p. 113.
[27] Fisch, p. 111. See also Franz Rosenzweig who calls the relation between God
and the World "creation", between God and man "revelation", between man and
the world "redemption". *Der Stern der Erlösung*, trans. I. Amir (Jerusalem, 1970.
Hebrew), part II, pp. 131–281, and Nahum N. Glatzer, *Franz Rosenzweig: His Life
and Thought* (New York, 1953), p. 303.

the relationship between Christianity and Judaism have to be reviewed.

To stress the contribution of Judaism to Christianity in general and to Puritanism in particular is to repeat well-known things. That Christianity is an amalgamation of Hellenic and Jewish beliefs and philosophies adapted to the pagan rites and thinking of the people converted is no longer disputed. The ancient Greeks vanished from history and nobody prevented the Christian Church from interpreting Greek philosophy and literature in such a way that it could be incorporated into Christianity and subordinated to its religious ethos. The Jews, on the other hand, survived the destruction of their state and temple, preserved their religious writings and beliefs, and remained a living influence in Western culture. They affected Christianity in several ways. First, as a mediating factor: it was Philo Judaeus who synthesized the neo-platonism of Greece with Judaism and influenced such thinkers as Augustine and Abélard, and it was the Aristotelianism of Maimonides which influenced Scotus and Aquinas. Second, insofar as their toleration in Christian countries[28] was a fulfilment of Scripture, the sufferings of the Jews in the course of history were, in the eyes of Christianity, a just punishment for their condemnation of Christ[29] and for their persistent rejection of His messiahship. In their refusal to admit that Christianity had advanced beyond Judaism or that the Mosaic law had been superseded by Christ's teaching, they acted as God's instrument to bring about the destined salvation and the eschatological end for which the world was waiting. The Jews were believed to have produced a significant religion prior to the rise of Christianity but since their refusal to accept the message of the Gospels, they had forfeited their right as God's chosen people.

Third, the Old Testament played an important role in the rejection of established orthodox doctrines. Reform movements such as the Waldensian, the Hussite, the Wycliffite, the Lutheran and

---

[28] For theological as well as for economical reasons, the Church has never sought to exterminate the Jewish race.
[29] For a recent reevaluation of the Jews' attitude to Jesus and the trial of Jesus in light of the known legal, political, and religious facts see Haim Cohn, *The Trial and Death of Jesus* (New York, 1971).

the Puritan, different though they are, had this in common: their reform involved emancipation from the Church's monopoly of Scriptural interpretation. Though predominantly anti-Judaic, most reform movements reverted to the sources of Christian faith for inspiration – that is, to Jewish literary sources. The very knowledge of the Biblical text in its original form led its readers to dissent. The anti-Trinitarianism of Michael Servetus as well as other unitarian tendencies during the Reformation were, in part, a result of the influence of Jewish monotheism as expressed in the Old Testament.[30] Such a Jewish influence is characteristic of most reform movements. Yet while Jewish ideas contributed to Christian reform movements, "Judaic" influence or "Judaizing" – as the word is frequently encountered – was a term of reproach and contempt. Since the Jewish religion was considered inferior by the Church and the Jew disliked for his rejection of Jesus, it was convenient to classify any heresy as Jewish. The term "Judaizing" was used as one of contempt by all Christian movements: the Catholic Church used it to condemn the Wycliffites and the Lollards; it accused Reuchlin, Luther, Melancthon, Zwingli and Calvin of "Judaizing". The Reformers too accused their opponents of Judaizing: Calvin accused Servetus; Luther accused Muenster and the Hebraists of the day.[31] Even such learned humanists as Erasmus feared that overmuch concern with Hebrew scholarship would mean a revival of Judaism among Christians.[32]

The Puritan movement in England had much in common with the Reform movements on the Continent. The English Puritans too believed in reliance upon the literal inspiration of the Bible. They felt a strong sense of identity with many figures in ancient history. This identification expressed itself in the desire to establish a theocracy, a Biblical commonwealth in England, in attempts to introduce the Mosaic law as a fundamental law of the land and to appoint seventy members of the Privy Council in accordance with the number of the "elders of Israel" who, together with Moses, gathered at the tabernacle of the congregation before God

---

[30] Louis Israel Newman, *Jewish Influence on Christian Reform Movements* (New York, 1925), especially pp. 435–645.
[31] Newman, pp. 2–3.
[32] Newman, p. 24.

(Numbers XI.16). All these reflect the Puritans' conviction that they were the "true Israel" allied in spirit with the ancient historic people of the Bible rather than with Jews or Judaism of their day. The attitude of English Puritans to contemporary Jews was more or less like that of Christendom all over Europe. In spite of Menasseh Ben Israel's visit to London and the Messianic expectations of the day, the Jews did not gain official permission to settle in England in Cromwell's days. The only Jews who, since the expulsion in 1290, lived in London were the Marranos who had started coming in the days of Charles I. These were Spanish and Portuguese Jews whom the Inquisition had forced to convert but who gradually reverted to Judaism, first secretly, then in the open. If liberal Puritans tolerated contemporary Jews, their tolerance was largely based on the belief that by converting, the Jews would help prepare for the advent of the Messiah. The expectations of the millennial kingdom of Christ to be brought about by the Saints in England was contemporaneous with the Messianic movement of Shabtai Zvi. Messianic enthusiasm was high throughout seventeenth-century Europe. On the whole, however, English Puritans drew a distinction between the Israelites of the Old Testament and their Jewish descendants: they identified themselves with the first (those who had been the chosen people) but looked with suspicion and disdain on their descendants – the successful merchants who had rejected their Messiah and were, in their eyes, heretics. If their preachers taught them to live according to the laws of Moses and to follow the Hebrew code of conduct, they interpreted this code in light of Christian morality, or, as Haller phrases it, they "recast for their own age Paul's digest of the laws of Moses, giving prominent place to the indispensible duties of Bible-reading and attendance upon sermons". The Hebrew code of conduct was of "practical application" as "interpreted and reinforced by the trenchant epitomizing genius of Paul".[33] Therefore, when Puritan preachers advocated the observance of the Laws of Moses by Christians, their motive was not the desire to return to Judaism but to turn to people away from what they considered the Church's idolatry to principles of morality. For

---

[33] William Haller, *The Rise of Puritanism* (New York [1938], 1957), p. 117.

them, the Old Testament never superseded the New; it vindicated it. If the motives behind the preachers' usage of the Old Testament aimed at laying down a moral pattern of day-to-day life for the people to follow, the motives of seventeenth-century learned hebraists were of a different order.

As they studied Greek and Latin primary sources, so they studied the Old Testament – as scholars with a humanist training. As they rejected scholastic methods in their study of the classics, so they rejected the Church's rendering of the Bible and turned instead to the texts of the Old and New Testaments themselves as well as to the writings of the early Fathers. This approach was not primarily anti-religious – there were few atheists in those days –[34] but, in theology as in literature and in philosophy, it was influenced by the literary and scholarly training they had received. As a result of the pro-Biblical atmosphere of the Reformation together with the interests of Renaissance humanists, the study of Hebrew became part of the necessary equipment of every enlightened scholar. Continental humanists like Ficino, Pico, and Reuchlin were accomplished hebraists who furthered the study of Hebrew for Gentiles and defended the freedom of pursuing Hebrew studies. Since the days of the Venerable Bede there had been Christian scholars, notably Alcuin and Roger Bacon, who knew Hebrew. But for those scholars living in England in the Middle Ages who had no access to Jewish teachers, physicians or converts, Hebrew studies had virtually remained a closed book. After the establishment of the Regius Professorships at Oxford and Cambridge in 1540, Hebrew scholarship flourished in England where it became associated with such names as Wakefield, Fagius, Tremellius,[35] Chappell, and Lightfoot. Men of learning like Selden

[34] No one called himself an atheist and no one denied the existence of God in those days, explains Don Cameron Allen in *Doubt's Boundless Sea* (Baltimore, 1964).
[35] For a good account of the people and books Milton had access to, see Fletcher, *The Intellectual Development of John Milton* (2 vols.). John Immanuel Tremellius succeeded Fagius at Cambridge at about 1550. His Latin translation of the Bible was a favourite with Milton. He was succeeded by Anthony Chevalier – tutor to Princess Elizabeth and author of a Hebrew grammar. All these were men of reputation in the field of Semitic studies. The man who directed Milton's Hebrew studies at Cambridge was also the tutor of John Lightfoot – who had left Cambridge before Milton's arrival – William Chappell. Fletcher, I, pp. 292–293.

the jurist (author of the "Hebrew Wife") and Newton the physician (author of a commentary on the Book of Daniel and the Apocalypse) were among the hebraists of the age. Their knowledge of Hebrew and Hebrew works was not derived from popular sermons: it was systematically acquired with the help of teachers and tutors. This learned interest in the Hebrew language and in the original text of the Bible is reflected in many of the translations of the sixteenth and seventeenth centuries from the Tyndale (through the Genevan and Bishops Bibles) up to the King James version.

This is the background against which Milton's knowledge of Hebrew literature and culture must be assessed. Three main motives then impelled John Milton to study Hebrew. The first was cultural, for like the study of Greek, the study of Hebrew had become part of the humanist education of the day; the second was religious, for the reading of the Old Testament in the original was motivated by the desire to understand the language of God aright. The third, to which we shall come back later, was literary. Milton appreciated the literary merits of the Old Testament and found in dedicated poet-prophets like Moses, Isaiah, and Ezekiel ideal models who spoke in a living language to his ears. Milton's conception of himself as a poet-prophet led him most naturally to identify with others who appeared to him in the same role.

Milton, it seems, spared no effort to acquire his knowledge. He himself mentions the "assiduous course of study" he entered in his youth, "beginning with the books of the Old and the New Testament in their original language".[36] At St. Paul's School he began his study of Hebrew with Thomas Young, with whom he later formed an interesting relationship, and continued with Gill the elder.[37] His education was completed at Cambridge where he studied Hebrew under the guidance of William Chappell. An impressive number of Hebrew texts were available at Cambridge by this time, and when Milton mentions medieval commentators quoted in the Rabbinical Bible or when he mentions portions of the Talmud and the two main Aramaic versions (Targumim) he quotes from first-hand knowledge. Had he been asked about his

[36] *The Christian Doctrine*, xiv. 4.
[37] *The Intellectual Development of John Milton*, I, pp. 264, 283.

knowledge of Hebrew, he would have answered that with all the "helps of Learning, and faithfull industry that man in this life can look for, and the assistance of *God*",[38] he was as good a hebraist as Young and Chappell, and he would have added that he advocated the study of the Hebrew tongue at an early age so "that the Scriptures may now be read in their originall: whereto it would be no impossibility to adde the *Chaldey* and the *Syrian* dialect".[39] As evidence that he had acquired a good command of Hebrew before he went to Cambridge, he might have shown his translation of the Psalms done at the age of 15.

Had Milton been asked about "hebraism" he would not have explained the word in nineteenth- or twentieth-century terminology – that is, in the abstract sense. He would have explained it in the Renaissance sense of the term, "an Hebraism" (plural hebraisms), meaning a Hebrew phrase or idiom characteristic of the Hebrew language. This is how Milton explains one of the ways "in which any person or thing is said to be known of God" – "God's approving or gracious knowledge" being "an Hebraism" and he proceeds to explain the meaning of the phrase in the Old Testament.[40] Similarly, he explains "sitting at right hand" as an Hebraism meaning "raised to a place of power".[41] Nowhere in his writings is the word used synonymously with Judaism. His attitude to Judaism is expressed unambiguously throughout his works. Even in the *Articles of Peace* where Milton argues in favour of religious toleration, he draws a distinction between toleration of Judaism and of Jews: "while we detest *Judaism*, we know our selves commanded by St. *Paul*, *Rom.* 11 to respect the *Jews*, and by all means to endeavor thir conversion".[42] Like other independent Puritans, he probably thought it might be "the duty of magistrates to permit the Jews, whose conversion we look for, to live freely

---

[38] *Of Reformation. Complete Prose Works of John Milton*, ed. Don M. Wolfe (New Haven, 1953), I, 568. Henceforth referred to as *Yale Prose Works.*
[39] *Of Education* (*Yale Prose Works*), II, p. 400.
[40] *The Christian Doctrine*, I. *The Works of John Milton*, ed. Frank Allen Patterson, 18 vols. (New York, 1931–38), vol. XIV, 121. Henceforth referred to as *Columbia Edition of the Complete Works.*
[41] *The Christian Doctrine*, I. 16. *Ibid.*, vol. XV. p. 313.
[42] *Articles of Peace* (*Yale Prose Works*), III, p. 326.

and peaceably amongst us".[43] Judaism is for Milton the "chaffe of overdated ceremonies" from which the doctrine of the Gospel has been winnow'd and sifted",[44] for the "whole Judaick law is either politicall, and to take pattern by that, no Christian nation ever thought itself oblig'd in conscience; or morall, which containes in it the observation of whatsoever is substantially, and perpetually true and good, either in religion, or course of life ... That which is thus morall, ... the Gospell, as stands with her dignity most, lectures to us from her own authentick hand-writing".[45] In spite of his assertion that Moses is "the only Lawgiver that we can believe to have been visibly taught by God",[46] Milton believes that on "the introduction of the gospel, or new covenant through faith in Christ, the whole of the preceding covenant, in other words, the entire Mosaic law, was abolished".[47] Had Milton been asked whether he thought there were any Judaic elements in his thoughts, he would have replied that though he found the Bible as easy as 'Symmachus', he was not "Judaized"[48] and that he was against all those who "in many points of religion had miserably Judaiz'd the Church".[49] If the word *Judaize* is used by Milton, as by most Christians, as a term of abuse[50] and contemptuously associated with *Idolatry* and *Papacie* – all of which the Protestant Reformation should "throw off"[51] – Milton never hesitates to use "Judaical" arguments whenever they suit his purpose[52] and, in his

[43] *Articles of Peace*, III, p. 326, note 79.
[44] *Of Reformation (Yale Prose Works)*, I. p. 519.
[45] *The Reason of Church Government*, iii *(Yale Prose Works)*, I, p. 764.
[46] *The Reason of Church Government*, I, p. 747.
[47] *The Christian Doctrine*, xxvii.
[48] Symmachus, a semi-Jew, is so called by Milton. *Of Reformation (Yale Prose Works)*, I, p. 567 and note 172.
[49] This is how he accuses "the defenders of tithes, after a long pomp and tedious preparation out of Heathen authors, telling us that tithes were paid to *Hercules* and *Apollo*, which perhaps was imitated from the *Jews*, and as it were bespeaking our expectation, that they will abound much more with authorities out of Christian storie, have nothing of generall approbation to beginn with from the first three or four ages, but that which abundantly serves to the confutation of thir tithes" *Means to Remove Hirelings (Columbia Edition of the Complete Works)*, vol. VI, p. 63.
[50] *An Apology (Yale Prose Works)*, I, p. 932.
[51] *Animadversions*, iv *(Yale Prose Works)*, I, p. 703.
[52] *Doctrine and Discipline of Divorce (Yale Prose Works)*, II, p. 332.

Doctrine and Discipline of Divorce, relies more than once on the authority of the "prudent Moses".

This anti-Judaic attitude is as characteristic of the Puritans in England as it is of other Reform movements. Paradoxically, it is reinforced by the Puritans' "pro-Israel" feelings and by their belief in themselves as the "true Israel". Like other Puritans of his age, Milton held that "God preferred Gentiles to Jews" but that at the Second Coming, salvation would be extended to Jews as well as to Christians and that the ancient tribes of Israel would be collected from their dispersion (*P.R.* II.34–35). The following lines of Milton's Christ "*Israel's* true King" (*P.R.* III.441) are primarily about the millennial kingdom:

> ... he at length, time to himself best known,
> Rememb'ring *Abraham*, by some wondrous call
> May bring them back repentant and sincere,
> And at their passing cleave the *Assyrian* Flood,
> While to their native land with joy they haste,
> As the Red Sea and *Jordan* once he cleft,
> When to the promis'd land thir Fathers pass'd;
> To his due time and Providence I leave them.
>
> P.R. III.433–440

Christ's realization that he doesn't need a kingdom "From *Egypt* to *Euphrates* and beyond", his calm assertion that Israel will be won back "in due time and providence" by spiritual rather than by physical might, reflect Milton's flash of historical insight into the nature of Old Testament faith. Gathered in this passage are references to three of the major events in the history of the people of Israel: the covenant with Abraham, the Exodus from Egypt, and the crossing of the Jordan before the children of Israel took possession of the promised land. Isaiah's prophecy that "the Lord shall set his hand again the second time to recover the remnant of his people which shall be left from Assyria and from Egypt ..." (xi. 11), alluded to in line 436, is the key to the passage for, according to the Christian interpretation of the chapter, Christ is the "branch out of the root of Jesse"; His is the peace-able kingdom to which Israel as well as the Gentiles will be restored. What we have here then is a typical example of one aspect of Milton's usage of Old Testament references or what may be termed his hebraism: allusions to Old Testament events of great historical importance and of universal ethical significance giving reality and validity to the Christian meaning of the passage. I have deliberately chosen this passage from *Paradise Regained* – with its unmistakable vision of the millennial kingdom – to show that an appreciation of hebraic references in Milton's poetry need not detract from the Christian meaning of his work.

Above all, it was the Old Testament and its commentators as literature that inspired the hebraism of Milton's poetry. And indeed in *Paradise Lost* this influence can be compared only with that of the classics. In a way both Hellenic and hebraic materials are receptacles for Milton's Christian philosophy. Both had a literary attraction for Milton, but there is a difference. In addition to the literary attraction which impelled Milton to read the prophetic poetry of the Old Testament, there was the religious motive, the Protestant belief that one must return to the literal text of the Bible in order to understand the language of God. According to his own testimony, the spring from which he drank the purest draughts was indeed Hebrew poetry. He would have objected to readers who, while seeking a rational principle of Christian theology in his works, tried to exculpate him from the charge of Old Testament influence. He would certainly have refuted the claim that his belief in the superiority of Hebrew poets to those of ancient Greece and Rome "in the very critical art of composition" was a "foolish notion" bred by "an enthusiasm of the moment" and a "perverse opinion".[53] His admiration for "*Sion's* songs, to all true tastes excelling", (*P.R.* IV.347) and for the prophets who are "men divinely taught" and better teachers "In their majestic unaffected style / Than all the Oratory of *Greece* and *Rome*" (*P.R.* IV.359–360) was natural and genuine.

The following chapters set out to examine the various functions

---

[53] C. A. Patrides, "*Paradise Lost* and the Language of Theology", *Language and Style in Milton*, p. 103. However, "poetry and theology", as Allen persuasively argues, "are not great bedfellows" and like him, I shall not force them to sleep together. *Doubt's Boundless Sea*, p. x.

of hebraism as a stylistic feature of the Puritan poet who read Old Testament poetry not as authoritative religion but as divinely inspired literature. It can be said of the hebraic element in *Paradise Lost*, as Milton did of Truth in *Areopagitica*, that it has "more shapes than one", for the hebraic elements function differently in the three areas in which the action of the poem takes place: hell, paradise, and heaven. With regard to the fallen angels, hebraic references and motifs operate ironically. They are intrinsic to the meaning of Milton's hell, for by evoking the conflict between the God of the Israelites and the false pagan gods of the Old Testament, they provide the moral yardsticks against which the fallen angels are measured. In the books on Eden, Milton adheres closely to the Genesis text and alludes to other books of the Old Testament to enhance the goodness and purity of our first parents. By balancing Old Testament echoes against classical ones, Milton successfully overcomes the difficulty of making credible to us the prelapsarian innocence as opposed to the postlapsarian sinfulness of Adam and Eve. Hebraic elements function even more directly in Milton's treatment of heaven for they express the religious and moral justification of God in council and in war. It is by means of Old Testament stories and figures like the chariot or the angel Abdiel that Milton projects his ideal of moral goodness and his concept of God as a hard but just Taskmaster. Michael's résumé of past history plays a double role: it unifies Old Testament allusions and concepts recurrent throughout the epic and validates Milton's view of man in terms of the Old Testament concept of history. The reader, like Adam, learns by analogy. It is in these last books that Milton's vision of man's predicament is most clearly presented. The fall having become an intellectual as well as an emotional reality for Adam, he now can, like the Old Testament patriarchs, put his faith in God and envision life as good and acceptable.

It may be asked whether the existence of these elements need be proved. Newton has already said that the 'Scriptural echoes' in *Paradise Lost* "are so evident, that it is almost superfluous to mention them. If we take notice of them, it is that every reader may be sensible how much of Scripture our author has wrought into that divine poem".[54] The recognition of hebraic elements is indeed only part of the story. The following chapters purport to show that a proper understanding of the function of these elements is relevant for some of the most crucial critical issues that twentieth-century scholarship has raised about *Paradise Lost*. They also set out to examine some Old Testament concepts that are closely related to the poem's total meaning and might be labelled hebraic. These however are not synonymous with the 'Hebraic heresies' Milton has been charged with. There is no doubt that some of these so-called heresies were influenced by the Old Testament way of thought and by hebraic interpretations of the Biblical word. Like most Protestants, Milton reverts to the Old Testament to support his repudiation of established orthodox doctrines. This is the case with his doctrine of divorce and may well also be the case with his mortalism and Arianism as well. Fisch's explanation of these heresies in terms of Milton's hebraism certainly carries conviction according to his wide definition of the term. Yet they do not necessarily affect Milton's Christianity in any significant way. They rather confirm Milton's belief in religious self-determination.[55]

It would therefore be dangerous to ask, "But was Milton strictly speaking, a Puritan? Can he be fitted into any pattern of Christian orthodoxy, medieval or modern?"[56] Milton was, of course, a Puritan, though independent and liberal.[57] It may perhaps be true that Milton does not fall into any medieval or modern pattern of Christianity, but he is certainly a good seventeenth-century Christian who belongs to the liberal Puritan Christian tradition. The following view of Milton as a hebraic writer seems debatable:

It all depends in a way from which end of the Bible one begins. Milton, if I am not mistaken, began from the Book of *Genesis* and went on steadily forward to the Book of *Judges* and *Job*.

---

[54] Thomas Newton on *Paradise Lost* IV. 421 (London, 1749).
[55] On this issue see also Maurice Kelley, "Milton and the Trinity", *HLQ*, XXXIII (1970), pp. 315–320.
[56] *Jerusalem and Albion*, p. 5.
[57] On Milton's Puritanism see Barker, *Milton and the Puritan Dilemma* (Toronto, 1942) and Haller, *The Rise of Puritanism* (New York, 1957, 1938).

Around those three works he wrote his major poems. One sometimes wonders whether he ever got as far as the *Epistles* of Paul, and he never wrote a full-length poem about the Crucifixion. The doctrinal Puritans on the other hand generally started from Paul's Letter to the Romans.[58]

There is nothing to stop a believer in the Epistles of Paul from being influenced by the heroic and ethical ideals projected by *Genesis* and *Judges*. The two are not contradictory but complementary. Indeed there is no reason why an assessment of the hebraic elements in *Paradise Lost* should cause us to shy away from Milton's fundamentally Christian Protestant faith. Hebraic elements – literary as well as conceptual – are there, yet to label *Paradise Lost* a "hebraic" poem would be to impoverish it, not to glorify it. Hebraic literary allusions and themes forcefully abound in Milton's work, but they constitute an element which has to be seen in terms of the Christian rather than the Jewish faith and in terms of the conflict between the two opposing strains felt by every writer and thinker of Milton's intellectual milieu.

Among the many currents of thought prevalent in his day, two opposing tendencies were at work. The first was religious. It was the Puritan Christian belief in theological sin which brought corruption to a world that God created good. The second was the humanist belief in man's dignity, spiritual faculties, and freedom of will. While Christianity attached more significance to man's sinfulness and dependence on God's providence, Renaissance humanism stressed man's nobility and the infinite power of his intellect. Milton tries to synthesize these two opposing currents of thought in his early writings.[59] In *Paradise Lost*, they are reconciled in a manner which makes it a Christian humanist poem par excellence, distinguishing it not only from Milton's other works

---

[58] *Jerusalem and Albion*, pp. 5–6.
[59] In *Of Education*, for example, Milton writes: "The end then of learning is to repair the ruins of our first parents by regaining to know God aright, and out of that knowledge to love him, to imitate him, to be like him, as we may the neerest by possessing our souls of true vertue, which being united to the heavenly grace of faith makes up the highest perfection" (*Yale Prose Works*, II, pp. 366–367).

but also from Spenser's poetry before him and Dryden's after.[60]
Neither the heroic values of chivalry nor the promise of Nature
provide the spiritual life and faith associated with "that great
Sabbaoth God" for the poet of the *Mutabilitie* Cantos. Whereas
Spenser, loathing "this state of life so tickle", can only pray to the
God of Hosts and hope for the Vision, Milton has the Vision and
firmly believes in Him. Hardly a generation later Dryden's mock-
heroic view of life and his political realism leave little room for
the "vision beatific". Milton is indeed, as Douglas Bush calls him,
the last and greatest of Christian humanists–the last who can use
the form of the classical epics for conveying the ideas and concepts
of Christian humanism; the greatest because the underlying
hebraic motifs in the poem reconcile the classical framework with
the Christian principles. The Old Testament ethical criteria expressed by the prophets exposing Idolatry and "Religions full of
Pomp and Gold" (I.372), the conception of the heroic expressed by
Old Testament characters "Not less but more Heroic than the
Wrath / Of stern *Achilles* on his Foe pursu'd / Thrice fugitive about
Troy Wall" (IX.14–18), the acceptance of the goodness of the
physical as well as the spiritual expressed in the affirmation of
marriage and love, and the concept of history based on the conviction of a purposeful course of events in which man plays a
significant role in which "the World is all before him" – these are
the major hebraic concepts which maintain the balance between
the humanist and puritan elements in Milton's thought. This is
the dynamic hebraic factor which synthesizes Milton's protestant
sense of providential care with his heroic humanist ideals. In this
sense it is closely related to Fisch's conception of Biblical humanism, to the vision of Jerusalem in seventeenth-century poetry
which, in his words, "is not a mythical ideal but rather capable
of resurrection in history through the exercise of our human faculties".[61]

Yet for all the hebraic concepts that are integrated in *Paradise*

---

[60] R. J. Zwi Werblowsky, *Lucifer and Prometheus, A Study of Milton's Satan*
(London, 1952) sees a conflict between these two opposed trends of thought in
Paradise Lost. He calls them "Hellenic" and "Hebraic".
[61] *Jerusalem and Albion*, p. 14.

Lost, for all the religious dissent that is expressed in his works, for all his heresies – that the Son is not co-eternal with the Father, that the Soul dies and is resurrected with the body, that the world is not created out of nothing, – for all the political conflicts he was involved in, Milton's outlook remains unified and coherent and *Paradise Lost* is, in the main, an orthodox poem. For all the option of choice regarding details, the traditional structure of the universe still had moral meaning for Milton. New religious ideas as well as new scientific discoveries are woven into the accepted cosmological scheme: both geocentric and heliocentric cosmology are clearly enunciated in the poem. None of this alters Milton's Christian Renaissance grasp of the divine order of things. With the syncretism characteristic of the late as well as the early Renaissance, Milton integrates and subsumes new political ideas, scientific discoveries as well as hebraic motifs to his Christian Protestant belief. They all serve his desire to write that poem which he intended to be "doctrinal and exemplary to a nation".

II

THE VALLEY OF HINNOM AND ITS INHABITANTS

1. THE VALLEY OF HINNOM

Hell is probably one of mankind's oldest concepts, for man has always tried to account for his experience of pain, evil, and death by creating imaginary worlds that he regarded as the source of his sorrows and woes. Yet the evils of Milton's hell, however imaginatively described, are the evils of our own world; his hell is neither Hades, the dwelling place of all the dead, nor Tartaros, located far beneath Hades and the place of punishment for those who oppose the will of the gods. Still, in many ways, Milton's hell belongs to the classical tradition. Its "four infernal Rivers that disgorge / Into the burning Lake thir baleful stream" (II.575–576) are four of the five rivers – Styx, Acheron, Cocytus, Phlegeton and Lethe – (II.577–584) that traditionally bound hell. The poet describes hell as a burning "Dungeon horrible" (I.61) but also as a watery place where Satan "Prone on the Flood" lay floating many a rood. Satan is chained on the "burning Lake" (I.210), and Moloch, in his speech for open war, counsels to leave that "forgetful Lake". This concept of hell as a watery place was traditional with the Renaissance and is common to many cultures,[1]

---

[1] In his new commentary to *Job* (*The Anchor Bible*, Garden City, 1965) Marvin H. Pope points out that "the watery character of the infernal region is abundantly stressed in the Old Testament". He explains the etymology of the word *shahat* in Job ix. 31, and shows that it designates not only the netherworld but carries the suggestion of moist or filth liquid. See also *JBL*, LXXXIII, iii (September, 1964), pp. 269–278. Quoting Ugaritic texts, Pope proves the watery character of Mot's abode. Elsewhere (*El in the Ugaritic texts* [Leiden, 1955]) he tells how El resides in aqueous and subterranean environs. In the O.T., *tehom, tehomot*, gener-

but it seems that in constructing his hell, Milton, like Dante, relied for the most part on the landscaping of Homer and Virgil. Thus, again, when Satan and Beelzebub leave the fiery lake, they are like Homeric heroes "Both glorying to have scap't the Stygian flood . . ." (I.239); when Milton appeals to the muse for inspiration to describe the fallen angels, his words echo those of Homer,[2] and the occupations of the devils after the council in Pandaemonium bring to mind the funeral games described in the *Iliad* and the *Aeneid*. Milton's classical references and borrowings are not surprising, for he was writing in the tradition of Virgil. Moreover, since there is no poetically suggestive picture of hell in the Bible, Milton very naturally turned for inspiration to scenes of hell in classical epics. Examples of classical echoes in words, phrasing, and concept are too numerous to be noted and are familiar to Milton students and scholars.

In all these, Milton's hell is traditional. What makes it unique is the hebraic imagery Milton has so adroitly used in describing it and its denizens. This is all the more surprising for the simple reason that there is no clear hebraic vision of hell. The Old Testament, having been carefully demythologized, has no equivalent for the Greek Tartaros. Since the whole world is God's creation and good, there is no room in Judaism for hell as a place of torture and punishment. *Sheol* is the dark abode of all the dead and not a place where the wicked are punished. *Gehenna* as a place of fiery torment is a relatively late concept in Jewish thought. The name is the Greek and Latin form of Ge-Hinnom (Valley of Hinnom; alternatively, the valley of the son of Hinnom, the valley of the sons of Hinnom) located south-west of Jerusalem. Because of the Canaanite child sacrifices performed at the place called *Tophet* at the junction of the valley and the river Kidron, the valley of

---

(*FOOTNOTE 1 continued*)
ally refer to subterranean supply of water as contrasted with the celestial reservoir, *e.g.* Gen. vii. 17, viii. 2, Dt. viii. 7, Prov. viii. 28 (*El in the Ugaritic Texts*, p. 63) and in Job xxxviii. 16–17, the abyss and the gates of hell are associated with the depths of the sea. Pope also points out that Babylonian texts allude to a river ordeal (*El in the Ugaritic Texts*, p. 70). One of the striking O.T. verses describing the watery character of hell appear in Ezekiel xxxi. 15.
[2] *Iliad*, I.1–6. *The Iliad of Homer*, trans. Richmond Lattimore (Chicago, 1961).

Hinnom became notorious as the valley of slaughter. In post-Biblical literature, it came to be identified with hell – the fiery place of punishment for the wicked – for the pagan rituals of cremation suggested the notion of a fiery hell.[3] This is the concept of Ge-Hinnom in later Jewish as well as in Christian tradition.

In spite of the fact that Milton's hell is Christian in its conception of moral evil, of pride, of worldliness, and of the defiance of God, it is significant that the richest cluster of Hebrew names and Old Testament allusions is found precisely in Books I and II of *Paradise Lost* rather than, say, in Books IV and V describing Eden, which surely could rely on the "authoritative reality" of the Genesis account. It is hard to believe that either the geographical descriptions of Palestine, the Hebrew phrases, words and metaphors, or the hebraic characterizations of the fallen angels are unconscious borrowings. The words and phrases culled from hebraic sources are as deliberate and apt as those inspired by Greek, Latin, or patristic sources. The very language of Milton in these books, though belonging to another family of human tongues, is notably hebraic. The referential meaning of Hebrew words and names is essential for understanding the poetry of hell. A case in point is Milton's powerful description of the valley of Hinnom "Tophet thence / And black *Gehenna* call'd, the Type of Hell" (I.404–405). The description of the place is in keeping with the traditional explanation of the word *tophet*[4] and its gruesome

---

[3] The notion of a fiery hell also appears in the New Testament, *e.g.* Matthew v. 22: "whosoever shall say, Thou fool, shall be in danger of hell fire." The idea of a punitive conflagration appears in earlier parts of the Old Testament, but it is only in the Greco-Roman period of Jewish history that the quite distinct concept of a blazing hell – a lake, or abyss, of fire – begins to emerge (Daniel 7:10, Enoch 18: 11–16, 27: 1–3 etc.). See *IDB* II, pp. 361–362 (New York, 1962).

[4] R. Solomon Yitzhaki (the eleventh-century commentator also known as *RaShI* by the initials of his name) understood the word as meaning "drum" and so did most interpreters. Hume too (on I.404) points out that the word is derived from *tof* (toph) = drum, timbrel. Recently, two new explanations have been suggested: 1) Pope in his commentary to Job on xvii. 6b, and in "A Note on Ugaritic ndd-ydd", *JCS*, ed. Albrecht Goetze, I (1947), pp. 337–341, suggests that the word *tophet*, especially as used in Job xvii. 6, has the primary meaning of *spitting*, and he translates the verse thus: "He has made me a popular byword, / One in whose face they spit." 2) On the other hand, Tur-Sinai, *The Book of Job. A New Commentary* (Jerusalem, 1957) (Hebrew), p. 278, believes *tophet* to be an originally Aramaic

rituals are so accurately conveyed as to give a living reality to Milton's hell. The passage evokes both auditory and visual associations of the place where children's cries are unheard "for the noise of Drums and Timbrels loud" (I.394).

It is also perhaps not fortuitous that Milton's valley of Hinnom is set in the midst of the lands of Moloch and Chemos, of Dagon and impious Pharaoh rather than in the lands of Achilles and Turnus. The Puritan poet must have sensed the clash between the morally strict, severely simple faith of the Israelites and the sophisticatedly sensuous, unashamedly material paganism of the Canaanites as recorded in the Old Testament,[5] and he uses hebraic references to provide the norms against which the values of hell are measured. Moloch is worshiped by the Ammonite

> in *Rabba* and her wat'ry Plain,
> In *Argob* and in *Basan*, to the stream
> Of utmost *Arnon*.
>   I.396–399

Like Moloch, Chemos is

> th' obscene dread of *Moab's* Sons,
> From *Aroar* to *Nebo*, and the wild
> Of Southmost *Abarim*; in *Hesebon*
> And *Horonaim*, *Seon's* Realm, beyond
> The flow'ry Dale of *Sibma* clad with Vines,
> And *Eleale* to th' *Asphaltic* Pool.
>   I.406–411

(*FOOTNOTE 4 continued*)

equivalent of 'the hearth (-stones) on which meat is put for cooking'. He accordingly translates Job xvii. 6: "He hath made me a prey to the peoples, / and I have become a firebrand for hosts." Eliezer Ben Yehudah too believes tophet primarily to mean site of conflagration. See *Dictionary and Thesaurus of the Hebrew Language* (New York, 1960) (Hebrew).

[5] This is part of the thesis of Kaufmann in *The Religion of Israel* (volume I, book 1) where he argues that the simple and morally austere monotheistic Israelite faith grew and developed as a reaction to a highly sophisticated and civilized pagan environment with which the Hebrews were in contact. He finds this reflected in the Old Testament. Yehezkel Kaufmann, *Toldot Ha-Emuna Ha-Israelit* (Jerusalem-Tel-Aviv, 1960 [1937]) (Hebrew).

Set, as it were, between the lands of the Ammonites and the Moabites, Milton's hell is, by inference, steeped in the heathen abominations practiced in those regions.[6] This is an effective means of contrasting the pagan ethos of the devils with the moral uprightness of the hebraic God. Whereas Jehovah is "thund'ring out of *Sion*, thron'd / Between the Cherubim", the fallen angels are invariably associated with the habitat of God's pagan enemies. They are like the "Memphian Chivalry" (I.307),[7] while God's people are called the "Sojourners of *Goshen*" (I.309).[8] The resounding name *Busiris* in I.307 is associated with ancient Egypt although the name is not to be confused with that of the Pharaoh

[6] These lines, incidentally, give a fairly accurate geographical description of the territories of the Ammonites and of the Moabites. Yet not all commentators seem to agree on all details. Most of Milton's commentators from Hume to Hughes think that *Abarim* is the name of a chain of hills. Hume, on I.408 writes: "of *Southmost Abarim*; Mountains of *Moab* bordering on the Desart Southward, and therefore wild, a wilderness, not far from Mount *Nebo*, Numbers 33, 47." On the same verse Hughes notes that the *Abarim* hills are conspicuous on Fuller's map. Allan H. Gilbert, however, believes *Abarim* is a plateau east of the Dead Sea (*A Geographical Dictionary of Milton* (New Haven, 1919), p. 7). Yet if Milton knew his Pentateuch, he had no need to go to Fuller's map, for Deuteronomy xxxii. 49, says: "Get thee up into this mountain *Abarim*, unto Mount Nebo, which is in the land of Moab, that is over against Jericho; and behold the land of Canaan, which I give unto the children of Israel for a possession." No one today knows exactly where this mountain called Abarim (or *'Avarim'* in Hebrew) is situated, whether it is identical with Mount Nebo or includes the latter, and the question has very little relevance to the understanding of Milton's lines.

Utmost Arnon (I.399) is, of course, the border of Moab and the names of the cities Milton mentions are found in Joshua xiii. Yet, even if the descriptions are mostly accurate, their main contribution lies in their referential meaning as well as in their giving the poem what Sims calls a sense of "authoritative reality" (*The Bible in Milton's Epics*, p. 8).

[7] On the "Memphian Chivalry", the association of Memphis with the royal seat of Busiris, and the etymology of the name, see John M. Steadman, "'Memphian Chivalry': Milton's Busiris, Etymology and Chronography", *UR* – Kansas City, vol. xxxvii (1971), pp. 215–231, Professor Steadman has kindly given me a copy of his excellent article after these pages had already been submitted for publication.

[8] *Goshen* is the name of the country where the people of Israel dwelt "and they had possessions therein, and grew, and multiplied exceedingly" (Genesis xlvii. 27).

who perished in the Red Sea.[9] If the devils come from the "Realm of impious *Pharaoh*" (I.342), the "Land of Nile" (I.343), they also come

> from the bord'ring flood
> Of old *Euphrates* to the Brook that parts
> *Egypt* from *Syrian* ground,
>
> I.419–421

and Pandaemonium is associated with the Temples of Babylon and Egypt (I.717–722). Beelzebub is well "known in Palestine" (I.80), Dagon "had his Temple high / Rear'd in *Azotus*" (I.463–464) but was "dreaded through the Coast / of *Palestine*, in *Gath* and *Ascalon* / And *Accaron* and *Gaza's* frontier bounds" (I.464–466), and Rimmon's "delightful Seat" (I.467) "Was fair *Damascus*, on the fertile Banks / Of *Abbana* and *Pharphar*, lucid streams" (I.468–469).

Milton's province of evil is not only described in terms of specific heathen localities. His vision of evil is frequently expressed through oblique Old Testament references. In describing hell, for example, he is inspired by Isaiah's personification: compare Isaiah v. 14: "She'ol has made its soul spacious and has opened

---

[9] Milton's identification of Busiris with the Biblical Pharaoh of Exodus is an interesting historiographical intuition. Ovid, in the *Art of Love* I tells the story of the Egyptian king who slaughtered foreigners and a similar version is found in Herodotus. See E. Cobham Brewer, *The Reader's Handbook of Allusions, References, Plots and Stories* (Philadelphia, 1883), p. 144. It is not unlikely that Milton read the story in Ovid and that he saw in it, as in other fables of mythology, a shadowy recollection of Biblical truth. D. C. Allen argued that Milton was misled by Melancthon's revision of the *Chronicle of Carion* ("Milton's Busiris", *MLN*, LXV (1950), pp. 115–116). In a more recent article, John M. Steadman has pointed out that Melancthon's comments on Busiris probably refer to an earlier Pharaoh, but that Milton's allusion to Busiris may derive from a combination of historiogaphical sources. Steadman also believes Milton may have been aware of what was considered the Hebrew etymology of the name in his days and suggests that the etymological significance of the name reinforces "the dominant idea – 'scattering' or dispersal – underlying the entire simile". See " 'Memphian Chivalry': Milton's Busiris, Etymology and Chronography", especially pp. 217–218, 227. On the other hand, Marvin H. Pope has pointed out to me that it was the name of a city in the Nile Delta – modern Abu Sir – and that it meant the House of Osiris.

its mouth wide beyond bounds" and Milton's "the void profound / Of unessential Night receives him next / *Wide gaping*" (II.438– 440) (italics mine); and again VI.874–875: "Hell at last / Yawning receiv'd them whole". Similarly, the phrases "Hell trembl'd as he strode" (II.676) and "Hell trembl'd at the hideous name" recall Isaiah xiv. 9, where hell becomes agitated at Lucifer's arrival. In VI.867–868, hell also "heard th'unsufferable noise, Hell saw / Heav'n ruining from Heav'n." Milton's insight and sensitive reading of Old Testament texts results in a lifelike and compelling characterization of the dark abyss.[10]

Hebrew words or words translated from Hebrew operate in a similar way: either directly by enhancing the moral meaning of the lines, or indirectly by enriching the associative background of the poem and conferring scriptural authority on the passage in which the words appear. The latter is the case when Milton writes of "Th' *Ionian* Gods, of *Javan's* Issue held / Gods," (I.508–509) for his use of *Ionian* for Greek suggests that he saw the connection between it and *Javan*, son of Japhet (Genesis x. 2), *Javan* and *Ion* being two versions of the same name. And when, in the invocation, Milton uses the phrase "chosen seed" (I.8), it brings to mind two scriptural phrases: *zera qodesh* (holy seed) and *am s'gula* (chosen people). Similarly, the "darkness visible" that pervades hell (I.63) reminds us of Job's description of the world of darkness and deadly shadows: "A land of darkness, as darkness itself; and of the shadow of death, without any order, and where the light is as darkness" (Job x. 22). The effect of utter darkness in Milton's hell is also conveyed by such expressions as "the palpable obscure" (II.406), which brings to mind the darkness that God sent to plague the Egyptians: "even darkness which may be felt" (Exodus x. 21), or, "If I wait, the grave is mine house: I have made my bed in the darkness" (Job xvii. 13). At times Hebrew phrases have a more direct impact, as when Moloch describes himself and the other fallen angels as "The Vassals of his [God's] anger" (II.90). The phrase used by Isaiah (xiii. 5) with regard to Babel, God's enemy and 'vessel of wrath', throws an ironic light on Moloch's words,

---

[10] Milton's characterization of hell bears much resemblance to Mot, the God of Death, whose ravenous mouth swallows Baal. See *Wörterbuch der Mythologie*, ed. Hans Wilhelm Haussig (Stuttgart, 1965), pp. 300–301.

and Milton seems to have had more than the Hebrew idiom in mind.[11]

This strange world of evil where fire is cold and light is dark is colorful and lively. One of the factors that contributes to this liveliness is Milton's use of Hebrew words and names to which we respond because of their evocative power and recognize because of their scriptural authority. These Hebrew words, proper names, and phrases that are so skillfully interwoven in the texture of the poetry describing hell also widen the scope of hell through auditory and visual associations.[12] T. S. Eliot may have been too categorical in claiming that Milton's imagination was only auditory, though it is true that the verbal music of Milton's poetry is outstanding. The poet must have felt that the continuous use of harsh Hebrew names would be euphonically detrimental to *Paradise Lost*, and this may be one reason – besides the sources from which he was drawing – why he often adopts Vulgate spellings, as he does in *Senaar* (III.467), or in *Oreb* (I.7), thus avoiding in the latter case the *h* which is a harsh guttural, semi-voiced sound which would be difficult to pronounce even as an aspirate after the preposition *of*, or in *Sion* for *Zion* in I.10; in *Siloa* for *Shiloah* (I.11);[13] in *Basan* (I.397); *Ascalon* and *Accaron* (for *Ashkelon* and

---

[11] In his edition of *Milton's Paradise Lost* (London, 1732), Richard Bentley suggests a good emendation on II,90: "vessels", but he lets the reader decide between *vessels* and *vassals*. Todd too accepts both possibilities. In either case, the idiom in Milton's mind, while he was dictating this passage, seems to have been a Hebrew one. The phrase "vessels of wrath" is closer to the Hebrew and yet "vassals of wrath," though not a translation, conveys a similar idea. The phrase "vessels of wrath" also appears in Romans ix. 22.

[12] The universality of Milton's hell has been discussed by several modern critics. See, for example, Louis Martz, *The Paradise Within, Studies in Vaughan, Traherne and Milton.* (New Haven, 1964), p. 111.

[13] Lauter has pointed out that John ix is a likely source for Milton's allusion and that the double reference there to "pool" of "Siloam" is more pertinent to Milton's passage than Isaiah viii. 6 ("Milton's 'Siloa's Brook'", *N & Q*, CCIII [1958], pp. 204–205). On the other hand, George W. Whiting and Ann Gossman think that though the pool of Siloam was regarded as a symbol of Christ, the allusion to the miracle of the pool is not relevant to Milton's muse. They argue that *Paradise Lost* is mainly an Old Testament epic, and that Milton, modifying the conventional classical invocation to the muses, invoked the heavenly muse who is here appropriately inspired by the waters of Siloa's Brook flowing by Mount Zion ("Siloa's Brook, the Pool of Siloam, and Milton's Muse", *SP*, LVIII [1961], pp. 193–205).

'*Eqron*) in I.465–466. Milton very often adopts the spelling of the Authorized Version where it is musically more effective; for example in *Palestine* (meaning *Canaan* in I.80) and in I.465 for *P'leshet* – the land of the Philistines. There seems to be no rule of thumb for determining Milton's spelling of Hebrew words: he transliterates almost accurately *Baalim* and *Ashtaroth* (I.422) but writes the singular *Astoreth* (I.438). Sometimes he gives the Greek form of a name as in *Azotus* for the Hebrew *Ashdod*.[14] But if Milton uses *Basan* for *Bashan*, he uses the Hebrew form of *Goshen* (I.309) and that of *Ahaz* (I.472). Words like *Leviathan* have become part of the English language and so has *Cherub* (I.324). It is perhaps significant that whereas the Authorized Version has *Seraphims* and *Cherubims* (*e.g.* Genesis iii. 24; Isaiah vi. 2), Milton gives the correct form of the plural *Seraphim* and *Cherubim* (I. 129 and I.665).

Regardless of the question of spelling, we find that the abundance of hebraic names gives a phonetic weight to the poetry. Any important word or name which sounds slightly different from the words our ear is accustomed to will attract our attention and bring to mind a new train of associations. Linked by sound and sense, *Sion* and *Siloa* evoke the heavenly inspiration of Old Testament poetry and are contrasted to the conventional "*Aonian* Mount" associated with the classical muses. In conferring the title *Sultan* on Satan (I.348) and including 'the Sultan in *Bizance*' (XI.395) in the visions of God, Milton again shows his mastery of meaningful allusion. By using this particular foreign word, he conjures up the picture of the pagan all-powerful Eastern ruler of his own day, thereby emphasizing the universality of hell in time as well as place.[15]

---

[14] Hughes on I.464 notes that this is the form used in Ortelius' maps.

[15] *Sultan* in Biblical Aramaic means "power"; the word is applied to divine power both beneficial (cf. Daniel iii. 33; iv. 31) and evil (Daniel iv. 19; vii. 6). The Turkish word *sultan* is derived from the Arabic word *sultan* (as the Hebrew *shilton* and the Aramaic *sholtan*) meaning power, authority, dominion.

Milton's commentators were well aware of the connotation of such words as *sultan, paynim*. Hume (on I.348) gives the Hebrew etymology of the word and notes that Milton used the word sultan because it was the title of the Turkish Emperors known "for their Cruelty and Tyrannick Government, well enough

Biblical names fulfil a similar function in the description of the Paradise of Fools in Book III where we find "The builders next of Babel on the Plain of Senaar" (III.466–467). There the windy outside of Milton's universe becomes somewhat more specific as we find it peopled by builders of Babel, philosophers, "Embryos, and Idiots, Eremites and Friars". Sim's argument that "the reader recognizes, through Biblical allusion, the truth that God will ultimately vanquish evil"[16] is valid for many passages in *Paradise Lost*. Where hell is concerned Milton seems to have wanted to soar even above the Sinai mount, to give more than an authoritative representation of Biblical truth; by using Old Testament materials inseparably from the context of hell, Milton powerfully brings to life the conflict between the arrogant, utterly depraved pagan ethos of the Ammonites, Moabites, Philistines and their like and the demanding, austere God of creation of Old Testament faith.

At this point it should be borne in mind that Milton's style in describing hell draws at least as much sustenance from classical sources as from hebraic ones. The allusions cannot always be neatly separated from one another for in some passages Milton simultaneously yet not fortuitously opposes and fuses pagan and Christian, Hellenic and hebraic materials. This fusion or mixing of allusions reflects the art of imitation of models, as one of the ways of *poesis*, consistently advocated and practiced by Renaissance and seventeenth-century writers. The technique is used deliberately by Milton, and the observation that "No English poet, perhaps no poet except Virgil, has ever cultivated with more assiduity the art of verbal integration, the art of coercing two or more passages from one or more authors into a kind of fruitful collaboration with one another" is well made.[17] This collaboration is fruitful not

---

(*FOOTNOTE 15 continued*)
apply'd to Satan". Todd (on I.764) suggests that Milton alludes to accounts of single combats between Saracens and Christians, of which the old romances are full, and Newton (on X.457) observes that the Devils are frequently described by metaphors taken from the Turks, the devil, the Turk and the Pope, being commonly thought to be nearly related and often joined together.

[16] *The Bible in Milton's Epics*, p. 16, with reference to Beelzebub's speech.
[17] Davis P. Harding, *The Club of Hercules* (Urbana, 1962), p. 96.

merely as one of the ways through which Milton conveys the
universal significance of the poem. Beyond the universal interest
they carry, the assimilation of allusions gives birth to new meanings. In the following passage, for instance, the devils chewing
"bitter ashes" are flawed by the moral significance implicit in both
sources used by Milton here. After the fall, while the applause of
the devils in hell turns to an "exploding hiss", nature too under-
goes a frightening metamorphosis:

> There stood
> A Grove hard by, sprung up with this thir change,
> His will who reigns above, to aggravate
> Thir penance, laden with fair Fruit, like that
> Which grew in Paradise, the bait of *Eve*
> Us'd by the Tempter: on that prospect strange
> Thir earnest eyes they fix'd, imagining
> For one forbidden Tree a multitude
> Now ris'n, to work them furder woe or shame;
> Yet parch't with scalding thirst and hunger fierce,
> Though to delude them sent, could not abstain,
> But on they roll'd in heaps, and up the Trees
> Climbing, sat thicker than the snaky locks
> That curl'd *Megaera*: greedily they pluck'd
> The fruitage fair to sight, like that which grew
> Near that bituminous Lake where *Sodom* flam'd;
> This more delusive, not the touch, but taste
> Deceiv'd; they fondly thinking to allay
> Thir appetite with gust, instead of Fruit
> Chew'd bitter Ashes, which th' offended taste
> With spattering noise rejected: oft they assay'd,
> Hunger and thirst constraining, drugg'd as oft,
> With hatefullest disrelish writh'd thir jaws
> With soot and cinders fill'd; so oft they fell
> Into the same illusion, not as Man
> Whom they triumph'd, once lapst.

X.547–572

This description is certainly not a crude allegory.[18] It is a typical Miltonic passage both in its mosaic of allusions and cross-references and in the powerful visual picture achieved by fusing hebraic and classical elements. It deserves closer attention. The "Grove sprung up with this thir change" is the mock counterpart of the Garden of Eden. The one forbidden tree turns here to a multitude of trees "to work them furder woe or shame". The tree of knowledge, like the sword discussed in chapter V, is here proliferated and its nature perverted. As Eve was waked by an "eager appetite" for the savory fruit, so the devils "fondly thinking to allay thir appetite with gust" plucked the fruits. Eve had eaten greedily and was satiate although she "knew not eating Death", whereas the serpents "Chew'd bitter Ashes". The perpetual torments of the damned are like those of Tantalus, but the "apples of the Tantalus myth are cross-grafted with those of the Dead Sea and tree of knowledge",[19] for the fruit itself is like that which grew "Near that bituminous Lake where *Sodom* flam'd" (X.562).[20] The perversion of values of the evil community of Sodom which is alluded to here enhances our sense of the fallen angels' moral evil: whereas the crime of Tantalus, in most legends, is that he steals the food of the gods and abuses the privileges which he had been granted, the people of Sodom have become an epitome of ungodliness and evil and the allusion to the bituminous lake also

---

[18] Waldock believes the technique of this scene "is exactly that of the comic cartoon". *Paradise Lost and Its Critics* (Cambridge, 1964 [1947]), p. 91. See also Hughes's annotation to X.545–572.

[19] See John M. Steadman's perceptive article, "Tantalus and the Dead Sea Apples", *JEGP*, LXIV (1965), pp. 35–40.

[20] Milton's description of that "bituminous Lake where *Sodom* flam'd" is in Hebrew tradition. Most commentators (see, for example, Todd on X.561) point out that Milton alludes to the Dead Sea passage as described by Flavius Josephus, but it is also possible that he borrowed the image directly from Genesis xiv. 10: "Now the Low Plain of Siddim was pits upon pits of bitumen." The fruit of ashes was most probably suggested to Milton by Josephus: "Adjacent to it is the land of Sodom now all burnt up ... Still too, may one see ashes reproduced in the fruits, which from their outward appearance would be thought edible, but on being plucked with the hand dissolve into smoke and ashes." *Wars*, IV, viii, 4. *Works*, trans. by William Whiston (London, 1845).

refers to the just punishment brought on them by God's messengers. Like Adam and Eve, the hospitable and righteous Lot and his family are saved, whereas the people of Sodom, like the fallen angels, are justly and irretrievably punished for their deeds.

There are many similar instances, but only a few will suffice to show Milton's method in fusing his sources effectively. One example of mixed allusions occurs when Satan, upon whose face "Deep scars of Thunder" (I.601) have left their mark, shines above the fallen angels like the sun darkened "In dim Eclipse disastrous" (I.597) and beholds the fellows of his crime. As Satan observes the fallen angels "faithful how they stood, / Thir Glory wither'd" (I.611–612), Milton likens them to a forest consumed by fire:

> As when Heaven's Fire
> Hath scath'd the Forest Oaks, or Mountain Pines,
> With singed top thir stately growth though bare
> Stands on the blasted Heath.
>
> I.611–615

Harding has indicated that "This is Virgil's 'dreadful consistory' – the Etnean brotherhood – adapted to the topography of Hell and the hopeless predicament of the Fallen Angels . . . In the *Aeneid*, the Cyclops are likened to trees which are alive and flourishing, not blasted and dying as are the forest oaks and mountain pines to which Milton compares the Fallen Angels."[21] If the simile of the forest was suggested to Milton by Virgil, it is also possible that the consuming fire, conceived as divine punishment, was suggested to him by the Old Testament. Thus Jeremiah predicts the punishment about to fall on the House of David: "And I will kindle a fire in the forest thereof, and it shall devour all things round about it" (Jeremiah xxi. 14). The Psalmist who prays that God may inflict punishment on the people's enemies uses the same simile: "As the fire burneth a wood, and as the flame setteth the mountains on fire" (Psalm lxxxiii. 14). And when Isaiah describes God's wrath, he describes it in the same terms: "For wickedness burneth as the fire: it shall devour the briers and thorns, and shall kindle in the

[21] *The Club of Hercules*, p. 62.

thickets of the forest and they shall mount up like the lifting up of smoke. Through the wrath of the Lord of hosts is the land darkened, and the people shall be as the fuel of the fire: no man shall spare his brother" (Isaiah ix. 18–19). The consuming fire as a punishment for God's enemies seems to be common to many ancient myths: we find it also in the thunder of Zeus as well as in the red right hand punishing Phaeton, but the heavenly fire in Milton's line is that of the hebraic Lord of Hosts.

Whereas the forest consumed by fire is a highly concrete simile fusing Virgilian and hebraic sources, there is, in Moloch's speech, another related simile, a hebraic one which leaves much more to the reader's imagination. Moloch advocates war and defies all consequences:

What fear we then? what doubt we to incense
His utmost ire? which to the highth enrag'd,
Will either quite consume us ...

II.94–96

The concept of the consuming ire of God is a vague but power-fully suggestive one. It releases many associations in the mind of the reader suggested by Biblical passages such as Exodus xxxii. 10: "Now therefore let me alone, that my wrath may wax hot against them, and that I may consume them"; or Isaiah xiii. 9: "Behold, the day of the Lord cometh, cruel both with wrath and with fierce anger, to lay the land desolate: and he shall destroy the sinners thereof out of it." Since the concept of burning and consuming ire is a recurrent one in the Old Testament, we may assume that it was the source of Milton's phrase. It is also one of the attributes of Milton's God.

Purely classical similes and allusions are strikingly absent from the books dealing with the heavenly host.[22] But significantly, classical similes fused with Old Testament allusions appear when-ever Satan is on the scene. When Satan, for instance, is about to resist Gabriel and his angels,

[22] See chapter IV.

> Th'Eternal to prevent such horrid fray
> Hung forth in Heav'n his golden Scales, yet seen
> Betwixt *Astrea* and the *Scorpion* sign,
> Wherein all things created first he weigh'd, . . .
>
> IV.996–999

The golden scales in battle are those of Homer in which were set two fateful portions of death (*Iliad*, VIII.69–70); they are also like Virgil's scales which Jupiter himself held aloft in the battle between Aeneas and Turnus (*Aeneid.* XII.725). Yet the concept of weighing the universe at creation appears too in the Old Testament.[23] Thus Isaiah conceives God at creation as weighing "the mountains in scales, and the hills in a balance" (Isaiah xl. 12). A related metaphor is used in Job xxviii. 25. The idea of a man's fate being weighed (like Satan's here) also appears in Job when he defends his integrity: "Let me be weighed in an even balance . . ." (xxxi. 6). Most relevant, however, for appreciating Gabriel's words to Satan,

> for proof look up,
> And read thy Lot in yon celestial Sign
> Where thou art weigh'd, and shown how light, how weak,
> If thou resist.
>
> IV.1010–13

are the words of Daniel to Belshazzar: "Thou art weighed in the balances, and art found wanting" (Daniel v. 27), for like that other vessel of God's wrath, Nebuchadnezzar, Satan has to acknowledge his defeat and has to recognize the powerful providence of the Creator.[24]

These and many other images drawn now from hebraic, now from classical sources, make hell with its frightful burning lake and its splendid Pandaemonium come alive. However, all this brilliant scenery serves only as setting for Milton's masterwork –

---

[23] Newton notes these allusions on IV.999.
[24] Unlike the present author, Harding, while admitting that "No reader could fail to catch the echo of the Book of Daniel and to perceive its significance in this place", nevertheless believes the Virgilian influence is paramount here (*The Club of Hercules*, p. 48).

the figures of the fallen angels. Whether describing it metaphorically or in concrete terms, Milton never allows his hell to obscure
its impressive tenants. For it is always the fallen angels, whether
they are like "scatter'd sedge / Afloat" (I.304–305) or like "great
Seraphic Lords and Cherubim" (I.794), who endow the opening
books of *Paradise Lost* with their majesty and power. And to them
we turn next.

2. THE FALLEN ANGELS

Hebraic as Milton's hell is, influenced as it is by the Old Testament
and its geography, it owes its structure, as we have seen, to the
classics rather than the Bible. Not so his fallen angels. If the concept of Satan as the head of the host of evil spirits does not yet
appear in the Old Testament[25] and if Milton found no story on the
fall of angels in the Old Testament narrative, he found in the poetry
of the prophets of Israel an impassioned condemnation of idolatry
and its immoral practices and scathing sarcasm directed against
a host of idols amongst which Baal, Moloch, and Astarte are the
most prominent. By using names, allusions, and references to the
poetry of the Old Testament prophets, Milton peoples his hell
with magnificent pagan deities that bear less resemblance to the
classical figures of epic tradition than we would have expected
from the humanist poet who was their creator. Though generally
acknowledged by Milton critics, this fact deserves more attention
than it has been given so far: a closer scrutiny of the literary function of hebraic elements would make not only for a sounder
understanding of the fallen angels but also for a deeper insight into
Milton's hell.

What I attempt to show here is that the hebraic allusions and
references with which the descriptions of the fallen angels abound

---

[25] Only in Job is he personalized as one of the Sons of God and in Zechariah 3 and
Psalm 9 as a roving secret agent who persecutes his victims. On the origin of the
concept of Satan in the Old Testament see, among many others: N.H. Tur-Sinai (H.
Torczyner), *The Book of Job. A New Commentary* (Jerusalem, 1957) (Hebrew), pp.
38–45; also Marvin H. Pope, *The Anchor Bible. Job* (Garden City, 1965), pp. 10–11.

contribute to Milton's dual vision of Satan and his compeers and
to his ironic presentation of the devils on the dramatic as well as
on the verbal plane. There is no discrepancy between Milton's
conscious and unconscious intentions, for while the fallen angels
are most impressive, their morality is consistently impugned by
the poet. The devils cut splendid figures – heroic in defeat, sublime
in courage – but their Hebrew names, the hebraic references and
allusions through which they are described give them away; for
through their names the poet condemns them both as characters
and as symbols.

Foremost among these is Satan. A great part of the criticism of
Paradise Lost has concerned itself with Satan and his role in the
poem. In the eighteenth century, critics, for the most part, praised
Milton for persuasively conveying his moral and took no offence at
his creation of a convincing and attractive devil. Johnson's comments in his *Life of Milton* are typical: "To make Satan speak as a
rebel, without any such expressions as might taint the reader's
imagination, was indeed one of the great difficulties in Milton's
undertaking, and I cannot but think that he has extricated himself
with great happiness. There is in Satan's speeches little that can
give pain to a pious ear."[26] Romantic critics, however, wrote about
Satan in a spirit of high praise, identifying his impiety and rebellion
with the character of his creator. By now, the issue is dead. But
whether one is 'Satanist' or 'anti-Satanist', one cannot help
admiring the brilliance, the vitality, and the fierce courage that
capture the imagination of all readers of Books I and II. One of
the most heroic characters of the English epic, Satan is an anti-
Christ clad in the armor of a classical warrior. But the matter
can easily be oversimplified for he is more than a conventional
hero in whom pagan and Christian elements are fused. Although
outwardly Promethean and heroic, Satan is primarily a Biblical
figure. This should not destroy the unity of the poem. There is no
reason why our moral objection to Satan and his psychological
attraction for us cannot live side by side. Milton actually created
a Devil large enough to embrace all evil: he is as brilliant and

[26] *Johnson's Lives of the Poets, Milton*, ed. K. Deighton (London, 1900), p. 59.

reckless as Phaeton, as abominable as Jehovah's enemies in the
Old Testament, as subtle as the serpent, as cruel as a vulture, as
ludicrous as the mediaeval devil, and as tragic as any human being
suffering from a "sense of injur'd merit", "Vaunting aloud, but
rackt with deep despair" (I.126). If Satan speaks the eloquent
language and uses the deceiving rhetoric of Milton's contemporaries, this only adds to the vividness and humanity of the majestic
portrait; it does not detract from the universality of the character.
Milton's fusion of these various elements in the creation of Satan is
what makes him a mythical figure since such figures, by definition,
are supernatural beings endowed with our own humanity.

   Throughout *Paradise Lost* Satan is associated with various
hebraic figures and events, some of them giving him the stature
of a powerful primeval monster, others degrading and belittling
him morally. At times, this degradation of the "hero" is achieved
through a single allusion; at times it is attained through repeated
metaphors identifying Satan with the defeated enemies of the
Old Testament God. One of the single allusions appears in Book
IV:

   So entertain'd those odorous sweets the Fiend
   Who came thir bane, though with them better pleas'd
   Than *Asmodeus* with the fishy fume,
                                         IV.166–168

The proleptic allusion comparing Satan to the Asmodeus of the
Book of Tobit affords a theme for irony, since Satan, though
pleased for the moment, will ultimately suffer an identical fate.
If the allusion compels us to compare the two figures, the comparison is not flattering to Satan, whose stature is here reduced to
that of a fleeing demon.

   Another hebraic allusion ironically pointing at the essence of
Satan's being is the Leviathan simile. When in I.200–220 Milton
compares the fallen Archangel to Leviathan, he clearly associates
Leviathan with the sea-beasts "whom the Fables name of monstrous size, / *Titanian*, or *Earth-born*, that warr'd on Jove" (I.197–
198). Yet Milton does not dwell at length on Hesiod's account
of Briareos for he believed, like other Christian humanists, that

the fables of classical mythology embodied only confused re-
collections of the truths found in the Bible. He prefers to compare
Satan with

> that Sea-beast
> *Leviathan*, which God of all his works
> Created hugest that swim th'Ocean stream:
>   I.200–202

and he has good reason to do so, for Leviathan is one of the names
of the primeval dragon subdued by Yahweh at the dawn of creation.[27] He is also the prince of the sea and the depths who reigned
over Sheol and wakened the other king-heroes that they might
assist him in his war against the God of Heaven and light.[28] Pope
describes the sea-dragon in detail, but only a few of its characteristics are pertinent here. He points out that the sea-serpent mentioned in Amos ix. 3 may refer to the same monster, that the
Hebrew "nahash" applied to Leviathan establishes with certitude
the serpentine character of the monster, and that Psalm civ. 26
has suggested to some interpreters that Leviathan is the whale.[29]
Such analogies might carry us far beyond the meaning of the text,
if we did not feel that Milton could have guessed most of this
when he read, with his poet's eye, the texts of the Old Testament
in Hebrew, and it is possible that his reading suggested to him
many characteristics which he attributed to his fallen angel. Thus
he knew, for example, that if the sea-monster was a whale in some
sources, he resembled a crocodile in others, and he describes him
as having a "scaly rind".

The many heads of the serpent Typhon were also for Milton
a shadowy recollection of the monster mentioned in Psalm lxxiv.
14: "Thou brakest the heads of leviathan in pieces." Isaiah xxvii.
1 too assigns to God the honor of slaying Leviathan: "In that day

---

[27] The name means the "coiled one, from לוה ; Arab. l-w-y, coil, wind". See
IDB, III, p. 116.
[28] Tur-Sinai, *Job*, p. 57, on Job iii. 8.
[29] M. H. Pope points out that his marine monster is called *Lotan* in the Ugaritic
myths (where Baal is given the credit for having subdued Lotan) and that there
were probably several versions of the major motifs of the myths and considerable freedom in their use; he cites two Ugaritic passages containing words and
phrases almost verbatim with Isaiah xxvii. 1 (*Job*, pp. 276–277).

the Lord with his sore and great and strong sword shall punish
leviathan the piercing serpent, even leviathan that crooked serpent; and he shall slay the dragon that is in the sea." Job xli. 1 as
well as iii. 8 allude to a similar marine monster.[30] The dragon is
mentioned apart from leviathan[31] in Ezekiel xxix. 3, xxxii. 2, where
it is applied metaphorically to Pharaoh, and this might have
been what led Milton to write that other beautiful simile about
Satan's crew and the *"Memphian* Chivalry". Biblical overtones
again come to the fore when Satan, in Book XII, is identified once
more with the Egyptian Pharaoh:

> Thus with ten wounds
> The River-dragon tam'd at length submits
> To let his sojourners depart.
> XII.190–192

Similarly, from Job xl, xli, Milton could have remembered Leviathan as "the prince of the sea" who was the first servant of the
Creator, built in the shape of a giant snake, who rebelled against
God. Allusions to Job serve another purpose, too. Throughout the
book, Job questions God's justice and refuses to resign himself to
his fate, to accept a God who punishes the righteous and lets the
wicked prosper. Job hardly expects God to answer his challenge
but when he gets an answer, it does not give him satisfaction nor
does it solve the problem of divine justice. God can explain himself to Job no more than He can explain himself to us. His answer
can only be in terms of His creation. Man's impotence, his
ignorance, and his need for faith are thrown into relief against
God's omnipotence and infinite knowledge so powerfully expressed in the description of Leviathan (Job xli).

At this point it is necessary to note that Milton chose to give

---

[30] For an excellent discussion of the Leviathan simile and its framework of allusion to Egypt and to the matter of Exodus, see Harold Fisch, "Hebraic Style
and Motifs in *Paradise Lost*", pp. 44–48.

It is also perhaps not irrelevant that Hobbes invests the name of the Biblical
sea-monster with political implications. On this subject see John Steadman,
"Leviathan and Renaissance Etymology", *J H I*, XXVIII (1967), pp. 575–576.

[31] In Apocalyptic literature (II Esdras, vi. 52; II Bar., xxix. 3–8) Leviathan is represented as destined to break loose from its bonds at the end of the present
era only to suffer a second and final defeat. See *IDB*, III, p. 116, footnote 18.

the first description of Satan's appearance (of which the leviathan simile is part), immediately after Satan's eloquent declaration,

> To do aught good never will be our task,
> But ever to do ill our sole delight,
> As being the contrary to his high will
> Whom we resist.
>
> I.159–162

Satan's assumption here is that he is the master of his own fate and that he can pervert God's ends. When, in the following description, Milton reminds us that Satan resembles "that Sea-beast / Leviathan, which God of all his works / Created hugest that swim th' Ocean stream" (199–202), he has two specific purposes in mind. Through the Biblical associations evoked by the leviathan simile, he ironically foreshadows the inevitable outcome of Satan's designs against God's Providence, and he already prepares us for his ultimate defeat. Also, by associating Satan with Leviathan, Milton returns to one of the main themes of the epic, the greatness and goodness of God the Creator and the sinfulness as well as the futility of such attempts "to grieve" Him and "disturb / His inmost counsels" (I.167–168). The inclusion of this simile into the composite image of the monstrous Typhon enhances the moral meaning of the description, revealing the poet's ironic vision of Satan. When, a few lines later, we find the Arch-fiend, huge in length,

> Chain'd on the burning Lake, nor ever thence
> Had ris'n or heav'd his head, but that the will
> And high permission of all-ruling Heaven
> Left him at large to his own dark designs,
> That with reiterated crimes he might
> Heap on himself damnation, while he sought
> Evil to others, and enrag'd might see
> How all his malice serv'd but to bring forth
> Infinite goodness,
>
> I.210–218

the words echo the book of Job again, for there too Satan plays the role of a prosecutor with a case against God himself – this, paradoxically, being part of God's design to test man. As soon as Satan speaks again (I.242ff.) we are carried away by his fierce temperament, his courage in defeat, and his proud pursuit of power. Although he is an evil character, his words capture the imagination, and Milton's ironic vision of him soon vanishes. In the first two books of the poem, the sense of God's omnipotence, of the goodness of his creation, is at times even dispelled by the various conflicts engendered by evil, by the sense of exaltation Satan's words convey. Yet, though we may forget the poet's warning comments on Satan (I.211–218), the leviathan simile, coming as it were between the lines, a momentary allusion, has left us with the perennial knowledge of God's omnipotence, of the ultimate goodness of his Creation outweighing the evil of this world. This vision of God, based upon the hebraic conception of God who "created the heaven and the earth" (Genesis i. 1), does not solve the problem of evil in the world or "justify" it in the narrow sense of the word, but it minimizes its significance, for the powerfully destructive Leviathan is only "that Sea-beast / . . . which God of all his works / Created hugest that swim th' Ocean stream."

Milton's hebraic allusions are not always so open. He meant to write a Christian epic, and it is natural that images and topoi derived from the New Testament and Christian literature are found throughout the poem. Yet at times Milton introduces striking Old Testament echoes and phrases into metaphors that seem purely Christian. It could be argued that this is part of Milton's Christianizing inclination and that he is merely indicating the parallels between the New Testament and the Old. But he is doing much more than this. He is deliberately echoing Old Testament words and phrases because of their richness, their post-figurative allusiveness which provides valuable insights into his descriptions. The following example will illustrate the point.

"Darkness visible" or invisible is shared by all the fallen angels; we enter the realm of light as we leave hell and its inhabitants. Light and darkness images are recurrent throughout the epic[32]

---

[32] These images pervade many of Milton's poems. See, for example, Rosemond Tuve's discussion of the symbol of light in *The Hymn on the Morning of Christ's Nativity* in: *Images and Themes in Five Poems by Milton* (Cambridge, Mass., 1962 [1957]), pp. 46–47).

and are both symbolic and concrete. Wherever he goes, Satan carries the darkness of hell within him and when "he fled / Murmuring" (IV.1014–15) from Eden, "with him fled the shades of night" (IV.1015). Satan's appearance and fall as an angel of light is part of this pattern of images in *Paradise Lost* and is one of the sustained images describing him. While the light and darkness imagery cannot be called either classical, Christian or hebraic, Milton's allusive use of the figure of falling light echoes not only the words and phrases of Isaiah xiv but calls up an old myth which Isaiah elusively hints at to portray the fall of the King of Babylon. Milton had the authority of the New Testament for associating Satan with falling light: "I beheld Satan as lightning fall from the sky" (Luke x. 18), or "Satan himself is transformed into an angel of light" (II Corinthians xi. 14). This metaphor also appears in Apocryphal literature, as in I. Enoch lxxxvi, which mentions a star falling from Heaven to earth. This image of falling light and brightness is one of the clues to understanding Satan, for there are numerous cross-references to the same image in *Paradise Lost*. When Lucifer first starts the rebellion in Heaven, his followers are called "Sons of Morn" (V.716). Lucifer was then still very influential:

> for great indeed
> His name, and high his degree in Heav'n;
> His count'nance, as the Morning Star that guides
> The starry flock, allur'd them, and with lies
> Drew after him the third part of Heav'n's Host:
> V.706–710

Satan's fall too is described in terms of falling light:

> Him the Almighty Power
> Hurl'd headlong flaming from th'Ethereal Sky
> With hideous ruin and combustion down
> To bottomless perdition.
> I.44–47

When Satan is confronted with Death, he

> like a Comet burn'd,
> That fires the length of *Ophiucus* huge
> In th' Artic Sky.
>   II.708–710[33]

And when God sends his Son to chastise Adam and Eve, Milton interpolates:

> So spake this Oracle, then verifi'd
> When *Jesus* son of *Mary*, second *Eve*,
> Saw Satan fall like Lightning down from Heav'n,
>   X.182–184

These passages allude to the myth of the fall of Heilel ben Shahar of Isaiah xiv. What is this myth about and what is its function in *Paradise Lost*?

The myth is that of fallen and vanquished gods. Variants of it appear in Isaiah xiv, Psalm lxxxii, and are frequently mentioned in other books.[34] It is an early myth, certainly earlier than the Rabbinic tradition which casts Satan out of Heaven on the sixth day of creation because he refused to do homage to man. The earlier myth, alluded to also in II Enoch xviii and xix, represents the rebel angel as being of highest rank, a prince, and a leader of an entire troop of angels. It tells of Satan's attempt to supplant God, the Lord of Light, as the ruler of the universe. It is obviously to this version of the myth that the New Testament refers in Luke x. 18, II Cor. xi. 14, Rev. xii. 7–9, Rev. xx. 1–7. In later literature, the two myths were fused into one, giving a two-fold motivation for the expulsion of Satan from Heaven. In addition, the myth of the Sons of God who descended to earth to consort with mortal women was later confused with the older myth telling about the

---

[33] On the comet simile and the influence of the supernova appearance on Milton's description see William B. Hunter, Jr., "Satan as Comet: *Paradise Lost* II.708–711" in *ELN*, V (1967), pp. 17–21.

[34] See a) Julian Morgenstern, "The Mythological Background of Psalm 82", *HUCA*, XIV (Cincinnati, 1939), pp. 29–126.; b) Marvin H. Pope, *El in the Ugaritic Texts* (Leiden, 1955); c) John L. McKenzie, "Mythological Allusions in Ezek. xxviii. 12–18", *JBL*, LXXV (1956), pp. 322–327. McKenzie questions Pope's theory that the same myth is reflected in Ezekiel xxviii.

rebellion of the angelic beings before creation.[35] Milton attributes
to Satan the pride of the angel who refuses to humble himself
before a mortal. He was also familiar with the myth of the fallen
Sons of God and with the reason for their fall, as appears in Book
V, when the poet observes of Eve ministering at table:

> O innocence
> Deserving Paradise! if ever, then,
> Then had the Sons of God excuse to have been
> Enamour'd at that sight; but in those hearts
> Love unlibidinous reign'd.
>
> V.445–449

The older myth of Heilel ben Shahar and his followers, however,
is clearly the story of their actual rebellion against the deity, and
Satan's attempt to set his throne above the throne of the Highest
and thus supplant Him as the ruler of the universe. The Vulgate
renders Heilel ben Shahar Lucifer and subsequent tradition has
identified Lucifer with Satan. All this evidence establishes that the
myth found in New Testament writings is identical with the myth
of Isaiah xiv. But this identification of Satan with Heilel ben
Shahar took place only after the period of the Chronicler – that
is, some time during the third century B.C. and more probably
during the second rather than during the first half of the century.[36]

The allusions to this myth must have appealed to Milton both for
their poetic suggestiveness and because they portrayed a radiant
angel, a superior divine being which proved "dramatically satisfy-
ing", for Milton wanted to create "at least the illusion of equality
between the two mighty opposites in his poem".[37] In addition, it
is also possible that Milton might have seen a connection between
the myth of Heilel ben Shahar and his followers with the Greek
myth of the Titans who stormed Olympus and sought to over-
throw the gods.[38] Furthermore, the metaphor of the fallen star was
also associated in Milton's mind with another bright rebel son
hurled from Heaven – Phaeton, for

[35] "The Mythological Background of Psalm 82", p. 98ff.
[36] *Ibid.*, p. 110.
[37] Harding, *The Club of Hercules*, p. 40.
[38] "The Mythological Background of Psalm 82", p. 112, note 153.

High in the midst exalted as a God
Th' Apostate in his Sunbright Chariot sat
Idol of Majesty Divine . . .

VI.99–101

Thus Satan led his troops to fight the faithful angels. Many commentators, including Jewish ones, interpret Heilel ben Shahar as the planet Venus – the last proud star to defy sunrise[39] – and when Milton describes Satan's rebellion in Book V.708–710, he uses the same image. After his fall, Lucifer, of course, ceases to be the bright day star; he is no longer the bright archangel, and his name as well as his nature changes with his fall:

Satan, so call him now, his former name
Is heard no more in Heav'n; he of the first,
If not the first Arch-Angel, great in Power,
In favor and preëminence, yet fraught
With envy against the Son of God, that day
Honor'd by his great Father, and proclaim'd
Messiah King anointed, could not bear
Through pride that sight, and thought himself impair'd.

V.658–665

Now it is true that this figure of Satan described in terms of falling light, though taking its origin in Old Testament texts, was adopted by the New Testament and by subsequent Christian literature and may be regarded as a Christian figure. Yet there are hebraic overtones in the manner in which it is apprehended and used by Milton for Satan here re-enacts or 'postfigures' the archetypal figure of the King of Babylon thereby giving it a new significance.[40] Whereas in the New Testament Satan appears as a powerful figure and his fall is treated as an event of great moment,

---

[39] Heilel ben Shahar is interpreted as the brightest morning star by Rashi (see chapter II, p. 26, note 4), Rabbi David Kimchi (known by his initials: *Radak*), Metsudat Tsion, and Metsudat David.

[40] It has already been pointed out that the Reformation and the Protestant concern with the Covenant tradition brought about a withdrawal from prefigurative exegesis and a concern with Old Testament characters as creatures of flesh and blood whose lives the Protestants felt they were re-enacting or "postfiguring" See Murray Roston, *Biblical Drama in England* (London, 1968), pp. 70–71.

the Old Testament prophet belittles the great king of Babylon, ridicules his proud aspirations, and mockingly prophesies: "Thy pomp is brought down to the grave, and the noise of thy viols: the worm is spread under thee, and the worms cover thee" (Isaiah xiv. 11). Isaiah believes that such is God's purpose, for "The Lord of hosts hath sworn, saying, surely as I have thought, so shall it come to pass; and as I have purposed, so shall it stand" (xiv. 24). The tone of the Hebrew prophet towards this king who came to be associated with Satan in Christian tradition is openly sarcastic. He ridicules the ambitions of the king who said in his heart, "I will ascend to heaven, I will exalt my throne above the stars of God: ..." (xiv. 13). By referring to this powerfully suggestive chapter, Milton emphasizes the concept of God as the ruling force of the world, thereby deliberately stressing Satan's limitations and shedding an ironic light on Satan's greatness. There can be little doubt that such was Milton's intention if we consider the following words of Satan to Beelzebub in Book I:

> If thou beest hee; But O how fall'n! how chang'd
> From him, who in the happy Realms of Light
> Cloth'd with transcendent brightness didst outshine
> Myriads though bright:
>
> I.84–87

These lines recall not merely what Aeneas says when he is faced with the vision of Hector's ghost (*Aeneid* II.275–276), but they are also reminiscent of Isaiah xiv. 12:[41] "How art thou fallen from Heaven, O Lucifer, son of the morning, how art thou cut to the ground, which didst weaken the nations!" As has already been indicated, as in other passages, Milton's fusion of the hebraic and the classic has a more than double potency.[42] Here, however, the irony of the allusion does not spring from the fusion of Isaiah and Virgil; it is rather derived from the dramatic situation for Milton puts in Satan's mouth the very words which are directed against the King of Babylon by Isaiah. The irony is also derived from the

---

[41] Most commentators noted only the reference to Virgil. Newton, in his 2 vols. edition of *Paradise Lost* (London, 1749), mentioned both.
[42] Douglas Bush, "Ironic and Ambiguous Allusion in *Paradise Lost*", *JEGP*, LX (1961), p. 633.

very verses of Isaiah xiv to which Milton obviously refers here – that is the function of this hebraic reference, for it infuses further meaning into the Christian figure of falling light. Such references are an integral part of Milton's whole design, for his treatment of Satan throughout the poem is pervaded with irony, dramatic as well as metaphorical, and hebraic allusions contribute not insignificantly to this treatment.

This is also true of the other fallen angels for all the characters of Milton's hell are associated with the pagan deities of the Old Testament; Milton calls on the Old Testament time and again to indicate the moral quality of hell and to counterbalance the magic of the alluring pagan figures and myths. These hebraic allusions project the immoral universe of the devils against the ethical justice and righteousness of God. It is through them that Milton creates irony because while the sentiments the fallen angels utter are outwardly noble and their appearance often deceptively attractive, their Hebrew names and the hebraic figures they are associated with indicate what their moral values really are.

For a true appreciation of the modes of irony in the books on hell, Milton's hebraic allusions have to be understood in their proper medium. The moral values that are assessed throughout the Old Testament are the assertion of God's justice, his supremacy over the heathen deities – or, in other words, the assertion of the supremacy of good over the temptations of evil. The gods of Canaan, Egypt, Syria and Babylon are consistently represented as examples of corruption and debauchery by judges, prophets, and priests; the chosen people are continually warned to resist their temptations. These values are obvious to any reader of the Old Testament. But their source, namely the Covenant between God and Israel, is all too often overlooked. This Covenant, the historic bond between God and Israel, may be said to be the 'indicative' of Israel's life.[43] It is therefore in the context of Old Testament faith

[43] See Edwin M. Good, *Irony in the Old Testament* (Philadelphia, 1965), especially pp. 241–247. The intention here is not to survey the various kinds of irony in the Old Testament but to indicate in what way Old Testament thought may have influenced Milton's ironic vision of hell and its inhabitants. For an examination of the Covenant between God and Israel and its role within the general framework of the 'corpus of law', see also Helen Silving, "Jurisprudence in the Old Testament", *New York University Law Review* XXVIII (1953), pp. 1129ff.

that the irony gains meaning, for implicit in Old Testament faith is a view of human life as it is lived projected against a vision of life as it ought to be lived.

This context of thought is the reason for the basic difference between Milton's hebraic poetic borrowings and the materials he culls from classical literature. There are other differences as well: first, classical myths are seen by Milton as shadowy versions of historical (*i.e.* Biblical) truths and, secondly, Milton consciously presents a new ideal – "Not less but more Heroic" (IX.14) – than Homer's ideal of individual glory or the ideal of Roman political virtue as set forth by Virgil in the *Aeneid*.[44] It is true that Odysseus and Aeneas were regarded as ideal heroes during the Renaissance, but by associating Satan and other fallen angels not only with enemies of these heroes – Turnus for example – but even with Aeneas himself,[45] Milton pits his new heroic ideal of faith against that of the classical epics which he, thereby, rejects. Moreover, as soon as Milton refers to Biblical passages, he drives home his message, for the ideal human type presented in the Old Testament is also the one Milton had in mind, namely, a "humble" hero whose sole strength lies in his faith in God, who knows that all God requires of him is "to do justly, and to love mercy, and to walk humbly with thy God" (Micah vi. 8); a man who like Moses, is "very meek, above all the men which were upon the face of the earth" (Numbers xii. 3). Although Adam was created in the image of God (Genesis i. 26), was made "a little lower than the angels", and "crowned with glory and honour" (Psalm viii. 5),[46] he must remember he is mortal "for dust thou art, and unto dust shalt thou return" (Genesis iii. 19). Therefore Milton invokes the heavenly muse

> that on the secret top
> Of *Oreb*, or of *Sinai*, didst inspire

---

[44] See C. M. Bowra, *From Virgil to Milton* (New York, 1965 [1945] and *The Club of Hercules*, pp. 24–39.

[45] Milton's description of Satan in terms associating him with Turnus is analyzed by Harding in *The Club of Hercules*, pp. 45–46 and passim. Harding also compares *Aeneid* I. 208–209 with *Paradise Lost* I.125–126. (*The Club of Hercules*, p. 37).

[46] Psalm viii. 6 in the Hebrew canon.

That shepherd, who first taught the chosen Seed,
In the Beginning how the Heav'ns and Earth
Rose out of *Chaos*:

> I.6–10

His song intends, indeed, to soar "Above th'*Aonian* Mount". But the main reason that may have inspired Milton to turn to the Old Testament in his descriptions of the fallen angels is the style of the Old Testament prophets who bitterly denounce both idols and idol worshipers and provide the simple and powerful language through which Milton ironically projects the false heroism of the fallen angels.

Let us begin with the description of the fallen angels as they appear "intrans't" on the burning lake:

Thick as Autumnal Leaves that strow the Brooks
In *Vallombrosa*, where th'*Etrurian* shades
High overarch't imbow'r; or scatter'd sedge
Afloat, when with fierce Winds *Orion* arm'd
Hath vext the Red-Sea Coast, whose waves o'erthrew
Busiris and his *Memphian* Chivalry,
While with perfidious hatred they pursu'd
The Sojourners of *Goshen* who beheld
From the safe shore thir floating Carcasses
And broken Chariot Wheels;

> I.301–311

In this complex simile, images from various sources are woven together, some pagan some Biblical. The "Autumnal Leaves" are reminiscent of Homer, Virgil, Tasso, and Dante, while the "scatter'd sedge" is that of the Red Sea which saw the destruction of Pharaoh's army in pursuit of the children of Israel. For Milton, the "autumnal leaves that strow the brooks in Vallombrosa" certainly stand for the beautiful even if that beauty is about to decay and die, and we can feel how splendid Busiris and his Memphian chivalry are. Then, suddenly, we are shocked into an awareness of what really is behind the beauty of the Etrurian shade–perfidious hatred. Busiris and his Memphian chivalry, like the autumnal leaves, thus qualify the fallen angels, brilliant in their decadence but soon to lose that brilliance. Only now can we see how the image of the floating wreckage grows out of the beautiful leaves and the sedge, and it finally comes very appropriately, identifying Satan's followers with another "perfidious" crew that defied God and perished. We can feel Milton's tone hardening in the alliteration of *k* and *r* sounds: "carcasses, broken Chariot wheels," especially because it stands in contrast to the Italian music of "Vallombrosa."[47]

A few lines later the fallen angels, roused by Satan's words, are compared to a cloud of locusts. Milton's simile illustrates their rising to Satan's call in the movement from the lifeless autumnal leaves and the carcasses and broken chariot wheels to the animated locusts:

> As when the potent Rod
> Of *Amram's* Son in *Egypt's* evil day
> Wav'd round the Coast, up call'd a pitchy cloud
> Of *Locusts*, warping on the Eastern Wind,
> That o'er the Realm of impious *Pharaoh* hung
> Like Night, and darken'd all the Land of *Nile*:
>
> I.338–343

The Biblical simile is appropriate because like the locusts, the bad angels are numberless and also bring darkness and destruction.

---

[47] Whaler ("The Miltonic Simile", *PMLA*, XLVI [1931], pp. 1034–74) has pointed out the patristic identification of Pharaoh and Satan, and Steadman ("The Devil and Pharaoh's Chivalry", *MLN*, LXXV [1960], pp. 197–201) has shown that the comparisons of the Red Sea to the fiery lake of hell and the destruction of the Egyptian army to the punishment of the rebel angels are also rooted in Christian exegetical tradition. He suggests that Milton's simile might be influenced by the commentaries of St. Jerome and Herveus on Isaiah xxxiv and also points out that Cowley anticipated Milton in describing Isaiah's leaves as autumnal in his "Pindarique Ode on the 34 Chapter of the Prophet Isaiah". Steadman believes that although "Milton's allusion to 'the Brooks in *Vallombrosa*' may indeed represent a 'memory of the Italian forests in autumn,' its chief value probably resides in its etymology."

Much has been written on the matter of Exodus and the function of the Exodus myth in *Paradise Lost*. The most valuable recent articles on the subject are: Harold Fisch, "Hebraic Style and Motifs in *Paradise Lost*", John T. Shawcross, "*Paradise Lost* and the Theme of Exodus", *Milton Studies II* (Pittsburgh, 1970), pp. 3–26; J. M. Steadman, "'Memphian Chivalry': Milton's Busiris, Etymology and Chronography".

Furthermore, they are associated with the story of 'impious *Pharaoh*" who proudly opposed God. Thus the three hebraic similes – the scattered sedge, the Memphian chivalry, and the cloud of locusts – are thematically linked. The scatter'd sedge, like the autumnal leaves, still has its beauty and glory; the Memphian chivalry and the locusts both represent an imminent peril to humanity. At the same time, however, we remember that the locusts were part of God's punishment of Pharaoh by means of Moses so that the stature of the bad angels is reduced for they are compared to creatures that bring destruction but have no more will or power of their own than insects. They are thereby associated with Satan who acts with the "high permission of all-ruling Heaven" (I.212).

Another instance of Milton's use of hebraic allusions operating ironically is also from Book I:

> With these in troop
> Came *Astoreth*, whom the *Phoenicians* call'd
> *Astarte*, Queen of Heav'n, with crescent Horns;
> To whose bright Image nightly by the Moon
> *Sidonian* Virgins paid thir Vows and Songs,
> In *Sion* also not unsung, where stood
> Her Temple on th'offensive Mountain, built
> By that uxorious King, whose heart though large,
> Beguil'd by fair Idolatresses, fell
> To Idols foul. *Thammuz* came next behind,
> Whose annual wound in *Lebanon* allur'd
> The *Syrian* Damsels to lament his fate
> In amorous ditties all a Summer's day,
> While smooth *Adonis* from his native Rock
> Ran purple to the Sea,[48] suppos'd with blood

[48] Marvin Pope called my attention to lines 450–452 which bring to mind the ancient river of Adonis – Nahr Ibrahim, today in Lebanon – on whose banks the Thammuz-Adonis rituals took place. In late antiquity, the site was famous for the shrine of Astarte-Aphrodite-Venus. According to legend, this was the scene of the embrace of Adonis and Aphrodite. The river, indeed, has its source amongst towering rocks and it runs rapidly into a deep gorge. See Pope, *El in the Ugaritic Texts*, pp. 75–81.

Of *Thammuz* yearly wounded: the Love-tale
Infected *Sion's* daughters with like heat,
Whose wanton passions in the sacred Porch
Ezekiel saw, when by the Vision led
His eye survey'd the dark Idolatries
Of alienated *Judah*.

I.437–457

In imagery and tone these lines form an artistic whole. They describe two fallen spirits: the first is Astoreth who, as Milton sarcastically implies, was called "Queen of Heaven" by the Phoenicians; in reality she is Queen of Hell. As a symbol of perverted fertility, she stands for lustful pleasures, and it is fit that the Sidonian virgins should pay their vows to this goddess at night when the outlet of man's "wanton passions" is shrouded in secrecy. The vows coming from the lascivious "Sidonian virgins", are a perversion of the solemn and religiously binding promises made when people dedicate themselves to one another or to God; the service the Sidonian women enter is clearly debauched. Such "dark idolatries" can only be practiced "nightly by the Moon". The moral blackness of the scene is illuminated by Astarte's "bright image", an image which has little in common with "Heav'n's purest light" (II.137) and which is not merely contrasted with the gloomy darkness of hell; it functions ironically and emphasizes the world of darkness which is hell. Furthermore, Astarte as worshiped by the "Sidonian virgins" is not real: they worship her bright appearance, her "image". So far, the satirical irony of lines 437–441 conveys an unequivocal meaning. But the lines also have another function which is revealed through the reference to Solomon as "that uxorious King, whose heart though large, / Beguil'd by fair Idolatresses, fell / to Idols foul" (lines 444–446). "Largeness of heart" is the Hebrew metaphor for wisdom,[49] and this phrase, which derives from I Kings iv. 29,[50] is used ironically here. The allusion to Solomon reveals the function of

---

[49] The same metaphor is used, ironically again, by Satan when he flatters Jesus, *Paradise Regained* III. 9.
[50] I Kings v. 9 in the Hebrew canon of the Old Testament.

the whole passage, which is to illustrate the connection between uxoriousness, idolatry, and the fall of man. Solomon was unable to resist the temptations of women, and his uxoriousness led to his worshiping "Idols foul". Subsequently, Astarte was "In *Sion* also not unsung", and her temple was erected on "th'offensive Mountain". The power of the passage lies in the implied comparison between the humble Solomon praying to God for wisdom and the fallen king "beguil'd by fair Idolatresses", a king who, in a way, foreshadows Adam though the latter was "not deceiv'd,/ But fondly overcome with Female charm." The lines describing Astarte have thus for their real subject the experience of the fall.

Lines 446–457 describe another fallen spirit, Thammuz-Adonis. The seasonal nature of his cult reflects the changeability, the unsteadiness of human nature. The light "*Syrian* Damsels" are "allured" by the gory wound which clearly has an erotic influence on them, for they proceed to lament his fate in "amorous ditties". They do not, like Dagon, mourn "in earnest" (I.458), and their gay and sensual laments do not last longer than a "Summer's day". The river is not really purple with the god's blood, implies the poet, but it has a hypnotizing effect on the Damsels (I.447). Milton's sarcastic view of this cult is further revealed by the use of the verb *infected* in I.453. To the Christian poet idolatry is a disease. But he carries the point further: such pagan worship is felt to have brought about the fall not only of men but of nations as well. To the Biblical poet-prophet of the Babylonian exile, Judah's alienation from God is the natural outcome of the "dark idolatries" of God's people. Ezekiel's scorn of the idolatrous "women weeping for Tammuz"[51] is based on the conception of history that regards the exile as the punishment for Judah's sins. To Milton, Ezekiel, who fought incessantly against idolatry and reproved the wayward daughters of Sion, is the symbol of holiness, justice, and righteousness, and the poet's conviction here is clearly that of the Hebrew prophet.[52] The harshness of the hebraic vision

---

[51] Ezekiel viii. 14. This verse is the only place in the Old Testament where Thammuz is mentioned.
[52] It is interesting to note that Rosemund Tuve, examining *The Hymn on the Morning of Christ's Nativity*, finds that Milton does not condemn pagan myths

expressed in the last lines is that of a poet who not only believes in an abstract hebraic God but also envisions Him as a hard task-master. This vision is antipodal to the vision originating in the world of pagan mythology. It is not that Milton condemns nature but that the myth is an example of a nature cult for its own sake and resulting in wanton passions. The next lines (457–466 and 469–471) ironically describing Dagon's fall and Elisha's cure of the leprous Na'aman are also related to this major theme in the poem, for pagan worship and man's yielding to his wanton desires are felt by Milton to have brought about the loss of Paradise, the fall of man and nations, and to have corrupted the human condition. Not only has Milton captured the tone of sarcasm character-istic of the Hebrew prophets but, for example, through the healing power conferred upon God's prophet, the poet has driven home his message stressing the goodness and supremacy of God over the heathen deities.

Let us now consider some of the most prominent and influential of the fallen angels who take part in the impressive council in Book II. Milton's use of hebraic materials in portraying these angels varies from character to character. Although they are primarily Christian figures, many of their names are either Hebrew or Aramaic names or nouns which Milton, in Renaissance rheto-rical tradition, uses imaginatively. More often than not there is, as Cassirer believes, an intrinsic connection between the names of the devils and the essence of their character.[53] A good example

(FOOTNOTE 52 continued)
there. He has "no word of condemnation for the erring worshippers, only the reiterated 'in vain ... in vain ... in vain.' From the line 'In vain the *Tyrian* Maids their wounded *Thamuz* mourn,' the two reiterated words enter each stanza, the more impressive because they are dry and final rather than triumphant and condemnatory ... It is quite as it should be that the *Hymn* not only abstains from condemnation of some aspects of pagan myth but has in certain stanzas a tone of sadness agreeing with the laments of the 'deities' Satan has used to his end." See *Images and Themes in Five Poems by Milton*, p. 68. The changes in Milton's mind over the years can indeed be illuminated by comparing and contrasting his use of the same figures and myths in his early and late poetry. There is no "tone of sadness" in *Paradise Lost* I, 446–457, where Milton definitely condemns the cult of Thammuz.

[53] On the rhetorical uses of names as a widespread scholarly device in the Renais-sance, see "Etymology in Tradition and in the Northern Renaissance", by Frank L. Borchardt in *JHI*, XXIX (1968), pp. 415–429.

is Mammon described in lines 678–688. The word *mammon* does not appear in the Old Testament, but it does appear in *Targumim* (Aramaic versions) and in some Hebrew translations of Ben-Sira xxxi. 8. The basic meaning of the word is wealth, riches, especially riches acquired by one's own effort. The ideas of safe-deposit, hoarding or concealing, or of being an object of worship seem to be secondary. The personification of mammon is a comparatively late dramatization appropriately reproduced in the vernacular versions of the New Testament. Milton, like Spenser, must have read vernacular versions, and it is possible that he also remembered Augustine's explanation of the word in his commentary "De Sermone in Monte II, XIV, 47". Augustine thought the word was Hebrew: "Quod Hebraei dicunt mammon, latine divitiae vocantur." In his personification of Mammon, which goes back to the New Testament (Matthew vi. 24; Luke xvi. 13), Milton follows the conventional Christian Mediaeval and Renaissance traditions which were well known to him mostly from Spenser's Cave of Mammon while he was also fully aware of what was then considered the "Hebrew" origin of the word.[54] Another example is Azazel who appears as a devil already in Enoch and is mentioned as one of the four standard-bearers in the kabbalistic writings of Agrippa, Reuchlin and Fludd.[55] Another case in point is Beelzebub who appears as the god of Ekron in the Old Testament (II Kings i. 1–6) in an episode expressing Israel's shameful infidelity to God and in which he is symbolically antipodal to God's true prophet, Elijah. Yet Milton's character seems rather to have been inspired by Christian writings where Beelzebub is equated with Satan (as in Matthew xii. 24, 27; Mark iii. 22), for his Beelzebub is Satan's "Companion dear" (V.673), and of all Satan's subordinates Beelzebub is always faithfully of one mind with him.[56]

[54] The Aramaic versions use *mammon* as translation for *kofer* (Exodus xxi. 30; Judges v. 19) and for *betsa* (Genesis xxxviii. 26). On the etymology of the word see Ben Yehuda, *Thesaurus* (Hebrew), pp. 3063–66, and A. M. Honeyman, "The Etymology of Mammon", *AL*, IV (1952), pp. 60–65.
[55] On the etymology of Azazel, see my note in *PQ*, XLIX (1970), pp. 248–249.
[56] The form of the name Milton adopts also substantiates the point that Milton does not refer to the Old Testament god *Baal-Zebub* or *Baal-Zebul*. He seems to personify the New Testament Beelzebub (as he also appears in Luke x. 15–18, for example), the chief of the demons. The form of his name is probably due to

At other times the character is presented by alluding to Old Testament phrases and episodes. Moloch, for instance, is presented this way:

> First *Moloch*, horrid King besmear'd with blood
> Of human sacrifice, and parents' tears,
> Though for the noise of Drums and Timbrels loud
> Thir children's cries unheard, that pass'd through fire
> To his grim Idol. Him the *Ammonite*
> Worshipt in *Rabba* and her wat'ry Plain,
> In *Argob* and in *Basan*, to the stream
> Of utmost *Arnon*. Nor content with such
> Audacious neighborhood, the wisest heart
> Of *Solomon* he led by fraud to build
> His Temple right against the Temple of God
> On that opprobious Hill, and made his Grove
> The pleasant Valley of *Hinnom*, *Tophet* thence
> And black *Gehenna* call'd, the Type of Hell.
>
> I.392–405

It is not insignificant that Milton opens the pageant of the apostate angels with a character of his own invention, for Milton is the first poet to have presented a fallen angel in the guise of the Canaanite Idol. The connotations of the name and the other names associated with it make Milton's rhetorical use of it very clear. In the lines quoted there are almost no classical allusions, no Homeric echoes, no Virgilian references. Instead, as Wimsatt writes, these lines (and lines 406–414) are a striking example of agnomination, and the sounds echoed in the lines are all linked with the hebraic names of the passage. Milton "mentions *abominations*, an *opprobious* hill, and *Chemos* th'*obscene dread of Moab's sons*, and at the same time the geographical places where the gods were worshiped, *Rabba, Argob, Basan* . . . Other emphatic *b*'s and *p*'s appear throughout the passage, *besmeared, blood, timbrels, worshipped*.

(FOOTNOTE 56 continued)
phonetic assimilation. On *Beelzebub* and *Beelzebul* see: *The Jewish Encyclopedia*, II, 387, 629; see also Pope and Röllig in *Wörterbuch der Mythologie*, ed. H. W. Haussig, p. 254.

There is a kind of extenuated pun, a fleeting shadow of pun, an extension of the ideas of obscenity and abomination through the echo of sounds."[57] One may add that the idea of abomination is expressed through the negative connotations implicit in the names as well as through the alliterative sounds. The names are almost all of pagan idols or those of their countries and places of worship, and when Solomon and Israel are mentioned in these lines, they are denounced for their infidelity to God. The cult of Moloch described in lines 392–405 was regarded by the prophets of Israel as a symbol of evil and the atrocious practice of sacrificing children to Moloch was one of the major pagan offences abhorred in the Old Testament.[58] Therefore even if Moloch appears as a Hellenic hero who fiercely advocates "open war" (II.51) and even if his oratory is dramatically convincing, the Hebrew name gives this warlike hero an additional dimension through its moral derogatory implications.

The next figure to be considered is neither an entirely original Miltonic creation nor is he a pagan idol. In the Old Testament, the word *Belial* is used in its abstract sense although in the Hebrew text of Nahum i, 11, the word appears as an attribute to a "wicked counsellor" (yo'etz b'liya'al). In the New Testament, Belial is already personified;[59] in the Middle Ages, he appears in sacred dramas and in the seventeenth century, Burton thinks of him as the prince of the third order of devils.[60] In his disparaging portrayal

[57] W. K. Wimsatt, Jr., *The Verbal Icon, Studies in the Meaning of Poetry* (New York, 1962), pp. 209–210.

[58] Hebrew *Molech* is mentioned several times in the Old Testament (*e.g.* Jer. xxxii. 35) as a Canaanite god. There are various theories about the name of the god, as well as about the sacrifice of children cremated in his honor. Eissfeldt (*Molk als Opferbegriff im Punischen und im Hebraischen und das Ende des Gottes Moloch* [Halle, 1935] did not consider the word a proper name, but suggested it was a noun meaning *vow, pledge*. He thought the sacrifice of children was common to Canaanites and Israelites alike before the Deuteronomic reform. Eissfeldt's philological argument has been refuted by Walter Kornfeld ("Der Moloch: Eine Untersuchung zur Theorie O. Eissfeldts", *Wiener Zeitschrift für die Kunde der Morgenländer*, LI [1952], pp. 287–313) as well as by W. F. Albright (*Archeology and the Religion of Israel* [Baltimore, 1942], pp. 162–164), who also thinks it is highly unlikely that "official Yahwism had ever sanctioned a rite which even the Assyro-Babylonians have given up".

[59] II Cor. vi. 15: "Further, what harmony is there between Christ and Belial?..."

[60] Merritt Y. Hughes, in his note to I.490–501, *Paradise Lost* (New York, 1962).

of Belial (I.490ff.) Milton is, however, inspired by Old Testament
episodes, and he shows an understanding of the exact meaning of
the Hebrew phrase "sons of Belial". The behavior of the Sodo-
mites (Genesis xix) and of Eli's sons (I Samuel, ii) is best described
as profligate debauchery, and the story of Gibeah is not only that
of a cruel rape: it reflects a baseness of character that befits the
lewdest spirit that fell from Heaven. In such wise Milton both relates the name of Belial to Biblical episodes where it is mentioned
and delineates his character by directing our attention to the affin-
ity between the depravity of Belial and the moral outrage implicit
in these episodes. The dramatic quality of Belial's speech, as
pointed out by Stoll,[61] gives Belial a "lofty charm"; the rhythm and
cadence of his speech reveal him as a well-bred, decadent son of
Epicurus. But, in additon, there are in Belial's speech further Biblical allusions that fulfill an ironic function. When Belial asks
rhetorically,

What if the breath that kindl'd those grim fires
Awak'd should blow them into sevenfold rage
And plunge us in the flames?

II.170–172

his question echoes Isaiah's prophecy on Assyria (xxx. 33): "For
Tophet is ordained of old; the pile thereof is fire and much wood;
the breath of the Lord, like a stream of brimstone, doth kindle
it."[62] What is referred to through the allusion to this chapter is the
punishment to be inflicted on another of God's enemies who also
serves as one of the rods of his wrath. There can be little doubt
that Milton, having that famous prophecy in mind, associates
Belial and the fallen angels with Assyria, particularly if we remember that he again relates the fallen angels with these enemies of
God when, in the ironical description of Pandaemonium, he compares its wealth and luxury with that of Egypt and Assyria:

Not *Babylon*,
Nor great *Alcairo* such magnificence

[61] E. E. Stoll, "Belial as an Example", *MLN*, XLVIII (1933), pp. 419–427.
[62] The English translation of that verse is that of Newton. Todd suggests that these
lines probably also echo Aeschylus, *Prometheus Bound* V.311.

Equall'd in all thir glories, to inshrine
Belus or *Serapis* thir Gods, or seat
Thir Kings, when *Egypt* with *Assyria* strove
In wealth and luxury.

I.717–722

Such references are by no means fortuitous for through them
Belial – like Balaam (Numbers xxii–xxiv) moved by a greater force
than himself – is convinced of God's ultimate victory over his
enemies and, like Isaiah in his prophecy, reinforces our belief
in the God of justice who punishes and defeats those who oppose
him. When Belial asks,

what if all
Her stores were op'n'd, and this Firmament
Of Hell should spout her Cataracts of Fire,

II.174–176

his question reflects not only his spirit "Timorous and slothful",
for the same expression is used with regard to the flood when God
opened not the stores of hell but those of heaven, and it rained for
forty days and nights. It is also ironical that in Belial's eyes, God
is a mocking tyrant who "from Heav'n's highth / All these our
motions vain, sees and derides" (II.190–191), this being the image
of God in the eyes of those who rebel against Him in Psalm ii,
the allusion suggesting that the opposite is true. Belial's concluding argument against war – that "if we can sustain and bear,/Our
Supreme Foe in time may much remit / His anger" – is in harmony
with his character but it also echoes another "false and hollow"
reasoning, namely that of Job's friends. Like Bildad the Shuhite,
he advises the fallen ones to look up to God (Job viii) and like
Zophar the Na'amathite, he counsels:

whence these raging fires
Will slack'n, if his breath stir not thir flames.
Our purer essence then will overcome
Thir noxious vapor, or *enur'd not feel*,
Or *chang'd at length, and to the place conform'd*
In temper and in nature, will receive

Familiar the fierce heat, and void of pain;
This horror will grow mild, this *darkness light*,
Besides what *hope* the neverending flight
Of future days may bring,
                    II.213–222 (italics mine)[63]

Thus, although Milton renders Belial very convincingly, although
he presents him as having "lofty charm", as being "graceful",
"humane", and "fair", the Biblical allusions in the speech enhance
Milton's comment that his "thoughts were low", and the qualities
attributed to him in Book I, self-indulgence and sensuality, are
indeed reflected in his speech in Book II. It further seems that
Belial's counsels of "slothful ease" cloth'd in reason's garb are
repudiated by Milton just as God finds that the friends of Job
"have not spoken of me the thing that is right, as my servant Job
hath". This Belial whose tongue drops "Manna"[64] is a supreme
achievement of characterization.

In summary, hebraic elements are so closely woven into the
texture of the books on Hell that an examination of the fallen
angels which fails to recognize them would result in a less than
comprehensive view of Milton's fallen angels. Hebraisms, whether
these be single references, names or sustained similes, by allusion
denigrating the fallen angels, serve the poet's purpose. Like other
humanist writers, Milton has recourse to such elements to create
one of the ironic contrasts that pervade the poem.[65] The values
against which these contrasts are set are those of the Old Testament for, through the identification of the fallen angels with the
pagan deities and other corrupt and base characters in the Old

---

[63] Compare Milton's lines with Job xi. 16–18: "Because thou shalt forget thy
misery, and remember it as waters that pass away: And thine age shall be *clearer
than the noon day*; thou shalt shine forth, *thou shalt be as the morning*. And thou
shalt be secure, because *there is hope*; yes, thou shalt dig about thee, and thou
shalt take thy rest in safety" (italics mine).
[64] This recalls Exodus xvi. 31: "And the house of Israel called the name thereof
Manna: and it was like coriander seed white; and the taste of it was like wafers
made with honey." The comparison of Belial's words to honey sweet "Manna"
(II.113) enhances the irony for behind them "all was false and hollow" (II.112).
[65] See Coleman O. Parsons, "The Classical and Humanist Context of *Paradise Lost*,
II, 496–505", *JHI*, XXXIX (1968), pp. 33–52.

Testament, the struggle at the core of *Paradise Lost* is seen as the eternal struggle between good and evil. Like the Old Testament prophets, Milton presents this struggle in an ironic mode and in the context of Old Testament faith which, as has been rightly pointed out, renders bearable all perceptions of incongruity.[66] This explains why though brilliant, unique and archetypal, the fallen angels, seen in light of the hebraic ethos, are not more impressive or "heroic" than Milton intended them to be.

---

[66] *Irony in the Old Testament*, p. 244.

III

ADAM AND EVE

In his setting for the story of Adam and Eve, Milton's first authority is the text of the Bible. His indebtedness to Genesis ii and iii is obvious. The description of his "Heaven on Earth"[1] is that of Genesis

> for blissful Paradise
> Of God the Garden was, by him in the East
> Of *Eden* planted;
>
> IV.208–210[2]

Eden is not only the name of the garden but also that of the geogra-

---

[1] The Old Testament mentions two gardens: the earthly garden of Genesis and the celestial garden of the God of Ezekiel; Rabbinical tradition also tells about two gardens – the terrestrial and the celestial one. For a brief account of the two gardens and the Rabbinical tradition, see U. Cassuto, *From Adam to Noah*, part one, pp. 72–83, and *The Jewish Encyclopedia*, ed. Isidore Singer (New York and London, 1906), V.38.

[2] "And the LORD God planted a garden eastward in Eden"; Milton's line is, incidentally, a syntactically exact rendering of Rashi's commentary on the verse: בְּמִזְרָחוֹ שֶׁל עֵדֶן נָטַע אֶת הַגָּן ‹. In lines IV.134–5 Milton, like Ezekiel, had located the garden on a hill, "a rural mound". It seems that Milton's geographical location of Paradise is in harmony with the map in the Bishop's Bible (1568) as well as with the description found in Raleigh's history. However, the sense of "Scriptural truth" is conferred upon his description mainly by the verbal echoes from Genesis.

Today there are various theories concerning the location of the garden of Eden. W. F. Albright, for example, bases his thesis on Weinheimer's "ingenious suggestion that the biblical tale is really a conflation of Egyptian ideas with Mesopotamian". Albright further claims that "the eastern localization is impossible" and finally concludes that Genesis ii itself states "that Eden lay in the far west". "The Location of the Garden of Eden", *AJSL*, XXXIX (1922–23), pp. 17–29.

phical region where it was planted. The Hebrew name's meaning
does not, of course, escape the poet when he talks of the delightful
aspect of the garden:

> in this pleasant soil
> His far more pleasant Garden God ordain'd;
>
> IV.214–215[3]

Devoted to the "truth of Holy Scripture", Milton is guided by the
Book in the description of the garden. Thus the tree of life is "The
middle Tree and highest that there grew",[4] higher than the "Cedar,
and Pine, and Fir, and branching Palm" (IV.139).[5] The lines

> Thus was this place
> A happy rural seat of various view:
> Groves whose rich Trees wept odorous Gums and Balm,
> Others whose fruit burnisht with Golden Rind
> Hung amiable, *Hesperian* Fables true,
> If true, here only, and of delicious taste:
>
> IV.246–251

---

[3] Patrick Hume notes on I. 4: " עֵדֶן , signifies Pleasure and Delight." But the
Anchor Bible, *Genesis*, on ii. 8 has "*Eden*. Heb. *'eden*, Akk. *edinu*, based on Sum.
eden 'plain, steppe.' The term is used here clearly as a geographical designation,
which came to be associated, naturally enough, with the homonymous but un-
related Heb. noun for 'enjoyment'."

[4] The Authorized Version reads: "the tree of life also in the midst of the garden"
(ii. 9). On IV.195 Hume comments: "*In the midst* is a Hebrew phrase, expressing
not only the Local Situation of this enlivening Tree, but denoting its Excellency,
as being the most considerable, the tallest, goodliest, and most lovely Tree in
that beauteous Garden planted by God himself; so *Scotus, Duran, Valesius*, etc.
whom our Poet follows, affirming it the *highest there that grew: To him that over-
cometh, will I give to eat of the Tree of Life, which is in the midst of the Paradise of
God, Revel.* ii. 7". Milton is thus following the accepted Christian translation of
Genesis ii.9. Actually the word בְּתוֹךְ could mean *inside* as well as *in the centre*,
but both Rashi and Onkelos understood the word as designating the central
location of both trees.

For the "high eminence" (IV.219) of the Tree of Life, it is possible that Milton
may have used an Old Testament authority referring to a garden in another
parable, for Genesis does not describe the Tree of Life as the highest: "Therefore
his height was exalted above all the trees of the field" (Ezekiel xxxi. 5).

[5] It may perhaps be significant that the trees in Paradise are not of the kind Milton
would have seen at Horton. While Satan drew nearer to Paradise, he "many a
walk travers'd / Of stateliest Covert, Cedar, Pine or Palm", all trees frequently
mentioned in the Old Testament.

are generally considered to be a blending of Genesis and Ovid's garden of the Hesperides. But a closer look reveals that although Milton has his Ovid in mind, he questions the veracity of the Hesperian fables. Whereas Sir Walter Raleigh in his *History of the World*[6] has no difficulty transferring Paradise "out of Asia into Africa" and simply identifies the dragon watching the apples with the serpent "which tempted Evah", Milton is unable to blend so fully the sources. The Hesperian groves are beautiful, indeed, but they are fables "If true", whereas the Biblical account is Scriptural truth.

Milton freely uses Hebrew materials to depict his Eden: similarly Heaven and Hell. But it would be tedious, here, to enumerate his many Old Testament allusions except where these serve a particularly literary function in the story as Milton chooses to tell it. And the story, as Milton tells it, is the story of the Fall of Man. The poet's fidelity and reverence towards the Old Testament do not stop his account of the Fall from being Christian Protestant in outlook. The identification of the treacherous serpent with Satan rebelling against God is essentially Christian. So is the idea of Adam's first disobedience being the beginning of all human transgression, involving all the cardinal sins.

But Milton, the discriminating moralist and sensitive poet, does not simply present Paradise through the eyes of the seventeenth-century Protestant church. His searching imagination probes between the lines of the scriptural text to create a Garden of Eden all his own. "Subservience to holy writ" was not, as has been claimed, "the last infirmity of noble Protestants"[7] from which Milton sought to liberate himself. Basil Willey thinks that "in assembling what seem to him relevant texts under each heading Milton has often treated the Bible in the old uncritical way as if it were one homogeneous texture throughout . . . in order to free his mind from the misinterpretations of others."[8] But Milton's "as-

---

[6] Sir Walter Raleigh, *The History of the World* (London, 1614), p. 86. See Hughes on IV.218–220.
[7] Basil Willey, *The Seventeenth Century Background. Studies in the Thought of the Age in Relation to Poetry and Religion* (New York [1934], 1953), p. 78.
[8] Willey, pp. 75–76.

sembling of relevant texts" can be defended on other grounds, and his earliest commentators often seem to have understood him better than modern students of seventeenth-century literature. In his note on the lines

> Indeed, hath God then said that of the Fruit
> Of all these Garden trees ye shall not eat,
> Yet Lords declar'd of all in Earth or Air?
>
> IX.656–658

Hume, for instance, remarks that the Hebrew particle *af* in Genesis iii. 1 "plainly shews, that the short and summary account that *Moses* gives of the Serpent's Temptation, has respect to some previous Discourse, which could, in all probability, be no other than what our Poet has pitch'd upon".[9] Hume is implying that Milton might have recreated the story that was the source of the first chapters of Genesis. When Milton expands the Old Testament narrative he indeed develops it as if he understood many of the stories and myths behind it. No epithalamion, for example, is mentioned in Genesis, but the climactic structure of chapter ii suggests that the original conclusion was suppressed by the author, that there was a pre-existing account of the creation of man and woman which had its climax and its conclusion in the consummation of sexual union. The conclusion was then suppressed in order to unite this account with that of the fall.[10] In *Paradise Lost*, as I read it, we have the fall and sin after the epithalamion, and the perversion of the relations between Adam and Eve in Book IX is enhanced by contrast with the innocence and purity of their love in Book IV.

---

[9] See appendix *Milton's Editors From Hume to Hughes*, p. 159.
[10] There are various theories explaining the sources and problems of the Genesis text. The most useful are: S. G. F. Brandon, *Man and his Destiny in the Great Religions* (Manchester, 1962); Cassuto, *From Adam to Noah*, vol. I, esp. pp. 71–177; J. Coppens, *La Connaissance du bien et du mal et le péché du Paradis* (Gembloux, 1948), Coppens, "L'interprétation sexuelle du péché du Paradis", *ETL* XXXIII (1957), pp. 506–508; Samuel Noah Kramer, *History begins at Sumer* (London, 1958); John L. McKenzie, "The Literary Characteristics of Genesis 2–3", *TS*, XV (1954), pp. 549–567; McKenzie, "Mythological Allusions in Ezekiel 28 12–18", *JBL*, LXXV (1956), pp. 322–327.

Milton has taken for his theme the well-known Biblical story. Being as familiar with other books of the Old Testament and Hebrew commentaries as he is with the classics, he has no difficulty in drawing motifs or images from any of these sources whenever he feels that it furthers his purpose. But though his theme comes from the Hebrew writings and many of his allusions are hebraic, his view of Paradise can hardly be attributed to Hebrew theology any more than to classical mythology. It remains essentially Christian Protestant. Far from detracting from his Protestant presentation of Eden, Milton's conversance with the Old Testament and its commentators helps him paint a live and convincing picture of his idea of Paradise. Only at times is the Hebrew ethos – and I mean its way of thinking rather than its theology – transmitted into the poem. Yet no serious study of the major critical issues connected with the garden and its inhabitants can be undertaken without an understanding of his hebraic references.

Since the end of the eighteenth century, several critics have agreed that in the books on Eden, Milton was faced with a difficulty inherent in the tendentious chapters of Genesis – the difficulty of describing the innocence and perfection of Adam and Eve in Books IV and V while preparing us for the inevitable Fall in Book IX. Thus Dr. Johnson felt that "to find sentiments for the state of innocence, was very difficult; and something of anticipation perhaps is now and then discovered".[11] While Tillyard evades the problem by saying that Adam and Eve are "virtually fallen before the official temptation has begun",[12] C. S. Lewis finds a lack of contrast in *Paradise Lost* between fallen and unfallen sexuality.[13] Tillyard argues that by creating an Adam and Eve who are imperfect in Books IV and V, Milton could account for the fall in Book IX. But then the fall loses impact and ceases to be the central event of *Paradise Lost*.

[11] Samuel Johnson, *Life of Milton*, edited by K. Deighton (London, 1900), p. 70.
[12] "The Crisis of *Paradise Lost*", *Studies in Milton* (London, 1951), p. 13. Davis P. Harding defines the problem this way: "Milton had two main problems: first, he had to provide substance for his skeletonic story, ... second, as an artist he had to motivate the Fall. He had to provide a psychological bridge between a state of entire innocence and a state of sin." *The Club of Hercules*, p. 68.
[13] C. S. Lewis, *A Preface to Paradise Lost* (London [1942] 1965), pp. 123–124.

This question is crucial for any examination of Milton's Eden. Basil Willey believes that Milton faced an insurmountable difficulty because, in his words, "Genesis, to which Milton must needs adhere, represented the Fall as due to, or as consisting of, the acquisition by Man of that very knowledge, the Knowledge of good and evil, by the possession of which alone Milton the humanist believed man could be truly virtuous", and also because "adherence to Genesis involved him in the necessity of representing man's true and primal happiness as the innocence of Eden".[14] Evans defends the perfection of prelapsarian Eden by saying it is not absolute but conditional. It depends on Adam's discipline and pleasant labour for he has to supervise and tend the garden.[15] At the same time, Milton does not manage to convince Willey that the prelapsarian life of Adam and Eve in the "happy garden" was genuinely happy. Strange, for it is hard to overlook Milton's enthusiasm in describing the "enormous bliss" of the garden in Books IV and V.

For critics like Johnson, Tillyard, and Lewis, Milton was primarily an epic poet who chose a Biblical theme, and they praised him or judged him according to how well they thought he had carried out his own intentions or, rather, their reading of the book of Genesis. The history of these critical views is a fascinating chapter of literary criticism, but that is another story. The point is that for most literary critics of Milton, the 1500 year-old exegetical tradition Milton was familiar with was not relevant. It may have comforted them to know that Milton's reading of Genesis had little importance for theologians.

Yet the Christian Protestant poet was certainly someone for whom the theological issues involved in the nature of Adam and Eve before the Fall, in the eating of the apple and in its consequences, were clear. He would have been rather surprised at those readers who, three hundred years later, doubted his intentions.

Milton's conception of the nature of Adam and Eve is a case in

[14] Basil Willey, *The Seventeenth Century Background*, p. 244.
[15] *Paradise Lost and the Genesis Tradition*, pp. 268–269.

point. Like the Rabbis and the Church Fathers before him, the poet appreciated the difference between the Adam created in God's image in Genesis i and the childlike, rather naive Adam described in Genesis iii, and he succeeds admirably in creating an Adam and Eve who are perfect and, at the same time, human.[16] Whereas he found the Church Fathers divided about Adam, some viewing him as childlike and immature, others making him angelic, there was no systematic Jewish doctrine in the Pentateuch and its Rabbinical commentaries. The Hebrew commentaries provided Milton with textual and narrative comments rather than with theological arguments. That is why there is no contradiction between Milton's Protestant doctrine of the Fall of man and his indebtedness to hebraic materials. In the Old Testament and in Rabbinic exegesis he found texts which supported his conception of our first parents. The twelfth-century Hispano-Jewish poet and exegete Ibn Ezra, in his observation on Genesis ii. 17, comments on the distinction between Adam's prelapsarian and postlapsarian knowledge. According to Ibn Ezra, Man was already full of knowledge or else God would not have addressed commands to him, neither would he have been able to bestow names on all the various creatures; in respect of one thing only did he not distinguish between right and wrong, and that was in respect of his wife who was with him in the Garden. Similarly Milton's Adam, whose account of his own creation to Raphael attests to his perfect intellectual knowledge of God and the world created by Him; this same intellectual knowledge seems to desert him in Eve's presence. This is the gist of Adam's moving confession:

> yet when I approach
> Her loveliness, so absolute she seems
> And in herself complete, so well to know
> Her own, that what she wills to do or say,
> Seems wisest, virtuousest, discreetest, best;

---

[16] Milton appreciated the literary differences between the various parts of the Genesis story though he could not know what we do about the ancient P and J texts that are behind it. His knowledge of the Bible is so good, however, that he grasps the contradictions in the text.

All higher knowledge in her presence falls
Degraded, . . .
VIII.546–552

The Adam of *Paradise Lost* is neither childlike nor angelic. Though responsible and intellectually mature, Adam is a human being:

> He created in him four higher attributes (literally: creations) and four lower ones: he eats and drinks like an animal, procreates like an animal, and execrates like an animal, and dies like an animal; but he stands like angels, talks like angels, thinks like angels, and sees like angels.[17]

One traditional Jewish view, substantiated by Maimonides in his *Guide to the Perplexed*, is that the knowledge Adam gains with the Fall is not intellectual but moral. Maimonides believes that perfection, the intellect, had been bestowed upon Man before he sinned: that is why he could be ordered to do or abstain from doing things (Genesis ii. 17), unlike animals or mindless creatures to whom no such orders would ever be addressed; and while he could intellectually distinguish between true and false, and aesthetically between beautiful and ugly, what he could not see was any blameworthiness in such matters as nakedness; it was only by way of punishment for succombing to the temptations of his eyes and his appetite (Genesis iii. 6) that he lost his purely intellectual and aesthetical conception and was immersed in complex conscientious scruples; and then he knew the extent of his loss and realised what had been taken away from him.[18] This is also how Milton's Adam sees it:

since our Eyes
Op'n'd we find indeed, and find we know
Both Good and Evil, Good lost and Evil got,
IX.1070–72

Now whereas this conception of Adam's perfection as a human

---

[17] *Genesis Rabba*, chapter VIII (Hebrew).
[18] Book I, chapter ii (Hebrew). I am indebted to Justice Haim Cohn for this free translation of the Hebrew text.

being is conspicuously absent in Paul's writings as well as in early
Christian commentaries, Milton supported his view with "Scriptural truth" by drawing on other Biblical passages and commentaries. One of the first instances of Milton's use of Scriptural echoes
occurs in Satan's second soliloquy. Here we view Adam and Eve
through the eyes of the fallen archangel who envies their bliss yet
has to admit the 'Divine resemblance' that shines through them:

> O Hell! What do mine eyes with grief behold,
> Into our room of bliss thus high advanc't
> Creatures of other mould, earth-born perhaps;
> Not Spirits, yet to heav'nly Spirits bright
> Little inferior:

IV.358–362

Giamatti, examining Milton's "allusive, elusive technique", calls
Milton's style in Eden "satanic" because it is "a means for reflecting
the way the devil works – while describing him at work"[19] and, relying heavily on Harding's study of *Paradise Lost*, he writes that "a
classical allusion in this Christian tale will always do two things;
it will invariably indicate the higher Truth and greater splendour
of the garden and of Adam and Eve; but it will also, obliquely,
by what it recalls and by the very fact it is there, prepare for a
context of falsity and disgrace."[20] But why shouldn't words or
phrases culled from the Old Testament or other hebraic sources
be just as functional and deliberate as those allusions associating
Eden with other classical or Renaissance gardens? In the lines
quoted above, Satan is, ironically and in spite of himself, forced to
praise those of whom he is jealous and whom he intends to destroy.
Psychologically, the situation is reminiscent of Balaam's in Numbers xxii–xxiv, for Satan's feelings are those of Balak but the words
that he utters are once more those of Psalm viii. 5: "For thou hast
made him a little lower than the angels, and hast crowned him with
glory and honour." Satan's envious admiration of Adam and Eve

---

[19] A. Bartlett Giamatti, *The Earthly Paradise and the Renaissance Epic* (Princeton,
1966), p. 298.
[20] *The Club of Hercules*, p. 80; *The Earthly Paradise and the Renaissance Epic*, p. 300
and note 5 on same page.

heightens our perception of their "Divine resemblance" and pre-lapsarian innocence.

Here is but one example of Milton's subtle but masterful use of literary allusion. Another suggestion of the goodness of Adam and Eve occurs after our first view of the "Fair couple": Milton describes the idyllic happiness surrounding them thus:

> About them frisking play'd
> All beasts of th' Earth, since wild, and of all chase
> In Wood or Wilderness, Forest or Den;
> Sporting the Lion ramp'd, and in his paw
> Dandl'd the Kid; Bears, Tigers, Ounces, Pards
> Gamboll'd before them, th'unwieldy Elephant
> To make them mirth us'd all his might, and wreath'd
> His Lithe Proboscis; close the Serpent sly
> Insinuating, wove with Gordian twine
> His braided train, and of his fatal guile
> Gave proof unheeded;
>
> IV.340–350

Hughes claims, with justice, that "Biblical illustrators liked to represent the friendly animals around Adam and Eve in the spirit of their description in popular poems like Samuel Pordage's *Mundorum explicatio* (1663)",[21] but Milton's lines are also an obvious allusion to Isaiah's prophecy: "The wolf also shall dwell with the lamb, and the leopard shall lie down with the kid; and the calf and the young lion and the fatling together; and a little child shall lead them. And the cow and the bear shall feed; their young ones shall lie down together: and the lion shall eat straw like the ox. And the sucking child shall play on the hole of the asp, and the weaned child shall put his hand on the cockatrice's den" (Isaiah xi. 6–8). It is no accident that this apocalyptic vision finds its way into *Paradise Lost* at this point for, like Virgil singing the new order of things when the lion shall lie down with the lamb, Milton, visualizing the prophecy about the messianic future, assimilates the vision of the Hebrew prophet to enhance the idyllic

---

[21] Hughes on IV.340–352.

pastoral quality of the prelapsarian Eden which is balanced against the serpent's "fatal guile". The eleventh chapter of Isaiah was, because of its allusion to a son of Jesse, well-known to Christians. It was thus natural for Milton to associate Eden before the fall with the days of Christ's coming to redeem the world. This allusion is characteristic of Milton's use of the Bible and other Hebrew sources in that he adapts those elements which are both poetically effective and in keeping with his Christian beliefs.

In emphasizing the goodness and purity of Adam and Eve before the fall, Milton draws much of his inspiration from the Psalms. When Eve asks Adam why the stars shine at night, Adam's answer echoes Psalms xix and xx:

> These then, though unbeheld in deep of night,
> Shine not in vain, nor think, though men were none,
> That Heav'n would want spectators, God want praise;
> Millions of spiritual Creatures walk the Earth
> Unseen, both when we wake, and when we sleep:
> All these with ceaseless praise his works behold
> Both day and night: how often from the steep
> Of echoing Hill or Thicket have we heard
> Celestial voices to the midnight air,
> Sole, or responsive each to other's note
> Singing thir great Creator:
>
> IV.674–684

The motif is that of Psalm 19:

> The heavens declare the glory of God;
> and the firmament sheweth his handywork.
> Day unto day uttereth speech,
> and night unto night sheweth knowledge.
>
> xix. 1–2

But the tone is more formal, and the structure less ritual, more elaborate. The hymn also recalls Psalms xlvi, xlix, xcii ("It is a good thing to give thanks unto the Lord, and to sing praises unto thy name, O most High:"), xcv–xcviii. Adam and Eve's prayer a little later has, as Hughes points out, much in common both with Psalm lxxiv. 16, Psalm cxxvii. 2 and with Aeneid II.269:[22]

> Thou also mad'st the Night,
> Maker Omnipotent, and thou the Day,
> Which we in our appointed work imploy'd
> Have finisht happy in our mutual help
> And mutual love, the Crown of all our bliss
> Ordain'd by thee, and this delicious place
> For us too large, where thy abundance wants
> Partakers, and uncropt falls to the ground.
> But thou hast promis'd from us two a Race
> To fill the Earth, who shall with us extol
> Thy goodness infinite, both when we wake,
> And when we seek, as now, thy gift of sleep.
>   IV.724–735

The morning hymn of Adam and Eve echoes again Psalm cxlviii:[23]

> These are thy glorious works, Parent of good,
> Almighty, thine this universal Frame,
> Thus wondrous fair; thyself how wondrous then!
> Unspeakable, who sit'st above these Heavens
> To us invisible or dimly seen
> In these thy lowest works, yet these declare
> Thy goodness beyond thought, and Power Divine:
>   V.153–159

Lines 159–160 recall the famous Psalm xix quoted above but, as Newton observes on V.153, the hymn is also an imitation of the "Canticle placed after *Te Deum* in the Liturgy, 'O all ye works of the Lord, bless ye the Lord, etc' which is the Song of the three children in the Apocrypha". While they address the sun, for example, Adam and Eve praise it in the words of the Genesis writer for whom God is He

---

[22] Hughes, on IV.724–735, refers to the passage where Aeneas talks about the quiet of the evening coming to bring the most welcome gift of the gods.
[23] See also Verity on V.153–208 and Hughes on V.156–169.

Who out of Darkness call'd up Light.
V.179[24]

And when they end their morning prayer, Adam and Eve invoke
God's creatures to witness their fidelity in the familiar words of
Psalm cxxxvii: "If I do not remember thee, let my tongue cleave to
the roof of my mouth . . ." (cxxxvii. 6).

It is not insignificant that in Milton's account of Eden, as in the
Genesis story, Eve's position changes sharply after the fall. In
Paradise Lost as in Genesis, her feminine vanity, when perverted,
leads her to sin. Milton grasped the contrast between Eve's role in
Genesis ii, when she is created, and her weakness in the temptation
scene and following it in chapter iii.[25] In chapter ii she is such that
"a man shall leave his father and mother and shall cleave unto his
wife: and they shall be one flesh." In chapter iii Eve almost becomes a symbol of human frailty who can only say in her own
defense: "The serpent beguiled me, and I did eat." The man who
was supposed to cleave to his wife is now punished for having
hearkened unto her voice. In chapter ii Man was alone and in need
of a wife; he was given woman by God as an honorable partner.
In chapter iii the woman becomes a pitiable creature, destined to
bring forth children in sorrow and to be subject to her husband's
desire (Genesis iii. 16).[26] Milton's treatment of Eve emphasizes
this contrast.[27]

In Books IV and V, Milton seems to follow the popular etymology
for Eve's name, connected with *to live*, as given in Genesis iii. 20.
Eve is often referred to by Milton as "Mother of Mankind" (I.36;
V.388). This popular etymology is also the traditional one. Thus

[24] The theme of God's revelation of himself through creation was a Renaissance
commonplace; but what is characteristic of Milton is his expressing it in Old
Testament language.
[25] See notes 10 and 16 above.
[26] Another explanation of Eve's curse is that she will be subjected to her husband
in her desire for him. See *Genesis*, edited by Hartom and Cassuto (Tel-Aviv,
1962 (9th edition)), on iii. 16 (Hebrew).
[27] Milton lets a long interval elapse between the pastoral idyl of Books IV and
V and the Fall in Book IX thus emphasizing the contrast between Eve before and
after the Fall.

the name Havva was also explained by Rashi.[28] When Adam
thanks his Creator for giving him a wife, his words also echo
Genesis:

Bone of my Bone, Flesh of my Flesh, my Self
Before me; Woman is her Name, of Man
Extracted; for this cause he shall forgo
Father and Mother, and to his Wife adhere;
And they shall be one Flesh, one Heart, one Soul.
VIII.495–499[29]

The relationship between Adam and Eve may seem voluptuous
by Augustinian standards or when envied by Satan who "Saw
undelighted all delight" (IV.286), but Milton's description of their
relationship is an idealization of marital love, physical as well as
spiritual. It is in keeping with Protestant tradition but backed up
by the basically hebraic attitude to life, by a belief in man's capabi-
lities, in the value of a wholesome sacred relationship between man
and wife.[30] If Harding's study of classical proleptic allusions relat-

[28] Kramer suggests that the origin of Eve's name is Sumerian: In the Sumerian
Dilmun poem, "One of Enki's sick organs is the rib. The Sumerian word for 'rib'
is *ti*. The goddess created for the healing of Enki's rib is called *Nin-ti*, 'the lady
of the rib.' But the Sumerian word *ti* also means 'to make live'. The name Nin-ti
may therefore mean 'the lady who makes live', as well as 'the lady of the rib'.
It was this, one of the most ancient and literary puns, which was carried over and
perpetuated in the Biblical paradise story, although here, of course, it loses its
validity, since the Hebrew word for 'rib' and that for 'who makes live' have
nothing in common." Samuel Noah Kramer, *History begins at Sumer* (London,
1958), p. 196.
   J. Renié, on the other hand, stresses the fact that in the Sumerian poem, Nin-ti
was not formed from Enki's rib, but was created in order to heal the sick rib of
the god. "Un prétendu parallèle sumérien de la création d'Eve", *Mélanges de
Science Religieuse* (Lille, 1953), pp. 9–12.
[29] Genesis ii. 23–24 and also Matthew xix. 4–6, Mark x. 6–8. "One Heart, one
Soul" is the poet's addition to the Genesis verse and its source is probably, as
Newton suggests (IV.483), Horace *Od.* I. iii, 8.
[30] B. A. Wright, "Note on *Paradise Lost* IV, 310", *N&Q*, CCIII (1958), p. 341,
comments on the fact that Milton considers physical love an essential and
inseparable part of human love at its best, as distinguished from the post-lapsarian
feelings of lust. Wright brings as evidence *Paradise Lost* IV.310, showing it is a
close translation of *Ars Amatoria*, II.718.
   There are more Ovidian references with regard to the married love of Adam

ing to Adam and Eve points to the "psychological bridge between a state of entire innocence and a state of sin", we have to turn to Old Testament references in order to see how Milton distinguishes between innocence and experience, for the primary function of the hebraic allusions in prelapsarian Eden is to stress the moral perfection of our first parents.[31]

But C. S. Lewis is not convinced. Like St. Augustine, he believes that sexual relations never took place in Paradise. He admits that both Milton and St. Augustine contrast the fallen sexuality which we know with unfallen sexuality. But, he goes on,

> for St. Augustine the unfallen sexuality is purely hypothetical: when he describes it he is describing what the act of generation *would have been* before the Fall, but he does not think it ever took place. Milton asserts that it did . . . He has dared represent Paradisal sexuality. I cannot make up my mind whether he was wise.

In a way Lewis, like Tillyard, believes that Adam and Eve are fallen before Book IX, that while Adam and Eve walked about naked in the garden, they should have remained sexually innocent. No child could be born in Eden. According to him, only after they tasted of the tree of knowledge did that knowledge engender shame, which engendered the fig leaves, which finally engendered the first child. But Milton describes a different Eden, and he was not only "wise" but courageous too.

It has long been recognized that Milton was influenced by Rashi in his description of the marital relations of Adam and Eve before the fall.[32] The point deserves to be explained. Rashi, in his comment on Genesis iv. 1, holds that Adam and Eve had children already before they sinned although the text mentions Eve's motherhood

---

(*FOOTNOTE 30 continued*)
and Eve, but these are always subservient to Biblical truths. For example, when Milton describes the purity of their married love, he does so through an overt allusion to Cupid's golden shafts (IV.763ff.), but in the same passage, the poet also echoes the Biblical injunction that "Our Maker bids increase".

[31] On Milton's concept of marriage and sexuality see also Fisch's illuminating discussion, *Jerusalem and Albion*, pp. 156–160.

[32] See, for example, Harris Fletcher, *Milton's Rabbinical Readings*, pp. 205–206.

only after their expulsion from the garden. He draws this conclusion from the tense used by the Genesis narrator – וְהָאָדָם יָדַע (to be distinguished from וַיֵּדַע אָדָם), which, as Rashi points out, applies to a far past. Indeed verse 25 of the same chapter tells about the birth of another son to Adam and Eve. Here the text reads: וַיֵּדַע אָדָם עוֹד אֶת אִשְׁתּוֹ .The English translations of the Bible make no distinction between the two tenses (King James Version to verse 1: "And Adam knew his wife ..." and to verse 25: "And Adam knew his wife again ..."). It is not improbable that Rashi's grammatical comment on this text shed life on the undertones of the story for Milton.

Arnold Williams, however, writes that Luther, too, strongly hints that Adam "knew" Eve before the fall, and he also indicates that Peter Martyr mentions the commentary of Rashi.[33] Whether Milton got the idea from Rashi directly, from Peter Martyr, from Luther's hint, or whether he understood it, like Rashi, from the text itself, we have no way of knowing. We do know, however, that Milton goes further than most commentators by explicitly writing about the "Rites Mysterious of connubial Love", for most commentators either thought Adam and Eve were virgins before the fall or considered the whole question as hypothetical. He also seems to have anticipated Lewis' criticism when he writes

Far be it, that I should write thee sin or blame,
Or think thee unbefitting holiest place,
Perpetual Fountain of Domestic sweets,
Whose bed is undefil'd and chaste pronounc't,
Present, or past, as Saints and Patriarchs us'd.
IV.758–762

The poet's words here echo Genesis xviii. 25: "That be far from thee to do after this manner, to slay the righteous with the wicked: and that the righteous should be as the wicked that be far from thee", drawing a distinction between courtly love, which is wicked, and conjugal love, which is righteous. Like St. Augustine, he knew that the command to be fruitful and multiply meant sexual rela-

[33] *The Common Expositor*, p. 89.

tionship, the end of which – to procreate – could not be sinful in itself.

His garden is a garden of love, but it is also a garden of dreams, of longing without which nothing worthwhile can be created. We get a subtle analysis of the states of mind of Adam and Eve, but they are never uneasy. His garden is not a garden of shame. The relationship between Adam and Eve is sensuous but not sensual. It is conjugal attraction, a love of body and soul. Its end is not the gratification of the senses, for in their harmonious physical relationship they are part of nature, and they fulfil God's purpose by contributing to the fruitfulness and plenitude of his creation.

While Milton's conception of marriage conforms with Protestant tradition, he goes further than the Protestant idea of marriage as an opportunity for spiritual effort.[34] The openly erotic description of the conjugal love of Adam and Eve needs no heavenly sanctification. Without being, as Patrides believes, an extension of celestial love, the relationship between Adam and Eve is sacred in itself.[35] The descriptions of Adam and Eve and the poetic dialogues between them are a blend of passion and purity not found in Protestant preachers and commentators. Milton's doctrine of conjugal love is, then, Protestant in its dogma. Yet in his prelapsarian garden it is presented as something far more human, which is distinctly hebraic, and derived from his reading of the Old Testament and its Hebrew commentators. At times he is as much indebted to other books of the Old Testament as he is to Genesis.

This is particularly so when he is describing Adam and Eve's pastoral happiness before the fall, when his familiarity with the Song of Solomon is much in evidence. What might at first seem surprising is that Milton turned so little for inspiration to these eight chapters of love-poetry, but they were not, after all, in the epic tradition in which he was writing. Significantly, Milton's

---

[34] On the Puritan attitude to marriage see William Haller, *The Rise of Puritanism* (New York, [1938] 1957), pp. 120–122, and William and Malleville Haller, "The Puritan Art of Love", *HLQ*, V (1942), pp. 234–272.
[35] See Patrides, *Milton and the Christian Tradition*, p. 176. The view expressed here is closer to that of Helen Gardner, *A Reading of Paradise Lost* (Oxford, 1965), pp. 85–86.

usage of the Song is as far removed from Christian as from Jewish hermeneutics; he reads it neither as a mystic allegory of a divine dialogue nor as a love-poem of the Church to Christ. Its main attraction for him must have been both sensuous and conceptual. Raphael's entrance to the "spicy Forest" of Eden is described in terms of the smells of the garden of the song "with all trees of frankincense; myrrh and aloes, with all the chief spices" (iv. 14):

> and now is come
> Into the blissful field, through Groves of Myrrh,
> And flow'ring Odors, Cassia, Nard, and Balm;
> A Wilderness of sweets; for Nature here
> Wanton'd as in her prime, and play'd at will
> Her Virgin Fancies, pouring forth more sweet,
> Wild above Rule or Art, enormous bliss.
>
> V.291–297

Conceptually, the poem must have attracted Milton because of the exalted idea of love it emanates. One of the most moving love-poems is Eve's:

> With thee conversing I forget all time,
> All seasons and thir change, all please alike.
> Sweet is the breath of morn, her rising sweet,
> With charm of earliest Birds; . . .
>
> IV.639–642

As Todd remarked, the expression "the breath of morn" might have been suggested by the original passage in Solomon's Song ii. 17 "Till the day breathe ..." (Todd annotating IV.641).[36] It is possible, however, that Milton was also influenced by chapter v

---

[36] Eve's beautiful lines to Adam are, in their cross references and melodious repetition of words and sounds, reminiscent of Milton's technique in *Lycidas* and the passage is, in essence, Miltonic. Keightley on IV.639 notes: "As Todd thinks, this idea may have been suggested by the verse, 'And Jacob served seven years for Rachel, and they seemed unto him but a few days for the love he had to her' Gen. 29.20". Todd does not mention this reference and Milton does not seem to allude to this episode here.

of the Song where the beloved bewails her separation from her lover.[37] Another passage similarly reminiscent of the Song is:

> Awake
> My fairest, my espous'd, my latest found,
> Heav'n's last best gift, my ever new delight,
> Awake, the morning shines and the fresh field
> Calls us; we lose the prime, to mark how spring
> Our tended Plants, how blows the Citron Grove,
> What drops the Myrrh, and what the balmy Reed,
> How Nature paints her colors, how the Bee
> Sits on the Bloom extracting liquid sweet . . .
>
> V.17–25

Keightley relates these lines to the Song of Solomon ii. 10–13: "Rise up, my love, my fair one, and come away. For, lo, the winter is past, the rain is over and gone. The flowers appear on the earth . . ." Milton here may also be indebted to the Song vi. 11: "I went down into the garden of nuts to see the fruits of the valley and to see whether the vine flourished, and the pomegranates budded." If lines 17–25 of Book V are inspired by the Song of Solomon, they do not seem to be, as Hughes notes,[38] "an obvious parody" of it. The garden of the Song of Solomon is referred to

---

[37] Todd also suggests that Adam's words to Raphael about Eve were inspired by Canticles:

> To the Nuptial Bow'r
> I led her blushing like the Morn:
> VIII.510–511

Todd comments that "Milton's is an elegant comparison in the Eastern style; the bride of Solomon being likened to the morning, Cant. vi. 10: "Who is she that looketh forth as the morning?" It is possible that Todd is right, but the metaphor of the blushing morning seems to be more Hellenic than hebraic. Similarly, the opening of Book V

> Now Morn her rosy steps in th'Eastern Clime
> Advancing,
> V.1–2

is reminiscent, as Hughes points out (on V.1), of the rosy-fingered Dawn of Homer. Morning is personified in both metaphors, but not precisely in an "eastern style".
[38] In his annotation to V.17–25.

again by Milton in a different context – just before the Fall – after two other negative comparisons. The garden of Eden before Satan's temptation of Eve appears to be a

> Spot more delicious than those Gardens feign'd
> Or of reviv'd *Adonis*, or renown'd
> *Alcinous*, host of *Laertes'* Son
> Or that, not Mystic, where the Sapient King
> Held dalliance with his fair *Egyptian* Spouse.
>   IX.439–443

In the same scene we also see Eve sustaining the drooping flowers

> Herself, though fairest unsupported Flow'r,

while

>   so thick the Roses blushing round
> About her glow'd, . . .
>   IX.426–427

In addition to the classical references of these lines, Milton may have had in mind other beautiful verses comparing the Shulamit to a flower amidst other flowers that next to her seemed like thorns:

> As the lily among thorns, so is my love among the daughters.
>   ii. 2

Such descriptions, evoking reminiscences of the delightful garden of the Song enhance the idyllic quality of Milton's Eden. Even Satan, beholding Eve's "graceful Innocence" (IX.459), is, for a brief moment, carried away by her chaste beauty and her holiness, "Stupidly good, of enmity disarm'd." But remembering his hatred, the pleasure of destruction overtakes him. The vision of the fair garden vanishes, and we return to the more prosaic and more familiar garden of trial with Satan beholding "alone/ The Woman, opportune to all attempts." Except for the motif of the alternation of absence and presence of the beloved echoed by Eve in her last love-poem to Adam (XII.615–619), the Song of Solomon is heard no more after the fall. But by then love has brought about their reconciliation.

Such echoes and resemblances are fairly obvious. What seems to have gone unnoticed so far is the connection between another comment of Rashi and an episode in Eden which has always been thought of as Ovidian. The relevant episode is the account of Eve's seeing herself mirrored in the lake. These are the words Milton puts in Eve's mouth:

That day I oft remember, when from sleep
I first awak't, and found myself repos'd
Under a shade on flow'rs, much wond'ring where
And what I was, whence thither brought, and how.
Not distant far from thence a murmuring sound
Of waters issu'd from a Cave and spread
Into a liquid Plain, then stood unmov'd
Pure as th' expanse of Heav'n; I thither went
With unexperienc't thought, and laid me down
On the green bank, to look into the clear
Smooth Lake, that to me seem'd another Sky.
As I bent down to look, just opposite,
A Shape within the wat'ry gleam appear'd
Bending to look on me, I started back,
It started back, but pleas'd I soon return'd,
Pleas'd it return'd as soon with answering looks
Of sympathy and love; there I had fixt
Mine eyes till now, and pin'd with vain desire,
Had not a voice thus warn'd me, What thou seest;
What there thou seest fair Creature is thyself,
With thee it came and goes; but follow me,
And I will bring thee where no shadow stays
Thy coming, and thy soft imbraces, hee
Whose image thou art, him thou shalt enjoy
Inseparably thine, to him shalt bear
Multitudes like thyself, and thence be call'd
Mother of human Race: what could I do,
But follow straight, invisibly thus led?
Till I espi'd thee, fair indeed and tall,
Under a Platan, yet methought less fair,

Less winning soft, less amiably mild,
Than that smooth wat'ry image; back I turn'd,
Thou following cri'd'st aloud, Return fair *Eve*,
Whom fli'st thou? whom thou fli'st, of him thou art,
His flesh, his bone; to give thee being I lent
Out of my side to thee, nearest my heart
Substantial Life, to have thee by my side
Henceforth an individual solace dear;
Part of my Soul I seek thee, and thee claim
My other half: with that thy gentle hand
Seiz'd mine, I yielded, and from that time see
How beauty is excell'd by manly grace
And wisdom, which alone is truly fair.

IV.449–491

The vision bears such a resemblance to Ovid's tale of Narcissus
that few critics have sought any other source. The Ovidian tale,
which was one of the fables for the Fall of man for the Renaissance,
has also been conveniently adduced to prove that we already feel
uneasy about Eve before the Fall. This is how Harding sees it:

> he [Milton] could not venture an out-and-out comparison
> with Narcissus, for that might well produce an impression of sin-
> ful vanity whereas Milton sought merely to establish a velleity.
> Eve is saved, as Narcissus is not, by a warning voice, and it would
> be a captious reader indeed who, recalling Eve's "unexperienc't
> thought," would be inclined to read too much into this trifling
> display of natural vanity. Milton himself invites the reader –
> virtually compels him, in fact – to underplay the vanity motif
> by permitting it to become swallowed up and almost lost in the
> professed moral of the episode ... But a certain amount of
> damage has been done. We can no longer feel altogether easy
> in our minds about Eve.[39]

Carried to its logical conclusion, this – pace Harding – reaffirms
Tillyard's belief that Adam and Eve are virtually fallen before the

---

[39] Davis P. Harding, *The Club of Hercules*, p. 74.

official temptation has begun. But to read the mirror scene as an evidence of Eve's feminine vanity and frailty is to misunderstand Milton's insistence on Eve's rejection of self-love, on her free choice of Adam, whom she claims as her "other half", as part of her Soul. Joseph Summers has noted the real difference between Eve and Narcissus:

> We should not take her initial narcissitic fascination with her own image as an indication of her "natural depravity" or "the fact that she has already fallen". . . . Love for one's own image is not always evil . . . Her fascination with her own image is a natural and inevitable potentiality for any free creature of perfect beauty . . . The point of Eve's narration is the contrast rather than the comparison with the original Narcissus. Narcissus had no "perfect" partner, no "other self", and he had no divine guide. Eve's early experience provides the crucial evidence that there could be no paradise for her apart from her relationship with Adam. She tells it to indicate her joy that she *has* found fulfilment, that she has not "pin'd with vain desire" (466).[40]

Another lead to the difference between Eve's reaction and that of Narcissus is found in Rashi's observation on Exodus xxxviii. 8: "And he made the laver of brass and the foot of it of brass, of the lookingglasses of the women assembling, which assembled at the door of the tabernacle of the congregation." The verse itself describing the people's offerings is irrelevant, but in his explanation of it Rashi includes a charming Midrash:

> The daughters of Israel had mirrors in which they used to look to beautify themselves and they did not refrain from bringing them as pious offerings to the Sanctuary. But Moses despised them and wanted to reject them since they exist to encourage the baser instincts. Said to him the Holy One, blessed be He, "Accept them, for they are to me the most acceptable offering

[40] Joseph H. Summers, *The Muse's Method* (London, 1962), pp. 97–98.

of all. For it was by means of them that the women of Israel provided many hosts in Egypt. When their husbands were utterly exhausted from their hard labour in Egypt, they would go and bring them food and drink and feed them. Then each of them would take her mirror and gazing into it together with her husband, would woo him saying, "See how much more beautiful I am than you are." Thus they roused the desire of their husbands who thereupon fulfilled their conjugal duties. Thus they conceived and bore children as it is said (The Song of Solomon viii. 5) "I roused thee under the apple tree." And from these mirrors was fashioned the brass laver, whose purpose it was to bring about peace between the husband and wife."

The similarity between this ancient Rabbinic gloss of the Tanhuma Midrash quoted by Rashi and the episode of Eve's discovery of her own beauty in the garden is striking not only for the corresponding details (the gazing into the mirror, the realization of the women that they are more beautiful than their husbands, the love scenes following both mirror episodes) but also for the corresponding implications of the two. As happens with Eve in *Paradise Lost*, the women in the Midrash are stimulated by their own beauty into arousing their husbands' desire. But there is nothing impure or sinful about this. On the contrary, feminine vanity is treated as a virtue, not a weakness. If indeed Milton did have this in mind, Eve's virtue is then enhanced rather than impugned by the mirror episode. The scene's poetic beauty is sharpened by the bisociation of this hebraic element thrown into a classical context.

Rashi, who centres on an apparently unimportant detail (the brass mirrors), makes a point of associating the women in this Midrash with the woman of the Song, and it may well have inspired Milton to write one of the most erotic conjugal love scenes in *Paradise Lost* right after the mirror episode:

So spake our general Mother, and with eyes
Of conjugal attraction unreprov'd,
And meek surrender, half imbracing lean'd
On our first Father, half her swelling Breast

Naked met his under the flowing Gold
Of her loose tresses hid:

IV.492–497[41]

The passage is as openly sensuous as many passages of the Song
and as pure. The conjugal love of Adam and Eve is of great simplicity and beauty. In a subtle way it conveys Eve's state of mind,
for it is precisely when she becomes aware of her own attraction
that she – like the women in the Midrash – yearns for her husband,
body and soul.

After the Fall, man's natural instincts – including sex – which
were previously good and positive in themselves share the general
corruption. Eve remains vain, but her vanity no longer brings
forth love. It leads to hypocrisy:

Hast thou not wonder'd, *Adam*, at my stay?
Thee I have misst, and thought it long, depriv'd
Thy presence, agony of love till now
Not felt,

IX.856–859

Then they "play / As meet is, after such delicious Fare" (IX.1027–
1028). Before the Fall, Adam with "gentle sway" wins Eve's response, and Eve yields

with coy submission, modest pride,
And sweet reluctant amorous delay.

IV.310–311

"Love will not be drawn, but must be gently led", as Spenser
puts it.[42]

After the Fall, Adam

---

[41] Joseph Summers believes that in this passage Milton "makes explicit the
continuing analogy between external nature and human sexuality which readers
in the age of Freud might naively consider unconscious". *The Muse's Method*,
p. 98. I think we have here rather a perceptive understanding of the ways of love
which is partly inspired by Rashi's observation.
[42] This motif recurs in Solomon's Song iii. 5 as well: "I charge you, O ye daughters
of Jerusalem, by the roes and by the hinds of the field, that ye stir not up, nor
awake my love, till he please".

>forbore not glance or toy
>Of amorous intent, well understood
>Of *Eve*, whose Eye darted contagious Fire
>   IX.1034–36

She inflames his senses with ardour to enjoy her. This lust for the body is far from the beautifully spiritual relationship of Book IV which brought about fulfilment and harmony with God's creation. Here is Milton, the discriminating moralist who feels that feminine vanity is a necessary part of womanhood and not to be condemned; it is only when fallen that love and sex are beset by wantonness and end in mutual frustration.

Up to the time of the Fall, hebraic references drawn almost invariably from the Old Testament are used to describe Adam and Eve and to confer on them spiritual purity and moral dignity. Hebraic references relating to them after the Fall are of a different nature. After Adam and Eve have become like everyman, most of Milton's references are derived from post-Biblical sources – that is, from the Apocrypha and various commentaries – the tenor of which is more realistic and closer to the everyday life we know. While before the Fall, for example, Milton follows the traditional etymology of Eve's name,[43] he associates it with "serpent" after the Fall. Though Rashi gives the popular explanation of the name Havva, Rabbinical exegesis has also joined the name to the Aramaic Hivya, "serpent". Cassuto follows "the scholars" in pointing out that the name is cognate with the Aramaic Hivya and the Arabic Hayya. He suggests that Adam named his wife Havva after the incident with the serpent.[44] D. C. Allen points out that the meaning of Eve's name was controversial in Milton's generation and that Milton could have read about the connection of the name with the serpent in the *Protrepticus* of Clement of Alexandria as well as in the *Praeparationis Evangelicae* Libri XV of Eusebius.[45] Allen suggests that Milton followed these sources when he tells Eve,

---

[43] See pp. 78–79 above.
[44] *From Adam to Noah*, p. 170.
[45] "Milton and the Name of Eve", *MLN*, LXXIV (1959), pp. 681–683.

> Out of my sight, thou Serpent, that name best
> Befits thee with him leagu'd, thyself as false
> And hateful;
>
> X.867–869

He believes that Milton put the name in Adam's mouth because Adam was angry at Eve and that Milton thus shows that this is the true meaning of the name. This theory of Eve's name is still controversial. Whether Milton learned about it from Clement of Alexandria, Eusebius, or Rabbinical commentaries is irrelevant to *Paradise Lost*. Milton was aware of the ambiguous meaning of Eve's name and made use of it very appropriately after the Fall. Whatever the source for this meaning of Eve's name, it certainly reflects the change Eve underwent after Book IV.

There is also a contrast in Adam's character before and after the Fall. Adam's perfection before the Fall is clearly expressed in the account of Adam's reception of Raphael in Book V. Three aspects of this meeting are implicit in the text: that angels come and visit humans and share their meals only when they deserve it; that Adam is mature enough to be told some of the mysteries of the cosmos and its creation; that at the same time, however, he is a human being who "might err in things too high", a mortal who treats his divine guest with respect and awe.

Adam receives Raphael amidst the oaks of Mamre,[46] here described as the spicy forest, recalling the garden of the Song of Songs:

> Him through the spicy Forest onward come
> *Adam* discern'd, as in the door he sat
> Of his cool Bow'r, while now the mounted Sun
> Shot down direct his fervid Rays,
>
> V.298–301

---

[46] The fact that Adam discerns his guest through the "spicy forest", is a suggestive detail indicating that Milton was aware of the meaning of the Hebrew words "Alonei Mamre" and preferred the "oaks of Mamre" in the original text to the "plains of Mamre" in the Authorized Version. This significant detail was first pointed out by Jason P. Rosenblatt, "Celestial Entertainment in Eden: Book V of *Paradise Lost*", *HTR*, LXII (1969), pp. 412–413, and I am indebted to him therefore.

and, while Eve hastes from each "bough and brake" "each plant and juicest gourd" to pluck such choice fruit to entertain their guest, Adam meets the angel:

> Meanwhile our Primitive great Sire, to meet
> His god-like Guest, walks forth, without more train
> Accompanied than with his own complete
> Perfections; in himself was all his state,
> More solemn than the tedious pomp that waits
> On Princes, when thir rich Retinue long
> Of Horses led, and Grooms besmear'd with Gold
> Dazzles the crowd, and sets them all agape,
> Nearer his presence *Adam* though not aw'd,
> Yet with submiss approach and reverence meek,
> As to a superior Nature, bowing low,
> Thus said . . .
>
> V.350–361

This encounter bears a strong resemblance to the story of Abraham and his divine visitors.

> And the Lord appeared unto him in the plains of Mamre: and he sat in the tent door in the heat of the day; And he lift up his eyes and looked, and, lo, three men stood by him: and when he saw them, he ran to meet them from the tent door and bowed himself toward the ground, And said, My Lord, if now I have found favour in thy sight, pass not away, I pray thee, from thy servant: Let a little water, I pray you, be fetched, and wash your feet, and rest yourselves under the tree: And I will fetch a morsel of bread, and comfort ye your hearts; after that ye shall pass on: for therefore are ye come to your servant. And they said, So do, as thou hast said. And Abraham hastened into the tent unto Sarah, and said, Make ready quickly three measures of fine meal, knead it, and make cakes upon the hearth. And Abraham ran unto the herd, and fetcht a calf tender and good, and gave it unto a young man; and he hasted to dress it.
>
> Genesis xviii. 1–7

The parallels between the two visits are striking.[47] Here again
Milton is using Hebrew materials for his poetic ends. The resemblance between Abraham's story and Adam's has a double purpose: it helps to make Adam a flesh-and-blood character and
gives an indication of his prelapsarian goodness (his "complete
perfections" V.352–353). Let us compare the two. Abraham and
Adam receive their visitors at "mid-noon" (V.311)[48] in contrast
with the "hour of Noon" (IX.739) when Eve gives in to the arguments of her tempter.[49] Both reveal hospitality and kindness.
Abraham does not know who the visitors are.[50] He "ran unto the
herd", "hasted" to dress the calf and enjoined his wife to "Make
ready quickly three measures of fine meal". His behaviour and
his words reflect his natural hospitality, his goodness, and also
the humility characteristic of the East ("if now I have found favour
in thy sight"). But most of all they signify his excitement and won-

[47] I believe this passage is based on Genesis xviii rather than on the conversation
between Adam and the angel in *Adamus Exul* as J. M. Evans believes. *Paradise
Lost and the Genesis Tradition*, pp. 212, 256.
  James Sims has observed most of Milton's allusions to the Genesis episode
(*The Bible in Milton's Epics*, pp. 202–204). Other parallels between the story of
Abraham and Adam have been studied by Mother Mary Christopher Pécheux
("Abraham, Adam, and the Theme of Exile in *Paradise Lost*", *PMLA*, LXXX
[1965], pp. 365–371) and by Barbara Kiefer Lewalski ("Structure and the
Symbolism of Vision in Michael's Prophecy, *Paradise Lost*, Books XI–XII",
PQ, XLII [1963], pp. 25–35). A thorough analysis of Milton's indebtedness to
Genesis xviii and to Rashi which substantiates the thesis presented here has been
written by Jason P. Rosenblatt, "Celestial Entertainment in Eden: Book V of
Paradise Lost".
[48] Harold Fisch points out that Milton's emphasis on the unusual heat of the sun
may have been suggested by Rashi, "Hebraic Style and Motifs in *Paradise Lost*",
p. 55.
[49] On the significance of the hour for the light-darkness symbolism of *Paradise
Lost*, see Jackson I. Cope, *The Metaphoric Structure of Paradise Lost* (Baltimore,
1962), pp. 130–133.
[50] Rashi may well have suggested the identity of Raphael to Milton. The importance of Rashi's commentary for understanding Raphael's mission has first been
perspicaciously commented upon by J. P. Rosenblatt, pp. 418–422. The fact that
Raphael's function is, according to Rashi, the healing of Abraham's wound of
circumcision is relevant here for, as Rosenblatt argues, Abraham's physical
discomfort carries no stigma. Adam and Eve are indeed no more guilty than
Abraham merely because they have been disturbed by Satan's dream. Like Rashi,
Milton makes Raphael "an agent of comfort and not of forgiveness".

der at the important visitors. Milton's Adam recognizes the "glorious shape" (V.309) of the Heav'nly stranger" (V.316)

> some great behest from Heav'n
> To us perhaps he brings, and will voutsafe
> This day to be our Guest
>
> V.311–313

and his eagerness to make his guest welcome ("bring forth and pour / Abundance, fit to honor and receive / Our Heav'nly stranger", V.313–315) resembles that of the faithful patriarch. The parallels are clear. What relevance has this similarity to the Genesis chapter? What differences are there between the two?

James Sims believes that the dramatic impact of the association of Adam and Abraham is important because, as he puts it:

> Without some such association, Adam might continue to be a perfect superman physically, mentally and spiritually, a character with whom it would be hard to sympathize and whose reality as a character would be difficult to accept ... This initial association of Adam with the Biblical Abraham foreshadows the Adam who pleads with God for a mate ... who too readily hearkens to his wife as Abraham did when Ishmael was conceived..."[51]

Harold Fisch, studying the hebraic influences on Milton's style, finds that the atmosphere of Adam's reception of Raphael is "domestic, even trivial", and that "the dominating domesticity of the atmosphere matches here the very nonepic, humble dignity of Adam and Eve as they converse with their angel guest".[52] Both Sims and Fisch attribute the dramatic realism of Milton's lines to the Genesis episode. That Milton was thinking of the Hebrew text when he composed the scene is supported by unmistakable textual references.[53] Adam here, as is generally agreed, is as human and real as the great patriarch. It is, however, more difficult to agree to the second part of Sims' argument – namely, that

---

[51] *The Bible in Milton's Epics*, pp. 202–203.
[52] "Hebraic Style and Motifs in *Paradise Lost*", p. 54.
[53] See note 51 above.

Adam's resemblance to Abraham foreshadows his human weakness and, to quote Fisch again, that "the low style" is bound up with the particular Biblical episode. Milton is careful to avoid just that. Though the poet here contrasts Adam's noble simplicity with the tedious pomp of princes, Adam, unlike the Biblical patriarch, was conscious of his own dignity and "complete / Perfections" (V.352–353). Adam is "our Primitive great Sire", and his "solemn" appearance when he meets his "god-like Guest" is far from the spontaneous and simple behaviour of the patriarch when he "lift up his eyes and looked, and, lo, three men stood by him". A low style is indeed found in *Paradise Lost*, and it does reflect domestic triviality and weakness but only after the Fall. Here the formalized style confers epic dignity upon Adam. It is true, the resemblance between the situations makes Adam real as a character, but I believe it is primarily intended as a further demonstration of his perfection and dignity. In the prelapsarian Eden, Adam is spiritually as close to God's messenger as Abraham was to his divine guests. In fact, Adam's reception of Raphael is reverent and cordial and evinces Milton's belief that decorum is always "the grand masterpiece to observe". This is also evidenced in the description of the meal. The Genesis writer briefly describes it thus: "and he stood by them under the tree, and they did eat" (Genesis xviii. 8). Milton's Adam is particularly ceremonious:

> A while discourse they hold;
> No fear lest Dinner cool; when thus began
> Our Author. Heav'nly stranger, please to taste
> These bounties which our Nourisher, from whom
> All perfet good unmeasur'd out, descends,
> To us for food and for delight hath caus'd
> The Earth to yield; unsavory food perhaps
> To spiritual Natures;
>
> V.395–402

The point, of course, is that Raphael partakes of the meal with his host as in Genesis[54] (unlike the same angel in the Book of

---

[54] On the eating of the angel, see also Rosenblatt, "Celestial Entertainment in Eden", p. 413.

Tobit who appears in a vision and neither eats nor drinks with men). Adam is so very ceremonious for unlike Abraham, he knows at once who their guest is and appreciates the fact that this is a real visit and not a vision. The festive meal thus conveys the harmony and close relationship between Adam and God's messenger. It also looks back to the Abraham figure in the council scene in Book III where the Son, interceding for justice,[55] borrows the words of the patriarch; it looks forth to the figure of the faithful patriarch, beneficiary of the covenant, going into exile with God's promise and the courage of his own convictions.[56]

This is not so in postlapsarian Eden, for when Michael's appearance in Eden is described, it is contrasted with another divine apparition:

Not that more glorious, when the Angels met
Jacob in *Mahanaim*, where he saw
The field Pavilion'd with his Guardians bright;
Nor that which on the flaming Mount appear'd
In *Dothan*, cover'd with a Camp of Fire,
Against the *Syrian* King, . . .

XI.213–218

Now "doubt / And carnal fear . . . dimm'd Adam's eye." Adam is guilty and much less conscious of his own worth than he was in Book V. It is perhaps also significant that the Archangel no longer appears in his "shape Celestial": fallen Adam is no longer worthy to speak with angels face to face, and Michael draws near "as Man / Clad to meet Man" (XI.239–240). Before the Fall, Adam is conscious of the gratitude he owes "our Nourisher" and invites the "sociable" Raphael to partake of the meal after thanking the "Celestial Father" who gives to all. After the Fall, Eve greedily "ingorg'd without restraint" (IX.791) and does reverence to the tree (IX.835). Both eat their fill (IX.1005), taking no thought and are so intoxicated by its fallacious fruit (IX.1008) that they "feel / Divinity within them breeding wings / Wherewith to scorn the Earth:" (IX.1009–1011). The realization of the serpent's prophecy

[55] See chapter IV, pp. 111–113.
[56] See chapter V, p. 154.

– "ye shall be as Gods" (IX.708) – brings with it the sins of gluttony, ingratitude, and idolatry.

In postlapsarian Eden, negative comparisons are no longer drawn with classical allusions but with episodes and figures from the Old Testament. After the Fall when the "heav'nly Bands" (XI. 208) light down from a sky of Jasper, Adam's eyes are dimmed by doubt and carnal fear (XI.211–212). The "glorious Apparition" (XI.211) is described as being

> Not that more glorious, when the Angels met
> *Jacob* in *Mahanaim* . . .
> Nor that which on the flaming Mount appear'd
> In *Dothan* . . .
>   XI.213–214; 216–217

Just as Jacob's dreaming of the ladder – symbol of promise and hope – and receiving God's promise is contrasted to Satan nearing Heaven but excluded from the world of God (III.510–525), so the figure of the courageous patriarch reappears here once more to point out Adam's realization of his Fall. Doubt and carnal fear dim his eyes whereas Jacob's eyes "were dim for age" (Genesis xlviii. 10).[57] Yet while pointing to Adam's changed nature, the lines also evince Milton's faith in the possibility of vision and courage for they allude to the story of the third patriarch, Israel (XII.-267), who was worthy to meet God's host at Mahanaim, who could wrestle with God and prevail, who received earthly as well as divine benedictions. We realize Adam's failure but we also realize that there is hope for men like Jacob who are, as Milton says, "beloved by God"[58] and through whom the divine will is to be enacted.

Milton's negative comparison is very apt in this context for it compels us to contrast the purpose and outcome of the two divine visitations as they are, indeed, contrasted by Adam:

> for I descry
> From yonder blazing Cloud that veils the Hill

---

[57] Genesis xlviii. 11 says Jacob could see his children. The chapter is a fusion of different texts and Milton, characteristically, identifies with the blind Jacob.
[58] *A Second Defense of the English People*, Yale Prose Works, IV, i, p. 587.

One of the heav'nly Host, and by his Gait
None of the meanest, some great Potentate
Or of the Thrones above, such Majesty
Invests him coming; yet not terrible,
That I should fear, nor sociably mild,
As *Raphael*, that I should much confide,
But solemn and sublime, whom not to offend,
With reverence I must meet, and thou retire.

XI.228–237

This shows once more how deliberate Milton's use of hebraic allusions is: whether these allusions are employed for positive or for negative comparisons, they are always intentionally related to the contexts in which they appear.

An interesting example of Milton's forceful use of Old Testament allusions is seen in Adam's words after hearing Michael's message:

This most afflicts me, that departing hence,
As from his face I shall be hid, depriv'd
His blessed count'nance;

XI.315–317

As Hughes notes on XI.316, Adam's reaction to Michael's message echoes that of Cain: "Behold, thou hast driven me out this day from the face of the earth; and from thy face shall I be hid" (Genesis iv. 14). Cain's fall, like that of Adam, is brought about by the victory of passion over reason and faith. As Raphael warned Adam, so God had warned Cain: "If thou doest well, shalt thou not be accepted? and if thou doest not well, sin lieth at the door. And unto thee shall be his desire, and thou shalt rule over him" (Genesis iv. 7). Neither Adam nor Cain, however, could "rule over" sin. Both lost faith and sinned, and the punishment of both significantly entails exile from Eden and "tilling the ground" which "shall not henceforth yield ... her strength" unto them (Genesis iv. 12). The words of Cain echocd by Milton's Adam describe the natural and inevitable outcome of the Fall – alienation from God. The Fall is no longer the unique experience of

Adam; through the reference to Cain, the Fall and its consequences become universal and, by falling, Adam becomes a "prototype" of humanity. Although the reader may identify with Adam when he decides to share Eve's fate and although he, partly at least, may feel that Adam acted nobly,[59] Milton still does not appear to have reached "a result the exact opposite of what he had intended."[60] If one is for a brief moment inclined to justify Adam when he was "fondly overcome with Female charm" (IX.999), the allusion to Cain compels us to compare their sins and strongly indicates that Milton conceived of Adam's sin as including all other sins.[61] Adam's sin of disobedience is, in Milton eyes, as deadly a sin as Cain's murder of Abel, and it is the cause of all other crimes as well. It is true that there is a clash between the human and dramatic moment of Adam's Fall and the theological message of the poem, but it was part of Milton's intention. This clash, moreover, dissolves when Adam recognizes the magnitude of his sin. By echoing Cain's words, Adam not only acknowledges his sin; his sincere grief at the loss of God also marks his acceptance of the just punishment meted out to him. It is perhaps not insignificant that a few lines later in the same scene, Adam, realizing his bitter fate, mourns that he will not be able to "relate" to his sons God's appearance before him (XI.319); he regrets his inability to fulfil the Biblical injunction of relating sacred events from father to son as laid down, for example, in Deuteronomy vi. 20ff. and in Joel i.2–3.[62]

Where Adam's realization of the Fall results in deep grief and is thus a direct reaction, Eve's reaction is less direct. She experiences jealousy for the first time:

---

[59] A. J. A. Waldock, *Paradise Lost and Its Critics* (Cambridge, 1964 [1947]), pp. 42–57.
[60] Waldock, p. 57.
[61] *Paradise Lost*, X.12–16.
[62] "And when thy son asketh thee in time to come, saying, What mean the testimonies, and the statutes, and the judgments, which the Lord our God hath commanded you? Then thou shalt say unto thy son ..." Deuteronomy vi. 20–21.

"Hear this, ye old men, and give ear, all ye inhabitants of the land. Hath this been in your days, or even in the days of your fathers? Tell ye your children of it, and let your children tell their children, and their children another generation". Joel i. 2–3.

what if God have seen,
And Death ensue? then I shall be no more,
And *Adam* wedded to another *Eve*,
Shall live with her enjoying, I extinct;
A death to think.

IX.826–830

Her words repeat Rashi's explanation of Genesis iii. 6 as well as Genesis Rabba xix. 5 almost verbatim:

"and she gave also to her husband – so that she would not die while he lived and took another wife."

(Rashi)

"R. Simlai: ... She said to him, What do you think? That I will die and another Eve will be created for you?"

(Genesis Rabba)

This jealousy triggered off by fear more than humanizes Eve. It points to her now sinful nature and is in contrast to the goodness and innocence she radiates before the Fall.[63] Quite significantly, envy, including sexual envy, is what brings anguish to Eve as it did to Satan.

Throughout *Paradise Lost* there is a close relationship between Milton's moral beliefs and the literary associations he evokes.

---

[63] Eve's jealousy is important methodically, for a variety of conjectured sources have been suggested for it. Whereas Saurat suggested the Zohar as a possible source for Eve's jealousy (Denis Saurat, *Milton et le matérialisme chrétien en Angleterre* [Paris, 1928], p. 98), Fletcher first suggested that the source for this motif was Yosifon (*Milton's Semitic Studies and Some Manifestations of them in his Poetry* [Chicago, 1926], pp. 133–135; but in *Milton's Rabbinical Readings*, pp. 206–207 he claims that Rashi's brief commentary on Genesis iii. 6 can also be connected with Milton, and Allen adds another Rabbinical source for the same theme ("Milton and Rabbi Eliezer", *MLN*, LXIII (1948), p. 262). On the other hand Arnold Williams traces the jealousy motif to Christian commentators (*The Common Expositor*, p. 123).

What we learn from this is that the Rabbinic idea of Eve's jealousy, because of its suggestiveness, seems to have become a commonplace idea, and Milton has recourse to it, very appropriately, after the Fall. It is probably not possible to determine the exact source Milton used; nevertheless it is pertinent to point out that where a hebraic idea or episode is found in Christian sources, it seems more probable that Milton should have gone there.

What we have tried to show in this chapter is that while proleptic allusions inspired by classical works tend to blur the distinction between the idyllic prelapsarian Eden and the fallen garden, the hebraic allusions as used and distributed by Milton tend to accentuate this distinction. In other words, the hebraic elements do not provide the central idea; they are not an end in themselves. Rather, they are a convincing means for bringing home Milton's Christian concept of moral truth and goodness expressed in his conception of the Fall as an event of great moment for humanity.

IV

MILTON'S GOD IN COUNCIL AND IN WAR

No aspect of *Paradise Lost* has been so harshly and frequently criticized as Milton's presentation of God and Heaven. Whether the poem is read against a Christian humanist background and admired for its message or whether it is praised for the beauty of its poetry, the God Milton paints is often found wanting.[1] Milton has been criticized for his "imperfectly anthropomorphic presentation", of God and, again, for his failure to achieve his poetic intention because he is committing himself to logic in his description of God.[2] Some readers, ignoring Milton's religious beliefs, claim the poem is good precisely because God is so bad.[3] My objection to this reading is not only that it is unhistorical[4] but that it is not

---

[1] Marjorie Hope Nicolson writes that "a modern reader of Book III feels rebuffed and repelled when he first meets Milton's God". She voices the opinion of many staunch admirers of the poem when she asks, "Great poet of light and sound as Milton was, could he not have made his God an awesome Presence, unmoved and unmoving, whom we feel, but whom our eyes – weaker than those of the Seraphim – cannot and should not see?" *John Milton. A Reader's Guide to his Poetry* (New York, 1966 [1963]), pp. 224–225. Helen Gardner, too, reluctantly admits that "it is impossible to deny that Milton's presentation of the Adversary and of Hell is far more impressive than his presentation of God and Heaven" (*A Reading of Paradise Lost*, p. 55).
[2] John Peter's first impressions of God are "strangely unfavourable" (*A Critique of Paradise Lost* [New York and London, 1960], pp. 12, 18).
   See also David Daiches, *Milton* (London, 1966 [1957]), p. 181.
[3] William Empson, *Milton's God* (London, 1965), revised edition, pp. 11, 13.
[4] In his essay on "Literary Criticism" in *The Aims and Methods of Scholarship in Modern Languages and Literatures*, edited by James Thorpe (New York, 1963), p. 59, Frye writes that academic criticism should be "partly historical, studying past literature in its original context, and partly an attempt to express what past literature can communicate beyond its own time to ours." Empson indeed claims a historical basis for this thesis. He believes that "the main European revolt

validated by what the poetry conveys. The view I wish to advance
here is that Milton's presentation of God and Heaven not only embodies his seventeenth-century theology; it is, on close examination, convincing in view of the various hebraic elements, thematic
and metaphorical, that are incorporated in Milton's descriptions
of God in council and in war. An appreciation of Old Testament
allusions and echoes is vital for the understanding of both the
conceptual link between the various scenes taking place in Heaven
and the analogical correspondence between Milton's circumfe-
rence and the human centre of the poem. The cosmic theme provides not only, as Helen Gardner says, "a comparison and a
contrast to the story of man's creation, fall and restoration";[5] it
also foreshadows the dramatic events in Eden which the poem
holds in focus. The greatness of Milton's Heaven consists in the
conceptual breadth and depth which it adds to the central theme
of the poem rather than in any inherent rhetorical power. And
this dimension depends upon Biblical allusions and echoes interwoven in the poem. It is also the Old Testament allusions which
give those parts of the poem dramatic intensity.

Milton uses Old Testament allusions not only for their poetic
suggestiveness but also because the language of the Bible was the
most appropriate for the description of God and Heaven. Like
other Renaissance and seventeenth-century writers,[6] he believed
that when

(*FOOTNOTE 4 continued*)
against Christianity does not date from the Romantic Movement but from more
than two centuries earlier, and the first name that occurs to one is Montaigne; ...
A person aware of this tradition ... is not likely to be 'embarrassed' by the
wickedness of Milton's God ... " (Empson, p. 14). This thesis is not substantiated
by the text.
[5] Gardner, p. 52.
[6] The theory of accommodation, as expressed by St. Augustine, for example,
was familiar to seventeenth-century readers. See Merritt Y. Hughes on "The
Filiations of Milton's Celestial Dialogue", in *Ten Perspectives on Milton* (New
Haven, 1965), pp. 123–125, and also William G. Madsen, "Earth the Shadow of
Heaven: Typological Symbolism in *Paradise Lost*", in *Milton. Modern Essays
in Criticism.* ed. by Arthur E. Barker (New York, 1965), pp. 246–263, and Leland
Ryken, "Milton and the Apocalyptic", *HLQ*, XXXI, 3, pp. 223–238.

we speak of knowing God, it must be understood with reference to the imperfect comprehension of man; for to know God as he really is, far transcends the powers of man's thoughts, much more of his perception ... Our safest way is to form in our minds such a conception of God, *as shall correspond with his own delineation and representation of himself in the sacred writings.* For granting that both in the literal and figurative descriptions of God, he is exhibited not as he really is, but in such a manner as may be within the scope of our comprehensions, yet we ought to entertain such a conception of him, as he, in condescending to accommodate himself to our capacities, has shewn that he desires we should conceive.[7]

(my italics)

Milton thus knew that it was best to avoid going "beyond the written word of Scripture" lest he "be tempted to indulge in vague cogitations and subtleties".[8] Helen Gardner believes that the theory of accommodation prevented Milton "from exercising his own power to suggest" and that "one reason why he 'wrote in fetters' when he wrote of Heaven is that there exist in Scripture images and fictions to describe Heaven which his own theory of Scripture told him were chosen by God to illuminate our understanding".[9] It is true that Heaven and its characters are described almost exclusively in terms of Scripture, but this limitation is not necessarily constrictive. As a matter of fact, the Scriptural passages Milton alludes to, those taken from the Old Testament, in particular, are powerfully suggestive, and it is they which make his Heaven so effective.

To the Books of Moses and to the writings of the prophets Milton could turn for ideal models of poetic personifications of God; in the unrhymed verses of the Psalms he could find the purest devotional poetry expressive of deep religious feelings. It is therefore natural that when he came to represent God, Milton turned to the verses of the Hebrew poet-prophets for inspiration. But the

[7] *The Christian Doctrine*, I.2.
[8] *Ibid.*
[9] Gardner, p. 55.

reason is not only poetic. Only the hebraic omnipotent God of the Old Testament is morally strong enough to defeat the fallen angels associated with the idols and heathen gods mentioned in the Old Testament. Had Milton created a more merciful God, a less hard taskmaster, he would not have been equal to his opponent in the poem. In the books on Hell, Milton invoked the atmosphere of the conflict between the God of the Israelites and the false gods as represented in the Old Testament. In the books on Heaven, Milton very appropriately invokes the image of the powerful Creator, the God of Justice as he is revealed in his dealings with his most devoted believers – Abraham, Moses, and prophets like Isaiah and Ezekiel. This image of God and the recurrence of Old Testament allusions and motifs create the thematic and conceptual link between the scenes which take place in Heaven.

The first scene to be considered is the heavenly council in Book III. Here Milton was faced with the problem of representing God as at once the powerful ruler of the universe, the Lord of Hosts, and as the essence of goodness and light. In terms of style, God had to be simultaneously idealized and rendered concrete. Milton achieves this end in the council scene, where God's first speech reveals his identity:

> Only begotten Son, seest thou what rage
> Transports our adversary, whom no bounds
> Prescrib'd, no bars of Hell, nor all the chains
> Heapt on him there, nor yet the main Abyss
> Wild interrupt can hold; so bent he seems
> On desperate revenge, that shall redound
> Upon his own rebellious head.
>
> III.80–86[10]

---

[10] Waldock believes these lines contradict Milton's own statement that Satan and his mate escaped the Stygian flood through the "sufferance of supernal Power". It is, however, difficult to accept his feeling of "impatience" with a poet "who, not content with a God who must, however matters are contrived, appear somewhat vindictive, goes out of his way to convict him on his very first appearance of flagrant disingenuousness and hypocrisy" (*Paradise Lost and Its Critics*, p. 101). Waldock seems unaware of the conceptions of God and Satan prevalent in the seventeenth-century audience for which Milton wrote.

The lines which Waldock objects to so strongly have been commented upon

This is the divine wrath of the Old Testament God that is also heard in the words of St. Paul and Revelations. And divine justice is turned against those who are wicked. God's attitude to man who broke the "Sole pledge of his obedience" is not only that of a judge punishing evil; it is mixed with paternal care:

> So will fall
> Hee and his faithless Progeny: whose fault?
> Whose but his own? ingrate, he had of mee
> All he could have; I made him just and right,
> Sufficient to have stood, though free to fall.
>
> III.95–99

These lines imply more than the mere affirmation of justice; they imply the hope that man might live up to the moral nature he has been endowed with, as well as a deep disappointment at his failure to do so. The eagerness to see man in his perfection and the regret at his moral fall are common to Milton and to the Old Testament prophets. Moreover, the sentiment expressed in Milton's lines here resembles that of the prophets blaming Israel for ingratitude to the creator; for example: "I have nourished and brought up children, and they have rebelled against me. The ox knoweth his owner, and the ass his master's crib: but Israel doth not know, my people doth not consider" (Isaiah i. 2–3).[11]

Although God's first speech ends with the promise "Mercy first and last shall brightest shine" (III.134), God's relationship to most of mankind is that of the Old Testament God of justice, and Milton forcefully expresses this in the words of the prophets. For those who "pray, repent, and bring obedience due", He promises His "ear shall not be slow", His "eye not shut", "for I will clear thir senses dark, / ... and soft'n stony hearts." But mercy is extended only to those who repent, and the words are harsh. It may

(*FOOTNOTE 10 continued*)

more justly by Christopher Ricks, who examines their diction and syntax, showing how they "compress his [God's] knowledge of Satan's single motive with his observation of his escape from Hell (*Milton's Grand Style* [Oxford, 1963], p. 60).
[11] Also Isaiah v. 1–7; Jeremiah ii. 5; iii. 10; iii. 20–21; Ezekiel v. 5–6; Micah vi. 2–8, and others.

be significant that the same metaphors are used by Isaiah in an opposite context: "Make the heart of this people fat, and make their ears heavy, and shut their eyes; lest they see with their eyes and hear with their ears, and understand with their heart, and convert, and be healed" (Isaiah vi. 10). Milton's God, too, has no mercy for the sinners:

> my day of grace
> They who neglect and scorn, shall never taste;
> But hard be hard'n'd, blind be blinded more,
> That they may stumble on, and deeper fall;
>   III.198–201

Patrick Hume notes (on III.200) that the allusion is to Pharaoh, the example of a sinner hardened by God's remitting his punishment, and he quotes Exodus viii. 15: "But when Pharaoh saw that there was respite, he hardened his heart, and hearkened not unto them; as the Lord had said." The correspondence between the sinners and Pharaoh has a double function here. The sinners are as proud and obstinate as Pharaoh and, like him, their hearts are hardened. But the recurring allusions to Pharaoh also have another significance, for throughout the Old Testament there are references to God's victory over the Egyptians and to the liberation of the Hebrews from Egyptian slavery. The recurrence of these references makes the Egyptians an archetype of God's enemies, secondary, perhaps, only to 'Amaleq.

When Milton expresses the irrevocability of God's punishments – the "desperate revenge, that shall redound / Upon his own rebellious head" (III.85–86) – the words as well as the concept are reminiscent of many Old Testament verses.[12] Milton's lines also reveal another important attribute of God – His jealousy.[13]

---

[12] For instance: Ezekiel xvii. 19; ix. 10. In His second speech (III.178–182), God promises that He will once more vouchsafe His grace to man. As Hughes indicates, line 180 echoes Psalm xxxix. 4: "Lord, make me to know . . . how frail I am."

[13] Lines 178–182 also express the idea of Exodus xx. 3. Verbally, they echo the verses of the poet-prophet to whom Milton alludes so often: Isaiah xlv. 5–6, 22. To isolate the reverberations from the Old Testament in God's speeches would not only be an injustice to Milton: it would be a misreading of the speeches of God in the context of the poem. These clear hebraic allusions make God come alive in the epic.

For Milton knew that only the jealous Lord of Hosts, the Almighty God who demands sacrifices from his prophets and who cruelly chastises his enemies, could be the counterpart to the evil adversary and the pagan deities described in the first two books.

The first speech of God, the Son's reply, and the ensuing speeches have been the subject of a heated dispute for, during the last century, most critics have found fault with God's logical arguments[14] and his rigid concept of justice; some have criticized the Son's more emotional plea for mercy. With respect to Milton's intention in presenting God as he does, two questions have to be clarified: the first is whether the distinction between the Old Testament God of vengeance and the merciful Jesus is co-extensive with the theme of the dialogue, in other words, whether there is an argument here between Milton's God (that is, Justice) and the Son (Mercy); the second is what concept of God emerges from the scene as a whole.

In one of the most recent critiques of the council scene, Hughes considers the tension between justice and mercy to be part of the tradition to which *Paradise Lost* belongs, for in the morality plays justice and truth plead for the prosecution, mercy and peace for the defense, and in the moralities "Mercy always prevailed with God for the repentant sinner."[15] Hughes believes that by "abandoning the debate between Justice and Mercy over fallen Man in favor of the dialogue between the Almighty Father and the Son, Milton

---

[14] See above p. 103. Daiches, for example, believes Milton "falls down in Book III" because "here he is committing himself to logic in order to achieve his poetic intention so that the reader, however much he wishes to read *Paradise Lost* 'as a poem', is forced to read it as this point as logical argument, and to answer back as he reads" (Daiches, p. 181).

[15] In his learned analysis of "The Filiations of Milton's Celestial Dialogue" Hughes reminds us that Milton had sketched the dramatic situation of the council (III.80–343) in an outline for a tragedy on the theme of *Paradise Lost*. Hughes traces this dramatic element to the morality plays in which God prejudged man's fate (*Ten Perspectives on Milton*, pp. 104–135).

The distinction between the Old Testament God of Justice and the merciful Jesus is well-rooted in English literature from the time of the mystery cycles, the plays of John Bale, and onward. M. Roston, *Biblical Drama in England* (London, 1968), pp. 60ff. examines the presentation of God and Christ in the Renaissance plays and the changes these figures underwent since the time of the mysteries.

found the way to a dialogue of distinct persons".[16] Hughes rightly rejects the theories of those modern critics who tend to polarize the Son and the Father by contrasting their characters. His thesis is that the debate on justice vs. mercy is a "dialogue in a more or less Platonic sense: the quest of truth" and that the "counterpoise of justice and mercy in the debate which Milton inherited from the theologians as well as from the morality plays was itself a forensic metaphor".[17]

The conversation between God and the Son is indeed a dialogue, but it seems that Milton was less inspired by theologians or by the dramatic justice vs. mercy antinomy found in so many morality plays than by two dialogues in the Old Testament – between God and Abraham and between God and Moses – in which the dichotomy between justice and mercy does not exist.[18] Hughes recognizes the Biblical allusions but fails to appreciate their significance. He writes, for example, that Milton "understood the difficulty of reconciling the passions of the anthropomorphic God of the Old Testament to the standards of human decency".[19] I believe the opposite is true – namely, that precisely by verbally echoing the dialogues of Abraham and Moses with their God, Milton was able to convey the true nature of his God, a God who stands for much more than "human decency", a God who loves His creatures, whose aim is to protect and save Mankind as well as the moral principles of Justice and Righteousness He stands for. In these Biblical episodes Milton very probably also found a model for what Hughes calls "a dialogue of distinct persons".

When the council scene in Heaven opens, we see God as the supreme and beneficent Creator and Father of the Universe:

> High Thron'd above all highth, bent down his eye,
> His own works and their works at once to view:
>
> III.58–59

---

[16] Hughes, p. 111.

[17] Hughes, pp. 113, 128 and 134.

[18] Hughes admits that the "Scriptural substrate of the speeches vindicated both their theology and their style". Referring to Sims he adds, "And actually by the most recent count of the unmistakable Scriptural echoes, there are no fewer than eighty-seven in 329 lines – enough to give every line the semblance of authentic divine utterance" (p. 122).

[19] Hughes, p. 123.

We then hear God explain two great truths that are paradoxes only to non-believers: good is creative and powerful but not powerful enough to destroy evil; the greatest good that was bestowed upon man ("All he could have" – III.98) is also the source of the greatest evil that may befall him. This good is Reason, man being "just and right, / Sufficient to have stood, though free to fall" (III.98–99).

When the Son answers God's speech, he neither argues with God nor does he flatter Him but – relying on God's partiality for His creation – he tries to soften man's sentence. His speech expresses mercy and goodness, but his words are those of another son of God who asks, in the name of divine justice, that God have mercy on His creatures. Abraham says: "That be far from thee to do after this manner, to slay the righteous with the wicked: and that the righteous should be as the wicked, that be far from thee: Shall not the Judge of all the earth do right?" (Genesis xviii. 25). So Milton's Christ pleads,

> For should Man finally be lost, should Man
> Thy creature late so lov'd, thy youngest Son
> Fall circumvented thus by fraud, though join'd
> With his own folly? that be from thee far,
> That far be from thee, Father, who art Judge
> Of all things made, and judgest only right.
> III.150–155

Milton not merely borrows Abraham's words and rhetoric; he assimilates them and subordinates them to the controlling idea of Christ's speech:

> Or shall the Adversary thus obtain
> His end, and frustrate thine, shall he fulfill
> His malice, and thy goodness bring to naught,
> III.156–159

No clash is intended between the God of Abraham and Milton's God here for, in the Son as in his patriarchal prototype, love of justice and mercy are fused with a boundless devotion to God. We might add that just as there is no true clash between Abraham and God, so there is no debate, no argument between God and the

Son. Like Abraham's intercession for the innocent people of Sodom, the Son's intercession for sinful man is motivated by absolute faith in God and a deep love for humanity. He "believed in the Lord" (Genesis xv. 6) is one of the leitmotifs of Abraham's life from the day God ordered him to "Get thee out of thy country, and from thy kindred ..." (Genesis xii. 1) until the moment of the supreme test: "Take now thy son, thine only son Isaac, whom thou lovest, and get thee into the land of Moriah ..." (Genesis xxii. 2). God understands Abraham's plea for Sodom which is a plea for justice as well as a plea for Abraham's own faith which needs to be reasserted. And just as God answers Abraham and spares the innocent family of Lot, so Milton's God readily complies with the Son's request, which also expresses His own will:

> O Son, in whom my Soul hath chief delight,
> Son of my bosom, Son who art alone
> My word, my wisdom, and effectual might,
> All hast thou spok'n as my thoughts are, all
> As my Eternal purpose hath decreed:
> Man shall not quite be lost, but sav'd who will,
> Yet not of will in him, but grace in me
> Freely voutsaf't;
>
> III.168–175

When the Son offers himself for the redemption of mankind,

> Behold mee then, mee for him, life for life
> I offer, on mee let thine anger fall;
> ... I for his sake will leave
> Thy bosom, ...
> ... on me let Death wreck all his rage;
>
> III.236–241[20]

---

[20] In his 1801 edition of *The Poetical Works of John Milton*, Todd (on III.236) quotes Newton, who noted that the frequent and vehement repetition of *mee* is very like Virgil when Nisus bravely offers himself and cries: "*Me, me*: adsum qui feci: in *me* convertite ferrum" (*Aen*, ix. 427).

Isaiah offers a perhaps more relevant prototype of the volunteer who is willing to sacrifice his own life for the sake of others but whereas the Son steps forward to "be mortal to redeem Man's mortal crime", Isaiah accepts a mission to the people to warn and heal them. Both act in answer to God's call:

his words echo those spoken by Moses when he pleads with God
to have mercy on the people who sinned against Him. Moses,
like the Son, argues that the enemy would achieve his aim –
vengeance – if God destroyed His own people.[21] Later on, when
Moses realizes how great is the sin which the Israelites have com-
mitted, he again intercedes with God and offers himself as a
scapegoat to save the people: "Yet now, if thou wilt forgive their
sin-; and if not, blot me, I pray thee, out of thy book which thou
hast written" (Exodus xxxii. 32). God's reply to Moses ("Whoever
hath sinned against me, him will I blot out of my book" [Exodus
xxxii. 33]) reflects an austere but moral concept of justice which
is less harsh than the "rigid satisfaction" mentioned by Milton's
God at the outset of the dialogue between Himself and the Son.
This "rigid satisfaction" is as far from the rigorous but righteous
Old Testament concept of justice as it is from the Christian doctrine of atonement[22] and forgiveness.

While Abraham the patriarch was the father of the chosen
people, Moses was their political and spiritual leader. Two of
his most significant character traits are revealed in the episode
of the burning bush (Exodus iii): the first is his humility ("And
Moses said unto God, who am I, that I should go unto Pharaoh
...?" [Exodus iii. 11]); the second is his complete identification with his mission. Both these traits are reflected in Exodus
xxxii. Like Abraham, Moses is concerned about God's own truth
and justice and selflessly offers himself for the sake of God's
people just as Abraham is ready to sacrifice his only son to God.

Now Hughes recognizes that "in Milton's scene [in Heaven]
the level is above fear or any passion except the love of mankind,

---

(*FOOTNOTE 20 continued*)
Say Heav'nly Powers, where shall we find such love,
Which of you will be mortal to redeem
Man's mortal crime,

                III.213–215

"Also I heard the voice of the Lord, saying, Whom shall I send, and who will
go for us?" (Isaiah vi. 8).
[21] See III.156–166 and Exodus xxxii. 12, as well as Numbers xiv. 13–19.
[22] Daiches, p. 182.

of truth, and of God's self ", and he contrasts it with Charlemagne's prayer to God in Ariosto.[23] On the other hand, he writes that one of the reasons why "Milton went as far as he did in developing the ambivalence of the suppliant figure of the Son" is that his "Italian studies had introduced him to the compound of severity and mercy which T. M. Greene recognizes as characteristic of the poetry and painting of the age which produced Vida's *Christiad* (1535) and Marino's *Gerusalemme Distrutta* (1632), with its painful portrayal of the Virgin pleading for God's mercy on the city."[24] I would argue that Milton's dialogue between God and the Son derives its power from verbal echoes in the dialogues of Abraham and Moses with their God, for these two episodes, as well as many others in the Old Testament in which God reveals Himself to His patriarchs or to the prophets, are permeated with a vision of God both as the benevolent and merciful Creator and as a just and moral God. It is in such poignant revelation scenes that men like Abraham and Moses are inspired with the spiritual courage to fulfil their moral duties in the spirit of their God. In such revelation scenes Milton found the "counterpoise of justice and mercy" that, indeed, is the key-note to his dialogue in Book III.

But there is also another reason which made the seventeenth-century prophetic poet turn to these Old Testament episodes for inspiration, and that is the personal relationship between man and God which they exemplify. Milton felt the need to convey this sense of personal relationship in the scene between God and Christ, and in these Old Testament scenes he found the perfect example of a relationship of man to God based upon absolute faith and devotion but not lacking the spiritual daring to search for justice and truth. Here Milton found what Hughes calls "the dialogue in a more or less Platonic sense: the quest of truth", and here he also found a dialogue of "distinct persons", a dialogue "above fear or any passion except the love of mankind, of truth and of God's self". Milton, as Greene suggests, was certainly familiar with the traditional debate in the morality plays as well

[23] Hughes, p. 118.
[24] Hughes, p. 120.

as with similar scenes in Italian literature, but he believed it "is better ... to contemplate the Deity, and to conceive of him, not with reference to human passions, that is, after the manner of men, who are never weary of forming subtle imaginations respecting him, but after the manner of Scripture, that is, in the way in which God has offered himself to our contemplation."[25]

Further evidence that Milton's dialogue between God and the Son was inspired by these Old Testament dialogues may be found in his resorting to many other verses from Exodus related to Moses throughout Book III. When the Son expresses the hope that he will see his Father's face upon his return to Heaven (III.262), the reference is again to Moses, for to him was it given to behold God's face. Milton had the figure of Moses as intercessor in mind, for he silently appropriates another allusion in his final description of the council:

> Thee next they sang of all Creation first,
> Begotten Son, Divine Similitude,
> In whose conspicuous count'nance, without cloud
> Made visible, th'Almighty Father shines,
> Whom else no Creature can behold;
>   III.383–387[26]

The shining of the Almighty Father is expressed in even stronger terms in lines 375–382:

> Fountain of Light, thyself invisible
> Amidst the glorious brightness where thou sit'st ...
>   III.375–376[27]

About the sources to these lines Harding writes that "the *Bible* contains many passages which associate God with intense light ... But nowhere in the *Bible* is the radiance about God described as being so intense that the eye cannot bear it."[28] We find, however,

---

[25] *The Christian Doctrine*, I.2.
[26] "And there arose not a prophet since in Israel like unto Moses whom the Lord knew face to face" (Deuteronomy xxxiv. 10).
[27] See Todd on III.377.
[28] Davis P. Harding, *Milton and the Renaissance Ovid* (Urbana, 1946), pp. 91–92.

a very intense light shining not from God but from the face of Moses, who himself possessed a divine quality when he descended from Mount Sinai: "And when Aaron and all the children of Israel saw Moses, behold the skin of his face shone; and they were afraid to come nigh him . . . And till Moses had done speaking with them, he put a veil on his face" (Exodus xxxiv. 30–33). The episode of Moses' shining face is likely to be an additional source to lines 380–383 besides the *Metamorphoses* and Isaiah vi, mentioned by Harding:

> Dark with excessive bright thy skirts appear,
> Yet dazzle Heav'n, that brightest Seraphim
> Approach not, but with both wings veil thir eyes.
>
> III.380–382

The problem is that God can neither be described nor conceived of in terms of any other character. This explains why the extended similes and metaphors found in Hell and Paradise are absent from the council scene in Book III. Milton's concept of God emerges from this scene – as it does from the whole poem – through the Old Testament allusions and phrases that have a specific poetic function: stressing God's righteousness, His might, and the certainty of His victory over His enemies. They reveal both the similarity and the difference between Milton's Christian God and the jealous but just Old Testament Lord of Hosts.[29] If, indeed, we read the council scene with the Old Testament in mind, we see that Milton's God is a hebraic God though none the less consistent with the Christian view for being hebraic.

The council scene in Book V is less austere and even more dramatic than the scene in Book III. The liveliness and power of this scene are reminiscent of various Old Testament passages such as Genesis xviii, Exodus xix, Micaiah's vision in I Kings xxii. 19, and in the council scene described in Psalm ii, whereas in the description of the council scene in Book III Milton conveys the sublime and the ethereal, Raphael's account to Adam of a previous

---

[29] There are also many Biblical allusions the function of which is to project New Testament beliefs into Old Testament episodes, but these are not to be considered hebraic. The best example of this category is Isaiah's prophecy (vii. 14) echoed by Milton in III.283–286.

council of God in Book V and of the war in Heaven in Book VI is
mainly rendered in human terms expressing the correspondence
between Heaven and Earth:

> By lik'ning spiritual to corporal forms,
> As may express them best, though what if Earth
> Be but the shadow of Heav'n, and things therein
> Each to other like, more than on Earth is thought?
> V.573–576

Milton's intention here is not, as in Book III, to contrast Heaven
and Hell but to compare Heaven and Earth.

After the meal the Seraph answers Adam's question about
Heaven and describes the council which incited Satan to rebel
against God. Here the drama heightens because Satan and his
consort play an active part in the council and because it explains
the cause of Satan's fall while foreshadowing the fall of Adam
and Eve. Now we see Satan as he, for the first time, openly dis-
obeys God by refusing to accept the principles God lays down.
The theological issues of Book III are thus brought to life. The
council scene as related by Raphael is also stylistically dramatic.

As in the council of God described in I Kings xxii. 19, there is
an impressive "Empyreal Host" standing by the throne of God.
The throne itself appears "Amidst as from a flaming Mount,
whose top / Brightness had made invisible" (V.598–599). The in-
visibility of God's brightness is extensively found in ancient epics
as well as in medieval, Renaissance, and baroque poems. But it is,
in the first instance, a Biblical concept. In *Paradise Lost* it is part
of the light versus darkness imagery which derives its power from
Milton's Biblical sources. The fallen angels had described God
"with the majesty of Darkness" round His throne (II.266). The
flaming Mount whose top is invisible is associated with the Mount
of Exodus xix. 16: "And it came to pass on the third day in the
morning, that there were thunders and lightnings, and a thick
cloud upon the mount, . . . so that all the people that was in the
camp trembled." Milton's description here does not produce fear,
but the vision is nonetheless awe-inspiring.

The simplicity and directness of God's speech derive a dramatic immediacy from a Biblical passage:[30] God's speech is almost a paraphrase of Psalm ii:

> Why do the heathen rage, and the people imagine a vain thing? The kings of the earth set themselves, and the rulers take counsel together, against the Lord, and against his anointed, saying, Let us break their bands asunder, and cast away their cords from us. He that sitteth in the heavens shall laugh: the Lord shall have them in derision. Then shall he speak unto them in his wrath, and vex them in his sore displeasure. Yet have I set my king upon my holy hill of Zion. I will declare the decree: the Lord hath said unto me, Thou art my Son; this day have I begotten thee. Ask of me, and I shall give thee the heathen for thine inheritance, and the uttermost parts of the earth for thy possession. Thou shalt break them with a rod of iron; thou shalt dash them in pieces like a potter's vessel. Be wise now, therefore, O ye kings: be instructed, ye judges of the earth. Serve the Lord with fear, and rejoice with trembling. Kiss the Son, lest he be angry, and ye perish from the way, when his wrath is kindled but a little. Blessed are all they that put their trust in him.

Milton had translated this Psalm in August 1653. Now, in *Paradise Lost*, his account of God's decree and the origin of Satan's rebellion is a dramatization based upon this Psalm, revealing the way he used Scripture for his poetic and dramatic purposes. In the Psalm, the rebellion of "the kings of the earth" precedes God's decree, but Milton's God does not declare His will to vex his enemies. The decree is the cause and not the result of the rebellion. The effect is thus one of dramatic irony, for if we remember verses 6 and 7 of the Psalm, we also remember the evil pride and the

---

[30] Newton (quoted by Todd on V.602) says: "We observed before, that Milton was very cautious what sentiments and language he ascribed to the Almighty, and generally confined himself to the phrases and expressions of Scripture; and in this particular speech the reader will easily remark how much of it is copied from Holy Writ, by comparing it with the following texts: *Psalm* ii. 6. 7; *Gen.* xxii. 16. *Phil.* ii. 10. 11." It is true that these texts are in the background of God's speech, but I shall try to show that Milton does more than merely "copy" from "Holy Writ".

futility of those who "rage" and invent a "vain thing". The "unsleeping eyes of God"[31] then witness the rebellion, and he takes
counsel with the Son. The Son's answer is not to be taken as a
"jeering ... as coarse as his Father's",[32] nor as representing an
Epicurean God equally indifferent to good and evil:

> Mighty Father, thou thy foes
> Justly hast in derision, and secure
> Laugh'st at thir vain designs and tumults vain,
> Matter to mee of Glory, whom thir hate
> Illustrates, when they see all Regal Power
> Giv'n me to quell thir pride, . . .
>
> V.735-740

In reality, God's laughter reflects neither His vindictiveness
nor philosophical indifference; it rather reflects, in anthropomorphic terms, the utter futility and vanity (Milton repeats
"vain" twice in line 737) of the rebels' efforts. Milton also alludes
to Psalm ii to enhance the moral significance of the council scene in
Book V, for the message of the Psalm is that "Blessed are all they
that put their trust in him." By referring to this Psalm, Milton
conveys his concept of an omnipotent but not vindictive God, a
God against whom it is "vain" to rage. Thus the scene very
dramatically ridicules the vain attempts of the fallen angels in
the war in Book VI to which we turn next.

St. John's revelation about "a great red dragon" whose "tail
drew the third part of the stars of heaven and did cast them to the
earth" (Revelation xii. 3–4) was Milton's authority for the rebellion in Heaven and for the historical truth of the war he described
in Book VI. The war itself, however, is in the classical tradition of
the battle between the Olympian gods and the Titans as told by
Hesiod.[33] Milton was thus following the allegorical tradition which

---

[31] Todd on V.647 quotes Newton, who suggests that "the unsleeping eyes of God"
echo Psalm cxxi. 4. "He that keepeth Israel shall neither slumber nor sleep" and
adds that "The author had likewise Homer in mind, *Iliad*. ii. 1."
[32] Empson, p. 96.
[33] Hesiod, *Theogony*, translated by Norman O. Brown (Indianapolis, 1953), pp.
53–82.

saw in the revolt of the Titans a pagan version, that is, a shadowy reflection of the revolt of the angels, and which identified the victorious Zeus with God.

But Milton's particular conception of this war in Heaven is reflected in his use of various Old Testament allusions throughout Book VI. These allusions are a unifying element in the account of the war. Milton's attitude to the war itself is not that of a classical poet glorifying heroism in battle. In Book XI Michael condemns the futility of war:

> For in those days Might only shall be admir'd,
> And Valor and Heroic Virtue call'd;
> To overcome in Battle, and subdue
> Nations, and bring home spoils with infinite
> Man-slaughter, shall be held the highest pitch
> Of human Glory, and for Glory done
> Of triumph, to be styl'd great Conquerors,
> Patrons of Mankind, Gods, and Sons of Gods,
>   XI.689–696

While Book VI glorifies God's host and the Son overcoming the rebel angels, there is no doubt as to the outcome of the war. Abdiel's words foretell it:

>   fool, not to think how vain
> Against th'Omnipotent to rise in Arms;
> Who out of smallest things could without end
> Have rais'd incessant Armies to defeat
> Thy folly;
>   VI.135–139[34]

And his stroke defeats Satan momentarily:

>   a noble stroke he lifted high,
> Which hung not, but so swift with tempest fell
> On the proud Crest of *Satan*, that no sight,

---

[34] The certainty of God's victory is a hebraic element (adopted by all monotheistic religions) for, in Greek mythology, none of the deities was assured of victory from the outset.

Nor motion of swift thought, less could his Shield
Such ruin intercept:

VI.189–193

This is more than a "Presage of Victory", for Abdiel is "in word
mightier than they in Arms" (VI.32), mightier than Satan who,
as in Book I, achieves gigantic dimensions:

> ten paces huge
> He back recoil'd; the tenth on bended knee
> His massy Spear upstay'd; as if on Earth
> Winds under ground or waters forcing way
> Sidelong, had pusht a Mountain from his seat
> Half sunk with all his Pines.

VI.193–198

The battle, thus, is not only between the heavenly host and the
rebel angels. It is a reflection of the war taking place in the
soul of man in that it is primarily a battle in which spirit overcomes force. This is the theme that is at the core of the war in
heaven, and an examination of it reinforces Joseph Summers'
thesis about the importance of Book VI.[35]

The Old Testament motif "Not by might, nor by power, but by
my spirit, saith the Lord of hosts" (Zechariah iv. 6) is the key
to Book VI, and it is best revealed in Milton's literary treatment
of the chariot throughout Book VI, for in *Paradise Lost* chariots
come to mean more than part of the conventional equipment used
in ancient warfare.[36]

In the first two books of *Paradise Lost*, the fall of Satan's host is
already associated with the destruction of Pharaoh's chariots for
Satan's fallen host is likened to the Egyptian "floating Carcasses /

---

[35] Joseph H. Summers, *The Muse's Method*, pp. 112–137.

[36] For the Kabbalistic treatment of the Merkabah vision and its influence on
Milton's chariot episode through Christian Platonists like Reuchlin and Pico,
see J. H. Adamson, "The War in Heaven: Milton's Version of the Merkabah",
JEGP, LVII (1958), pp. 690–703.

Chariots, in their conventional meaning, occur often in *Paradise Lost*; see, for
example, II.885–887.

And broken Chariot Wheels" (I.310–311).[37] These chariots are conventional ones but they are symbolic of Pharaoh's futile warfare and defeat. In Book III we learn that the Son of God overcame his enemies in a unique chariot, a flaming one:

> thou that day
> Thy Father's dreadful Thunder didst not spare,
> Nor stop thy flaming Chariot wheels, that shook
> Heav'n's everlasting Frame, while o'er the necks
> Thou drov'st of warring Angels disarray'd
>
>   III.392–396[38]

But we do not yet know how the Son overcame the warring angels or how his chariot differs from the conventional war chariots. Clearly contrasted in Book VI, however, are two kinds of chariots: that of the Son of God on the one hand, and all the others on the other hand.

On his way to the Mount of God, Abdiel beholds

> all the Plain
> Cover'd with thick embattl'd Squadrons bright,
> Chariots and flaming Arms, and fiery Steeds
> Reflecting blaze on blaze,
>
>   VI.15–18

This description is Homeric, and although the chariots are those of armed saints, they do not seem to differ from the chariots of the

---

[37] The same episode of chapter xiv of Exodus is mentioned again in Michael's history of mankind related to Adam, XII.210.

[38] Another flaming chariot is alluded to by Milton in Book III. When Satan is on his journey to Earth, he sees the gates of Heaven and

> underneath a bright Sea flow'd
> Of Jasper, or of liquid Pearl, whereon
> Who after came from Earth, sailing arriv'd,
> Wafted by Angels, or flew o'er the Lake
> Rapt in a Chariot drawn by fiery Steeds.
>
>   III.518–522

The vision is reminiscent of the one Elisha had when there appeared "a chariot of fire, and horses of fire, and parted them both asunder; and Elijah went up by a whirlwind into heaven" (II Kings ii. 11).

warriors in the *Iliad*.[39] As for Satan, he

> High in the midst exalted as a God
> Th' Apostate in his Sun-bright Chariot sat
> Idol of Majesty Divine,
>   VI.99–101

The chariot is that of the Sun-God, and Satan's exaltation is like that of the ambitious Phaeton. He is, significantly, described as an "Idol" of Divine Majesty. His chariot is thus associated with that other one which brought about chaos and destruction to the world until its proud charioteer was struck down by Jove's thunderbolt. But Satan's rash ambition is humbled for he cannot, any more than can Phaeton, "equal God in power" (VI.343), and wounded by Michael's sword, he is borne back to his chariot (VI.338). The first day of battle ends and

> all the ground
> With shiver'd armor strown, and on a heap
> Chariot and Charioteer lay overturn'd
> And fiery foaming Steeds; . . .
>   VI.388–391

Satan still thinks that God can be deemed fallible (VI.428) and he plans, the next day, to send forth

> Such implements of mischief as shall dash
> To pieces, and o'erwhelm whatever stands
> Adverse, that they shall fear we have disarm'd
> The Thunderer of his only dreaded bolt.
>   VI.488–491

At first it seems that Satan is overcoming God's host, for

> down they fell
> By thousands, Angel on Arch-Angel roll'd;
>   VI.593–594

---

[39] See, for example, *Iliad*, VIII.562–565, translated by Richmond Lattimore (Chicago, 1951), p. 197. Todd, on VI.18, refers to Homer and adds: "But it is probable that Milton had in view a very magnificent description of this kind in I *Maccabees*, vi. 39."

And Milton adds, "The sooner for thir Arms" (VI.595) since force alone cannot overcome evil. It is thus significant that on the third day of battle God sends forth not Michael and his host with implements from the "Armory of God" (VI.321), but His Son:

> Go then thou Mightiest in thy Father's might,
> Ascend my Chariot, guide the rapid Wheels
> That shake Heav'n's basis, bring forth all my War,
> My Bow and Thunder, my Almighty Arms
> Gird on, and Sword upon thy puissant Thigh;
>
> VI.710–714

These lines echo the descriptions of Homeric battles, but they also include a Biblical element: whereas Phaeton did wrong in insisting upon riding Jove's chariot, Milton's God invites His Son to "ascend my Chariot". The contrast between the God-Christ and the Jove-Phaeton situations is the more striking for the similarity of the vocabulary God uses to that attributed to Jove by writers from Homer to Ovid:

> bring forth all my War,
> My Bow and Thunder, my Almighty Arms
> Gird on, . . .

Moreover, since Christ rides the chariot at the request of his Father, it is not – as in the hands of Phaeton – an instrument of destruction and chaos; it brings about peace and order in Heaven:

> At his command the uprooted Hills retir'd
> Each to his place, they heard his voice and went
> Obsequious,
>
> VI.781–783

And when Christ appears, Milton does not describe another battle scene. Instead he describes a spiritual revelation:

> forth rush'd with whirl-wind sound
> The Chariot of Paternal Deity,
> Flashing thick flames, Wheel within Wheel, undrawn,
> Itself instinct with Spirit, but convoy'd

By four Cherubic shapes, four Faces each
Had wondrous, as with Stars thir bodies all
And Wings were set with Eyes, with Eyes the Wheels
Of Beryl, and careering Fires between;
Over thir heads a crystal Firmament,
Whereon a Sapphire Throne, inlaid with pure
Amber, and colors of the show'ry Arch.
Hee in Celestial Panoply all arm'd
Of radiant Urim, work divinely wrought,
Ascended, . . .

VI.749–762

This revelation is the climax of Book VI as well as of the war in Heaven. It deserves some consideration.

As has been indicated by previous editors,[40] the chariot revelation is inspired by the vision of the prophet Ezekiel (i. 4–28). Milton, as well as the hexaemeral poets before him,[41] had the authority of St. John for identifying the divine image of the chariot with Christ, but Milton's description is much closer to the original revelation of the Old Testament poet-prophet. Although his lines condense the Ezekiel chapter, at times he slightly diverges from it and emphasizes, as we shall see, those elements that are necessary for his poetic purposes. For example, Milton's chariot "forth rush'd with whirl-wind sound", whereas Ezekiel first beholds a whirlwind coming out of the north and, in the midst of it, he then sees a chariot (i. 4). Ezekiel sees a cloud, a brightness about it, and "out of the midst thereof as the colour of amber, out of the midst of the fire" (l. 4), while Milton expresses the brightness and the fire in the onomatopeic phrase, "Flashing thick flames" (VI.751).

---

[40] See Hume, Newton, and Todd. Todd on VI.749 refers to Ezekiel i. and, quoting Newton, adds: "Or perhaps Milton here drew Isaiah likewise to his assistance, lxvi. 15." On VI.755, Todd quotes Ezekiel i. 16 and 13 and adds: "Milton has again described this part of the prophetic vision, and with additional sublimity, ver. 848."

[41] Referring to G. McColley's *Paradise Lost*, pp. 36–38, Hughes (on VI.750–759) notes that at least one hexaemeral poet before Milton, Rupert of Deutz in the twelfth century, had used the vision of Ezekiel as a symbol of Christ triumphing spiritually over the rebel angels.

Milton follows Ezekiel when he emphasizes that the chariot has
"Wheel within Wheel, undrawn, / Itself instinct with Spirit": "and
their appearance and their work was as it were a wheel in the middle of a wheel. When they went, they went upon their four sides;
and they turned not when they went . . . Whithersoever the spirit
was to go, they went, thither was their spirit to go: and the wheels
were lifted up over against them: for the spirit of the living creature
was in the wheels" (i. 16, 17, 20). Milton's four "Cherubic shapes"
(VI.753), however, are an idealized form of the "living creatures"
of Ezekiel (ḥayyot) as well as of the beasts which appear in St.
John's revelation (iv. 6). Milton may well have been influenced by
Isaiah's initiatory vision, for the beasts in Revelation have six
wings like the *seraphim* in Isaiah vi. 2. The living creatures of
Ezekiel have wings as well, but only four. It is also possible that the
"Cherubic shapes" of Milton were suggested to him by chapter x of
Ezekiel where we find cherubim in a similar vision at the centre
of which is the "likeness of a throne": "This is the living creature
that I saw under the God of Israel by the river of Chebar; and I
knew that they were the cherubims" (Ezekiel x. 20). The "four
Faces each / Had wondrous" (VI.753–754) are like the four faces
each "living creature" had in Ezekiel's vision whereas in Revelation, each of the beasts has a different face (iv. 7).

The light, radiance and fire predominant in Milton's lines are
also derived from Ezekiel's chapter. The wings as well as the wheels
are set with eyes, but the sight is not as dreadful as Ezekiel's vision:
"As for their rings, they were so high that they were dreadful; and
their rings were full of eyes round about them four" (i. 18), nor is the
"crystal Firmament" over Milton's chariot (VI.757) the "terrible
crystal" of Ezekiel i. 22. But the chariot of Christ is resplendent
with light: the wheels are of Beryl (VI.756) as in Ezekiel i. 16 and
the throne is of Sapphire (VI.758) as in Ezekiel i. 26. The "careering
Fires" (VI.756) are like the flashes of fire and lightning of Ezekiel
i. 13–14.[42] Christ is armed with bow and quiver and "three-bolted

---

[42] On VI.751 Hume quotes the Ezekiel chapter "out of which Chapter this noble
Description is taken". Milton's lines indeed follow the order of Ezekiel's description, which begins with the chariot, the living creatures, and ends with the throne.
In Revelation iv, the description begins with "a throne was set in heaven, and one
sat on the throne" (iv. 2) and ends with the description of the beasts and the
elders worshiping the Lord. There is no chariot in the vision.

Thunder'' (VI.764), but the nature of his divine armor is symbolized by the ancient and radiant *"Urim"* worn on the breastplate by the Hebrew high priests.[43]

We may conclude, then, that if Milton had wanted to present a powerful Lord of Hosts destroying and routing His enemies, he could easily have found authoritative sources for such a conception.[44] But as long as the battle between Heaven and Hell was described in terms of war, no poetic distinction was possible between the forces of Heaven and the forces of Hell. So Milton chose to present the manifestation of God's might not in terms of power but in a scene intense with light and spirit, radiant with glory. The very splendor of Christ's chariot and the light it radiates denigrate Satan exalted as a god in his sun-bright chariot and render all the devilish machinations (VI.504) powerless. The great thematic image of the chariot thus emphasizes the key theme of Book VI, for the power of Ezekiel's as well as Milton's fiery chariot is that it is instinct with spirit and moved by divine force; it is this divine force which renders the power of God's enemies futile. The chariot scene thus, by its very nature, serves as the poetic distinction between the powers of Heaven and the powers of Hell. Here, rather than in the council scene of Book III, does Milton become, like the Hebrew prophets and like Dante, a visionary of God.

The essence of the divine chariot having been revealed, Milton turns to the actual war, for the wrath of the jealous Lord of Hosts is now turned against his enemies. The "smoke and bickering flame, and sparkles dire" (VI.766) are like a raging fire that consumes everything in its path.[45] The divine chariot is no longer alone; it is now part of the multitude of chariots forming God's host. The description is reminiscent not only of Homer but also of Psalm 68, which is echoed by Revelation vii:[46]

[43] As Todd indicates (VI.760), Milton has the authority of Ephes., vi. 11 for Christ's divine armor, but the mysterious Urim are those we find on Aaron's breastplate (Exodus xxviii. 30). See also Hume on VI.760.

[44] See, for example, the fierce description of the Day of Judgment of Joel ii. 1–11.

[45] See Nahum i. 6; Isaiah ix. 18–19 (Hebrew canon: Isaiah ix. 17–18); II Samuel xxii. 9. Hume's annotation to VI.766 refers to Psalm xviii. 8 (xviii. 9 in the Hebrew canon) and to Psalm 1. 3.

[46] Newton, quoted by Todd on VI.767, refers to both Psalm lxviii. 17 and Revelation vii. 4, and, characteristically, observes: "Let it be remarked how much of his sublimity, even in the sublimest part of his works, Milton owes to Scripture".

> Attended with ten thousand thousand Saints,
> He onward came, far off his coming shone,
> And twenty thousand (I thir number heard)
> Chariots of God, half on each hand were seen:
> VI.767–770

When Christ appears on the battle field, the metaphor of the throne merges with that of the God who, like Baal riding the clouds, is described by David as He "rode upon a cherub, and did fly: and he was seen upon the wings of the wind" (II. Samuel xxii. 11). But He does not, at first, manifest his wrath by destruction, and His appearance is not described in destructive terms as that of the Babylon prophecy (Isaiah xiii), for "At his command the uprooted Hills retir'd / Each to his place, they heard his voice and went / Obsequious, Heav'n his wonted far renewed" (VI.781–783). Order and harmony are thus the manifestation of God's might.

Yet the "hapless Foes" (VI.785) are still insensate, "obdur'd" and, like the Egyptians, "hard'n'd more" against the might and glory of God. And it is at this stage that Christ's appearance becomes that of the wrathful God of Deuteronomy (xxxii. 35)[47] for "Vengeance is his, or whose he sole appoints" (VI.808). And "since by strength / They measure, all, of other excellence / Not emulous" (VI.820–822), He reveals his might in battle,

> and into terror chang'd
> His count'nance too severe to be beheld
> And full of wrath bent on his Enemies.
> VI.824–826

Like the jealous God of Israel, Milton's God punishes and destroys those who disobey Him. The enemy, now "all resistance lost, / All courage; down thir idle weapons dropp'd" (VI.838–839) and "wish't the Mountains now might be again / Thrown on them as a shelter from his ire" (VI.842–843). Their fear is like that of the kings of the earth (in Revelation vi. 15–16) and also echoes the fear of the sinners on the Day of Judgment described by Isaiah (xiii. 7–8): "Therefore shall all hands be faint, and every man's

---

[47] See Hume and Todd on VI.808.

heart shall melt: and they shall be afraid": When Christ vanquishes his enemies, the chariot is again the element Milton emphasizes, and he effectively echoes the awe-inspiring passages of the Ezekiel chapter:

> from the fourfold-visag'd Four
> Distinct with eyes, and from the living Wheels,
> Distinct alike with multitude of eyes;
> One spirit in them rul'd, and every eye
> Glar'd lightning, . . .

VI.845–849[48]

Thus the power of God is mostly represented in spiritual terms recalling Ezekiel's vision, and to the chariot itself – both as reality and as symbol – is attributed a new significance in the mythical war in Heaven. Thus whenever the might of God is manifested in terms of war, the allusions echo Old Testament passages where a jealous but righteous God punishes those who persist in their sins so that although the war in Heaven follows classical tradition, its religious and moral justification is poetically expressed through hebraic allusions.[49]

One set of such allusions functions through one of Milton's angels who is a unique Miltonic figure. He is different from the others in that he is an original creation of Milton. His name is not reminiscent of any Biblical or hebraic figure.[50] It is, however, a

---

[48] See Hume on VI.848.

[49] Todd stresses the idea that the Son "meant / Not to destroy", and on VI.853 ("Yet half his strength he put not forth") he writes: "This fine thought is somewhat like that of the Psalmist lxxviii. 38. 'But he, being full of compassion, forgave their iniquity, and destroyed them not; yea, many a time turned he his anger away, and *did not stir up all his wrath*.' And it greatly exceeds Hesiod, who makes Jupiter, upon a like occasion, exert *all* his strength, *Theog.* 687."

[50] The name *Abdiel* ('Avdiel – עַבְדִּיאֵל) appears only once in the Old Testament (I Chronicles v. 15), referring to a human being. Another version of the same name – Abd'el ('Avd'el – עַבְדְּאֵל) is also mentioned once (Jeremiah xxxvi. 26) with reference to another person. See also Hughes on *P.L.* V.805. On Abdiel see also Robert H. West, *Milton and the Angels* (Athens, Georgia, 1955), pp. 124, 152–154; G. Davidson, *A Dictionary of Angels* (London–New York, 1968), p. 4; M. Schwab, *Vocabulaire de l'Angélologie* (Paris, 1897), p. 207; *Sefer Raziel* (Amsterdam, 1701), f. 4b, 34b; Jack Goldman, "Insight into Milton's Abdiel", *PQ*, XLIX (1970), pp. 249–254.

Hebrew name meaning the "Servant of God" (VI.29). Abdiel's character and zeal for God suggest why Milton chose a Hebrew name for him. In his faith in Christ and his loyalty to the Son of God, Abdiel is a Christian figure. His words to Satan (V.835–845), for example, about the creation through Christ echo, as Hughes indicates, Colossians i. 15–17, but the terms in which Abdiel conveys his zeal for the Son are often hebraic. In his speech to Satan, for instance, he warns that the

> Golden Sceptre which thou didst reject
> Is now an Iron Rod to bruise and break
> Thy disobedience.
>
> V.886–888

This iron rod, as Hume points out (II.327), is an allusion to Psalm ii. 9: "Thou shalt break them with a rod of iron." It also reminds us of the words of Beelzebub when he warns the fallen angels that God

> In highth or depth, still first and last will Reign
> Sole King, and of his Kingdom lose no part
> By our revolt, but over Hell extend
> His Empire, and with Iron Sceptre rule
> Us here, as with his Golden those in Heav'n.
>
> II.324–328

Beelzebub has learned that Abdiel's warning has become reality. As Newton remarks (quoted by Todd on V.835) Abdiel's first speech ends on the note of Psalm ii (verses 10–12):

> Cease then this impious rage,
> And tempt not these; but hast'n to appease
> Th'incensed Father, and th'incensed Son,
> While Pardon may be found in time besought.
>
> V.845–848

The second speech also ends with an Old Testament allusion. Abdiel's zeal could not save the rebel angels just as Moses' warning could not prevent the just punishment that befell another faithless band destroyed by God's ire:[51]

> Well thou didst advise,
> Yet not for thy advice or threats I fly
> These wicked Tents devoted, lest the wrath
> Impendent, raging into sudden flame
> Distinguish not:
>
> V.888–892

The words of God to Abdiel show best how Milton infuses Old Testament allusions in Christian contexts:

> Servant of God, well done, well hast thou fought
> The better fight, who single hast maintain'd
> Against revolted multitudes the Cause
> Of Truth, in word mightier than they in Arms;
> And for the testimony of Truth hast borne
> Universal reproach, far worse to bear
> Than violence: for this was all thy care
> To stand approv'd in sight of God, though Worlds
> Judg'd thee perverse:
>
> VI.29–37

As Hughes indicates (VI.29) the greeting to the man in the parable of judgment (Matthew xxv. 21) mingles here with St. Paul's cry, "I have fought a good fight", but these lines also silently appropriate Isaiah's description of God's servant: "He is despised and rejected of men; a man of sorrows, and acquainted with grief: and we hid as it were our faces from him; he was despised, and we esteemed him not" (Isaiah liii. 3). To Milton's Abdiel, the fervent defender of Christ, are thus attributed some qualities associated with prefigurations of Christ yet, significantly, he is more hebraic than Christian. He is, like the Old Testament Messiah, God's instrument for the punishment of the wicked. The character of the angel "in word mightier than they in Arms" embodies the Old Testa-

---

[51] Newton (quoted by Todd on V.890) points out the allusion to Numbers xvi. 16: "And he [Moses] spake unto the congregation, saying, Depart, I pray you, from the tents of these wicked men, and touch nothing of theirs, lest ye be consumed in all their sins."

ment concept of spiritual superiority over physical strength, which is the central theme of the war in Heaven. In this connection it must be mentioned that though Abdiel evinces the central Christian virtue of meekness, the conduct of the war in Heaven exemplifies the superiority of spiritual might rather than that of spiritual meekness. This hebraic element of spiritual might lives again in Milton and is one of the factors which keeps the balance between the Humanist and the Puritan in his thought. It is spiritual might and not the traditional spiritual meekness which is made evident in Book III, in the scenes describing Christ in battle, God in council, and in figures like the chariot or the angel Abdiel.

V

"FUTURE THINGS": THE VISION OF HISTORY

The vision of life that emerges from Milton's poem is based on his belief in man's ability to transcend the imperfect reality he lives in through faith in providence and in the world's goodness and reason. Eden has been lost. What man has to face now is "good with bad" (XI.358), "supernal Grace contending / With sinfulness of Men" (XI.359–360). But even if this world seems alien to Adam, it is no "despicable gift" (XI.340), for despite the inevitable presence of evil everywhere, God's benign and righteous order still rules the universe:

> *Adam*, thou know'st Heav'n his, and all the Earth,
> Not this Rock only; his Omnipresence fills
> Land, Sea, and Air, and every kind that lives,
> Fomented by his virtual power and warm'd:
> All th' Earth he gave thee to possess and rule.
> XI.335–339

After the fall, Adam instinctively grasps the great principle that life in itself is good and must go on. Although shattered by misery and despair (X.720–844), he is nevertheless able firmly to reject Eve's proposal to commit suicide (X.1013–46), like Job who rebukes his wife for her advice to give up his integrity: "curse God, and die" (Job ii. 9). But Adam still has far to go before he can become a morally mature and responsible individual who will have the strength to overcome despair and to

> learn
> True patience, and to temper joy with fear

And pious sorrow, equally inur'd
By moderation either state to bear,
Prosperous or adverse:

XI.360–364

This is the message of Michael's vision and his subsequent account of history. But Michael's prophecy does more than invest Adam with the stoic spirit of acceptance. It may be noted here that Adam's spirit of acceptance is antipodal to the attitude of Stoic detachment adopted by the classically educated Cavaliers; Adam's acceptance, the result of his faith in God's plan and purpose, is characteristic of the Biblical view of history which influenced Old Testament-reading Protestants.[1] It leads to a conscious, emotional as well as intellectual, acceptance of good and evil:

Henceforth I learn, that to obey is best,
And love with fear the only God, to walk
As in his presence, ever to observe
His providence, and on him sole depend,
Merciful over all his works, with good
Still overcoming evil, and by small
Accomplishing great things, by things deem'd weak
Subverting worldly strong, and worldly wise
By simply meek; that suffering for Truth's sake
Is fortitude to highest victory,
And to the faithful Death the Gate of Life;

XII.561–571

This acceptance, which is one of the keynotes of the poem, transcends classical stoicism, for it derives from the belief that to "obey is best", that God is merciful, and that suffering leads to the "highest victory" rendering worldly evil powerless.

It is significant that Adam comes to terms with the concept of "suffering for Truth" at the end of Book XII when Michael's vision

---

[1] Hughes (on XI.363) fails to make this distinction. On the collision in European culture between the classical Greek and the Biblical view of history, see Tom F. Driver, *The Sense of History in Greek and Shakespearean Drama* (New York, 1960), pp. 19–66, and also Ruth Nevo, *The Dial of Virtue* (Princeton, 1963), p. 76.

of history is unfolded to him. This vision helps Adam develop a new relationship to Time and makes him realize that he is part of a large community and that his own life and death can have no meaning if they do not take their place in the history of mankind.

In the widest possible sense, the conception of the history of mankind Milton projects in the last books of the poem is hebraic and has its roots in the historical consciousness reflected in the Old Testament. In the following pages I shall discuss this concept of history, comparing it with the Christian view of history, and calling upon Michael's story of the future to illustrate my thesis.

The general consensus among historians and theologians is that whereas a sense of human history was not characteristic of Greek thought since the nature-oriented Greek mind was concerned with what is permanent (above and beyond the changes wrought by man), an historical awareness coalesced in Judaeo-Christian thinking stemming from man's belief in creation and in his consequent responsibility to the Almighty.[2] Common to both Judaic and Christian traditions is an historical orientation. The starting point of both traditions is the idea of creation *ex nihilo*. Also common to both is the belief in Providence which becomes the Judaeo-Christian alternative to Fate, distinguished from the latter by purpose, creativity and choice. This is where complete similarity ends.

One of the fundamental principles of Judaism is the doctrine of election under the covenant. The three stages in the development of this doctrine all point to the national character of the covenant. The first is the election of Abraham called upon to leave the foreign land that was his home and settle in the land of Canaan. The promise to Abraham "to give him this land to inherit it" (Genesis xv. 7) confirmed with the covenant is reiterated to Isaac and Jacob and kept in the memory of the people and its prophets. The second stage is the election of Israel as a people at Mount Sinai, where the settlement of the promised land is reaffirmed (Exodus vi. 4–8). The election under this covenant works two

---

[2] See, for example, R. G. Collingwood, *The Idea of History* (Oxford, 1946). Throughout this section I am indebted to Driver, *The Sense of History in Greek and Shakespearean Drama*, especially pp. 3–66.

ways: God elects his people and the people take it upon themselves to keep the laws. Failure to keep the laws will bring about calamities (Exodus xxxii) but will not abrogate the covenant. The third stage is the election of the servant of God (Isaiah xli ff.).[3] Two themes are at the core of this election: the suffering of God's servant (referring to the destruction of the First Temple and the subsequent exile), and the salvation as a result of the renewal of the covenant (Jeremiah xxxi. 31).

The raison d'être of election under the covenant is God's peculiar love for Israel.[4] Though it does not imply any merit on Israel's part[5] or entail any privilege, the idea of election under the covenant does involve the people's obligation to uphold the law and implies Israel's moral mission on earth. As a religious and national concept, the covenant characterizes Israel's faith, for from the time of Abraham, the concern of patriarchs, leaders, and prophets was to preserve the "children of Israel" as a select community chosen by God to keep his covenant (Deuteronomy xiv. 2) and be a source of light to other nations (Isaiah ii. 35). This idea of the covenant is largely responsible for Israel's characteristic awareness of the importance of historical events for its identity.

This doctrine of a chosen people was understandably rejected by Christianity, which upheld not the Israelite covenant between God and Abraham that was renewed at Sinai but the universal covenant between God and Noah. For Paul's followers, the grace of God only had meaning insofar as it was incarnated in the God-man: the love and grace of God is no longer simply "given"; it is "given you by Jesus Christ" (I Cor. i. 4).[6] Christianity, moreover, regarded the Israelite covenant as a covenant of the law that was

---

[3] According to Biblical tradition, God's servant is the people of Israel. See, for example, Leviticus xxv. 42; Isaiah xli. 8–9; xlii. 19; liv. 17; lxiii. 17; lxv. 8, 15; lxvi. 14. Christianity based its concept of Christ as the servant of God mainly on Isaiah liii.

[4] See George F. Moore, *Judaism in the First Centuries of the Christian Era. The Age of the Tannaim.* (Cambridge, Mass., 1932 [1927]), I, p. 398.

[5] This point has also been made by C. A. Patrides, *Milton and the Christian Tradition*, p. 199.

[6] Patrides, pp. 198–199.

superseded by a "better covenant" established on "better promises" (Hebrews viii. 6).

> For Christ is the end of the law for righteousness to every one that believeth. For Moses describeth the righteousness which is of the law, that the man which doeth those things shall live by them. But the righteousness which is of faith speaketh on this wise, Say not in thine heart, Who shall ascend into heaven? . . . The word is nigh thee, even in thy mouth, and in thy heart: that is, the word of faith, which we preach:
>
> Romans x. 4–8

By rejecting traditional hebraism and Christianizing the universal elements of the Old Testament, Paul and his followers laid the foundations of a universal religion that was soon adopted by the Gentile world. Having broken with Judaism, they believed that they were now the true heirs of God's covenant which Israel had rejected. Throughout centuries, the Christian churches believed Israel's role to have ended with the Jews' refusal to accept Jesus as the Messiah although some Puritans in seventeenth-century England such as the Levellers, believed that the English nation was the successor to Israel's covenant with God and likened the Puritan Revolution to the Maccabean revolt against Antiochus.[7] The discussion of the covenant in Western thought sometimes tends to emphasize the universal rather than the national aspect of the Israelite covenant as expressed in Isaiah and Deutero-Isaiah.[8] True, the idea of a universal covenant with "nations that knew not thee" (Isaiah lv. 5) is clearly expressed by the prophet in exile. Yet it is always subordinated to the idea of the national covenant between God and Israel. Whereas the salvation of Israel comes

---

[7] In his early prose works Milton too expressed the idea that the English were a chosen people whose mission it was to reform the Church. See *Doctrine and Discipline of Divorce* (*Yale Prose Works*, II, p. 232); *Areopagitica* (*Ibid.*, p. 553); *Tetrachordon* (*Ibid.*, p. 707). But if this was his belief in his militant days, it was no longer so for the poet of *Paradise Lost*. See also *Jerusàlem and Albion*, p. 125.

On Milton and the Levellers, see *Yale Prose Works of John Milton*, vol. III, pp. 22–38.

[8] See, for example, Harold Fisch, *Jerusalem and Albion*, pp. 93–114.

from God, the salvation of all other nations will come by means of God's servant, Israel.[9] This universal aspect of the covenant through which Deutero-Isaiah explains the sufferings of Israel and the nation's mission among the Gentiles assumes a cardinal importance for Christianity, which sees Christ as God's servant who will bring salvation to mankind.

Characteristic of hebraic thought is also the sense of temporal perspective. As Driver writes, the Hebrews had "the typically Western concern to understand oneself in terms of one's past . . . Their objective . . . was to see the relationship of present to past, which means that their historical concern was not academic but existential."[10]

This historical orientation brings with it the idea of the new expressed in the Bible as the Creation.[11] The same element continues into the New Testament in the apocalypse of John who sees "a new heaven and a new earth . . . And he who sat upon the throne said, 'Behold I make all things new'."[12] But in conceiving of Jesus as the Messiah who will come again to bring about the summation of history and the final judgment, Christianity diverged from Judaism. The Jews never saw the Messiah as a manifestation of the divine and never looked upon his advent as the centre of history.[13] By building its doctrine around the idea of Incarnation, Christianity reshaped historical perspective, thereby, in Driver's terms, softening the linear element in the hebraic idea of time and turning history into a drama.[14] The Christian ordering of history around the Incarnation and the Resurrection – that is, in a pattern which is visible in Christ – is an ordering of time, a limiting factor which renders Christian history dramatic and distinguishes it from the open concept of the future central to hebraic thinking.

---

[9] Isaiah xlix. 6; lx. 3.

[10] Driver, *The Sense of History in Greek and Shakespearean Drama*, p. 44.

[11] Driver, p. 49.

[12] This is hardly surprising since the apocalypse of John is much more hebraic than the synoptic gospels.

[13] Scholars are generally agreed that the messianic idea was of relatively late development among the Hebrews and in its later forms dates only from the Exile. Before this, the Messiah was regarded as human.

[14] *The Sense of History in Greek and Shakespearean Drama*, pp. 58 and 63.

It should be added here that the dogmas of Incarnation and the Last Judgment derive their poignancy from the Christian concept of original sin. By magnifying Adam's sin and the gravity of his fall and by removing the precept of election under the covenant, Christianity developed a different view of history and a different attitude to man. While the doctrine of national election conferred heavy responsibilities upon each Jew, its ethical demands lent meaning and purpose to his life both as an individual and as a member of his community.[15] On the individual Christians, on the other hand, fell the burden of original sin and a painful awareness of the loss resulting from the fall. This leads us back to the new idea of the Messiah. The Christians put faith in Christ and hope in his second coming to bring salvation to the faithful thus making Christ the apex of history.

Milton scholars are generally agreed that his reading of history is in the Judeo-Christian tradition. But the idea that it may be more hebraic than Christian is rarely encountered. On the contrary. In his excellent study *Milton and the Christian Tradition*, Patrides writes that "*Paradise Lost* is a 'comedy' involving a divine mystery best understood – if it can be understood at all – in terms of the ineffable work of grace on both man and the universe at large."[16] He believes that for Milton as well as for other Christian historians, Jesus Christ stands at the centre of universal history, that the "vision of the future in *Paradise Lost* unfolds . . . in terms of faithful individuals (such as Abel, Enoch, Noah, Abraham, Isaac, Moses, Joshua and David), culminating at last in the incarnation of the Son of God whom Adam accepts as his redeemer 'by faith alone.'"[17] The vision of the future thus embodies, above all, the

---

[15] Hence the strong social and ethical principles of solidarity that for centuries have kept Jewish communities from disintegrating in spite of persecution.

The responsibility which gives purpose to the life of every individual stems from the traditional belief that all men are stamped by God with the seal of Adam and is expressed in the saying: "Therefore every man is bound to say, On account of *me* the world was created." That is, as Moore explains, "every man is to feel himself responsible, as though the whole human race depended on his conduct" (George F. Moore, *Judaism*, I, p. 445).

[16] Patrides, *Milton and the Christian Tradition*, p. 10.

[17] Patrides, p. 128. Joseph H. Summers too believes that the plan of the last two books is overwhelmingly Christian. See *The Muse's Method*, pp. 186–224.

universalistic and Christocentric view of history. Yet Patrides concedes that "the consensus, after all, appears to be that Milton had 'no profound belief in the incarnate Christ', that his account of the Incarnation is 'only an incident in the long history' of the world, that the redemption is 'sketched, hastily and prosaically, in the Twelfth Book', and that the mere 'hundred lines' allotted to it even there is 'surely insufficient treatment'."[18] The views of Raleigh, Tillyard and Daiches which Patrides advances here assist the argument that Milton's view of history calls for further examination.

What, in effect, emerges from the views of these critics is that it would be possible to take the references to Christ's Incarnation and Resurrection out of the poem without basically changing its meaning or the reader's response to it. Not that one could approve of such deletions for this would violate the poem's Christian framework, but these critics' conclusion certainly fits with the theory that Milton's view of man and history is hebraic in essence. And, paradoxically, it is perhaps in Milton's treatment of Christ that this can best be seen.[19] True, he describes Christ as the "greater Man" who "will restore us and regain the blissful Seat" (I.4–5), that Christ offers his life to redeem Man (III.236–241); he is the "Messiah" and "anointed King" (VI.718), the seed of Abraham, the "great deliverer, who shall bruise / The serpent's head" (XII.149–150). But the Messianic figure who will endure man's punishment "by coming in the Flesh / To a reproachful life and cursed death / Proclaiming Life to all who shall believe / In his redemption" (XII.405–408) is not at the centre of *Paradise Lost* nor does he occupy a central position in the historical résumé of the last two books. Indeed, the figure of Christ on the Cross taking upon himself the sins and sufferings of all those who believe in him is strikingly absent from the poem.[20] But though Patrides realizes

---

[18] Patrides, pp. 259–260. Patrides studied the Christian view of history in greater detail in *The Phoenix and the Ladder* (Berkeley and Los Angeles, 1964).

[19] On the other hand, the poem would be severely affected were all the hebraic references omitted.

[20] The Crucifixion is briefly described in XII.413–416, but the Cross itself is not a central image in the poem.

Milton's concern in *Paradise Lost* is with Man, he does not believe
that Milton's philosophy is anthropocentric, for, he writes,

> the story told is not a sentence in the history of the world, it is a
> parenthesis in eternity that opens with Raphael's account of the
> "great Year" before the creation, and closes with Michael's
> vision of the end of time. Within and without this span stands
> the God-man, making *Paradise Lost* Christocentric and securing
> for Milton an honoured position in the long line that stretches
> from Eusebius to Augustine, thence to Jerome and Orosius,
> Isidore and Bede, Otto of Freising and Vincent of Beauvais, and
> finally to Dante and the Renaissance.[21]

The Christian idea of history, it is true, certainly provides the
background against which the narrative is enacted but Milton,
while accepting this, has shifted the emphasis. The Christocentric
view of history minimizes the importance of the individual whereas
Milton's poem holds in focus precisely the story of man, of Adam
and Eve. It is in this respect that Milton is closer to the Old Testament idea of history which sees the Creator as a universal Almighty
God and considers life in this world worth living simply because it
was created by God. By attributing to Christ the central and divine
function of being the Saviour of mankind, the Christocentric view
reduces the weight of all events that do not foreshadow or prepare
Christ's coming to bring about eternal salvation and rest. This does
not present any ideological problem for the Old Testament-reading
poet, for though *Paradise Lost* reflects Milton's belief in man's fall,
the poet's strong positivism[22] and his faith in man modifies this
conception. That is undoubtedly one of the hebraic factors in the
poem for, as Fisch defines it, "Hebraism is indeed a doctrine of
salvation, but of salvation which we may behold as a condition of
our existence in this world".[23] Indeed, Milton creates in *Paradise
Lost* a world very similar to the world in which we live. We still

[21] *Milton and the Christian Tradition*, pp. 262–263.
[22] The term as used here does not, of course, refer to the logical positivism associated with Auguste Comte.
[23] *Jerusalem and Albion*, p. 14.

read the poem with pleasure not because Milton stands "in the long line that stretches from Eusebius to Augustine"[24] etc. but because he tells us of each man's own experience of despair and love. When the poem ends, the world is neither saved nor lost. With all its vicissitudes, it is still good.

One of the basic tenets of Christianity is the necessity of faith in Christ for man's redemption:

> Even the righteousness of God which is by faith of Jesus Christ unto all and upon all them that believe: for there is no difference: For all have sinned, and come short of the glory of God; Being justified freely by his grace through the redemption that is in Christ Jesus:
>
> Romans iii. 22–24

However, inherent in Milton's Weltanschauung is the belief in man. Like the Hebrew prophets, the humanist poet believes men who have sinned are capable of bettering their moral nature. It is when Adam and Eve fall lowest and humbly confess their sin that they are most worthy of God's redemption.[25] Like the Old Testament characters, Milton's Adam and Eve show that "Humiliation and elevation . . . belong basically together."[26] While Christianity attached the greater significance to the weakness of the flesh and Renaissance humanism stressed man's dignity and intellect, the Old Testament deals with men who, however great, are not without human flaws. In the simple Biblical narratives which Milton summarizes in the last two books, he projects his own anti-heroic ideal of man. Both his Renaissance humanism and his Christian belief derive their strength from the spirit of the Old Testament. The ethical humanism of *Paradise Lost* is the major conceptual hebraic factor in the poem.

Now, it may be argued that there is a contradiction between Milton's positive attitude to man and his Christian belief in man's

---

[24] *Milton and the Christian Tradition*, pp. 262–263.
[25] Judaism not only believes that each man may redeem himself but attaches great moral significance to the repentance of the sinners. See, for example, *Berakhot*, 34b: "Where the penitent stands even the righteous cannot stand."
[26] Erich Auerbach, *Mimesis* (New York, 1957 [1946]), p. 15.

fall and its results. The answer is that Milton was aware of this contradiction and therefore felt the need to "justify the ways of God to men". It is only in the last books of the poem that the conflicting doctrines of acceptance and hope for salvation on the one hand and the idea of the positive value of living on the other are reconciled imaginatively. For in Michael's account of history, Milton pinpoints the hebraic view of history which recognizes, at one and the same time, divine goodness and the inevitable presence of evil in the world. It acknowledges both the frailty and the nobility of human nature made "a little lower than the angels,... crowned ... with glory and honour".[27] This is why Milton's imaginative grasp of Biblical history as revealed to Adam has a much deeper significance than the prophecies of history in the epic tradition Milton was following. Adam, in a way, is like Homer's Odysseus, who has to learn from the experience of the dead before he can return to the living, or like Aeneas, who has to learn from Anchises about the heroic destiny of Rome,[28] but what Michael teaches Adam through the visions and the narrative is not heroism, courage, or a sense of the destiny of one nation; it is, rather, an acceptance of man's life within the panorama of history.

Until the fall, Adam and Eve understood everything subjectively. At the end of Book X, they become aware of each other but it is the Archangel Michael who opens up the whole world before Adam's eyes just as God himself, according to a Rabbinic commentary, showed Adam the "book of the generations".[29]

It is through Michael's account of events like the Exodus that the sense of temporal perspective is relayed.[30] Though purporting

[27] Psalm viii. 5. The frailty of man is partly explained by the "evil drive", for the "imagination of man's heart is evil from his youth." (Genesis viii. 21).
[28] On the vision of the future as a convention in epic poetry, see also T. Greene, *The Descent from Heaven* (New Haven, 1963), p. 163.
[29] Genesis v. 1: "This is the book of the generations of Adam." Sforno (1475–1550) comments that this is the book of the account of the history of mankind. See also the opinions of the elders of the Tosafot.
[30] My reading of the Exodus episode in Book XII differs from that of John T. Shawcross, who has recently examined the function of the exodus myth in the poem ("*Paradise Lost* and the Theme of Exodus", *Milton Studies II*, [Pittsburgh, 1970], pp. 3–26). I do not believe that Milton's presentation is mythopeic here.

to have great moral significance, it in fact simply recounts a
sequence of events. This is how Michael tells the story: Joseph
dies and

>   leaves his Race
> Growing into a Nation, and now grown
> Suspected to a sequent King, who seeks
> To stop their overgrowth, as inmate guests
> Too numerous; whence of guests he makes them slaves
> Inhospitably, and kills thir infant Males:
> Till by two brethren (those two brethren call
> *Moses* and *Aaron*) sent from God to claim
> His people from enthralment, they return
> With glory and spoil back to thir promis'd Land.
> But first the lawless Tyrant, who denies
> To know thir God, or message to regard,
> Must be compell'd by Signs and Judgments dire;
> To blood unshed the Rivers must be turn'd,
> Frogs, Lice and Flies must all his Palace fill
> With loath'd intrusion, and fill all the Land;
> His Cattle must of Rot and Murrain die,
> Botches and blains must all his flesh imboss,
> And all his people; Thunder mixt with Hail,
> Hail mixt with fire must rend th'*Egyptian* Sky
> And wheel on th' Earth, devouring where it rolls;
> What it devours not, Herb, or Fruit, or Grain,
> A Darksome Cloud of Locusts swarming down
> Must eat, and on the ground leave nothing green:
> Darkness must overshadow all his bounds,
> Palpable darkness, and blot out three days;
> Last with one midnight stroke all the first-born
> Of *Egypt* must lie dead. Thus with ten wounds
> The River-dragon tam'd at length submits
> To let his sojourners depart, and oft
> Humbles his stubborn heart, but still as Ice
> More hard'n'd after thaw, till in his rage
> Pursuing whom he late dismiss'd, the Sea

Swallows him with his Host, but them lets pass
As on dry land between two crystal walls,
Aw'd by the rod of *Moses* so to stand
Divided, till his rescu'd gain thir shore:

XII.163–199

The references to the Exodus appearing in the first books of the
epic have, as we have seen, a literary suggestiveness which enhances
the message of these books.[31] It is therefore of cardinal significance
that similar references to the Exodus fulfil a different function in
Book XII. Egypt's ruler is called a "sequent King" (XII.165) and is
reduced to the size of a historical figure. Nor does the "*River-
dragon* tam'd at length" have the mythical dimensions of "that Sea-
beast Leviathan" (I.202–203). Compare also the factual description
of the plague of the locusts

A darksome Cloud of Locusts swarming down
Must eat, and on the ground leave nothing green:

XII.185–186

with the powerful simile describing the same plague in Book I:

As when the potent Rod
Of Amram's Son in Egypt's evil day
Wav'd round the Coast, up call'd a pitchy cloud
Of *Locusts*, warping on the Eastern Wind,
That o'er the Realm of impious *Pharaoh* hung
Like Night, and darken'd all the Land of *Nile*:

I.338–343

Similarly, the brief account of the drowning of the Egyptian host

till in his rage
Pursuing whom he late dismiss'd, the Sea
Swallows him with his Host, but them lets pass
As on dry land between two crystal walls

XII.194–197

is contrasted with that allusive simile

---

[31] Chapter II, section b.

> scatter'd sedge
> Afloat, when with fierce Winds *Orion* arm'd
> Hath vext the Red-Sea Coast, whose waves o'erthrew
> *Busiris* and his *Memphian* Chivalry,
> While with perfidious hatred they pursu'd
> The Sojourners of *Goshen*, who beheld
> From the safe shore thir floating Carcasses
> And broken Chariot Wheels;
>
> I.304–310

The same notes are struck but in a different key: what is emphasized in Book XII is not the mythical size of God's enemies; the defeat of Pharaoh and his host is briefly described as a historical event indicating once more God's supremacy over his enemies. Furthermore, the emphasis here is not on Pharaoh but on the God who intervenes in history, the God who is revealed as acting in history for a moral purpose:

> Such wondrous power God to his Saint will lend,
> Though present in his Angel, who shall go
> Before them in a Cloud, and Pillar of Fire,
> By day a Cloud, by night a Pillar of Fire,
> To guide them in thir journey, and remove
> Behind them, while th' obdurate King pursues:
> All night he will pursue, but his approach
> Darkness defends between till morning Watch;
> Then through the Fiery Pillar and the Cloud
> God looking forth will trouble all his Host
> And craze thir Chariot wheels: when by command
> *Moses* once more his potent Rod extends
> Over the Sea, the Sea his Rod obeys;
> On thir imbattl'd ranks the Waves return,
> And overwhelm thir War: the Race elect
> Safe towards *Canaan* from the shore advance
> Through the wild Desert,
>
> XII.200–216

This manifestation of God within the interplay of God and man in the order of events (which Milton paraphrases here with such fine economy) is the central theme of Exodus xiv and is, in fact, vital to the hebraic faith.[32]

Milton also follows Hebrew tradition in seeing the Exodus as the beginning of Israel's history as a nation: the "Race growing into a Nation" will in the Wilderness

> found
> Thir government, and thir great Senate Choose
> Through the twelve Tribes, to rule by Laws ordain'd:
>   XII.223–226

But he does not visualize the Exodus as having a typological significance. The story is not presented as foreshadowing the Crucifixion or the Resurrection, and Pharaoh is not described here as a type of Satan. It therefore would seem wrong to claim that Milton views all history in terms of a pattern which is visible in Christ. What we have, rather, is a historical treatment of Exodus, or, as Harold Fisch writes about Isaiah "a determined movement from myth to history".[33]

What applies to such significant episodes in history as the Exodus also applies to isolated allusions which evidence the same movement from myth to history within *Paradise Lost*. A pertinent illustration is Milton's use of the sword metaphor. After Satan's dramatic speech advocating war "open or understood", the fallen archangel speaks

> and to confirm his words, out-flew
> Millions of flaming swords, drawn from the thighs
> Of mighty Cherubim; the sudden blaze
> Far round illumin'd hell: highly they rag'd
> Against the Highest, and fierce with grasped Arms
> Clash'd on thir sounding shields the din of war,
> Hurling defiance toward the Vault of Heav'n.
>   I.663–669

---

[32] Patrides rightly recognizes that the God of Israel is a living God, "not an impersonal abstraction, dwelling beyond the confines of the universe and utterly incommunicable" (*Milton and the Christian Tradition*, pp. 221–222).

[33] "Hebraic Styles and Motifs in *Paradise Lost*", p. 41.

Todd suggests that the source of the image of the "Millions of flaming swords" is Tasso, *Gerusalemme Liberata* V.28:

Quasi in quel punto *mille spade ardenti*
Furon vedute fiammegiar insieme.

Keightley rightly adds the reference to Genesis iii. 24 which is relevant here: "the flaming sword which turned everyway." In Hebrew, the phrase says "the flame of the turning sword",[34] and this powerful image could well have been in Milton's mind when he described the fallen angels.[35] In Book VI while describing the battle between Satan's legions and Michael's angels, the sword of Michael is a decisive agent in the battle. The battle was hanging in "even scale" until the moment Satan saw

> where the Sword of *Michael* smote, and fell'd
> Squadrons at once, with huge two-handed sway
> Brandisht aloft the horrid edge came down
> *Wide wasting*;
>
> VI.250–253 (italics mine)

The passage is telling, for it reveals Milton's understanding of the Hebrew word he uses. In Hebrew the word *sword* is a derivative of a root which also means "to dry up", "to ravage", "to lay waste", "to destroy". The poetic power of Michael's sword which comes down "wide wasting" is enhanced through the connotations of the word in Hebrew.[36] Michael is aware of the divine power of

[34] Ben Yehudah, *Thesaurus*, p. 2629, explains the word *lahat* in this context (Genesis iii. 24) as edge.
[35] Speiser suggests that the "fiery revolving sword" could also be derived from Mesopotamian tradition. Most of the gods of that land had distinctive weapons of their own such as the dagger of Ashur or the toothed sword of Shamash. Speiser points out an illustration of the image in the concluding lines of the *Enuma Elish* and suggests that the fire seems to characterize the weapon, a metaphorical description apparently of a glinting blade like a bolt of lightning. The magical weapon was all that stood between the insurgent gods and their goal (E. A. Speiser, translator and editor, *The Anchor Bible*, *Genesis* [Garden City, 1964], p. 24.)
[36] On the connotations of this Hebrew word see Ben Yehudah, *Thesaurus*, p. 1734. It is not impossible that Milton had the same Biblical sword in mind when he wrote, in *Lycidas*, of "that two-handed engine at the door . . . / . . . ready to smite once, and smite no more . . ." (ll. 130–131).

his weapon and he warns Satan that he shall go to hell

> Ere this avenging Sword begin thy doom,
> Or some more sudden vengeance wing'd from God
> Precipitate thee with augmented pain.
>
> VI.278–280

His threats, however, do not awe Satan, and the two angels renew
their godlike struggle:

> Now wav'd thir fiery Swords, and in the Air
> Made horrid Circles; . . .
>
> VI.304–305

>   but the sword
> Of *Michael*, from the Armory of God
> Was giv'n him temper'd so, that neither keen
> Nor solid might resist that edge: it met
> The sword of *Satan* with steep force to smite
> Descending, . . .
>
> VI.320–325

Finally, when the battle is over and Satan's forces are defeated,
Michael places "in Guard thir Watches round, / Cherubic waving
fires" (VI.412–413). These "Cherubic waving fires" are, as in
Genesis, intended to bar those who are unworthy from entering.[37]
The image is thus thematically the same, but it is also multiplied
by Milton's imagination and the one powerful "flame of the revolving sword" has become many "waving fires" that seem to illuminate
the darkness of Night's "cloudy covert" whilst Satan is "Far in the
dark dislodg'd, and void of rest" (VI.415).

In Books XI and XII Milton uses the sword image as it appears
in Genesis. At the end of *Paradise Lost* as in Genesis, the angels
of the Lord and the sword – here *wide waving* – guard the Tree of
Life, acting as agents of God. In Book XII the sword of God is no
longer "wide wasting", it is only "wide waving"; it is not intended

---

[37] The same sword of divine justice also appears in Ezekiel xxi. 9–17, where the
fiery swords in the air "Made horrid Circles" (VI.305). A sword also appears in
the hands of Jesus's disciple in Matthew xxvi. 51 and, in John xviii. 10, the same
episode is referred to and the disciple identified as Peter.

to destroy Adam and Eve, its only function being to bar the way to the Tree of Life. In Book I, conversely, the "millions of flaming swords" belong to those of Satan's cohorts, who rage "Against the Highest". God entrusts Michael with the task of coming to Adam and Eve to

> send them forth, though sorrowing, yet in peace:
> And on the East side of the Garden place,
> Where entrance up from Eden easiest climbs,
> Cherubic watch, and of a Sword the flame
> Wide waving, all approach far off to fright,
> And guard all passage to the Tree of Life:
>
> XI.117–122

Michael fulfils the function assigned to him and shows Adam the guards

> By mee encampt on yonder Hill, expect
> Thir motion, at whose Front a flaming Sword,
> In signal of remove, waves fiercely round;
>
> XII.591–593

And when Adam and Eve leave the garden,

> The brandisht Sword of God before them blaz'd
> Fierce as a Comet;
>
> XII.633–634

It is interesting to speculate on how Milton's imagination works through his constant use of the sword image. In Book VI, the one sword becomes an infinite number of "fiery swords". In Book I, we see how evil proliferates that same sword into "Millions of flaming swords" but here again we have an instance of Milton's irony: the cross references in *Paradise Lost* point out the contrast between the sword of Michael – identical in purpose with the sword of Genesis iii. 24, the sword of divine providence and just punishment – and the sword that, in the hands of the fallen angels, becomes an instrument of destruction with which they hurl "Defiance toward the Vault of Heaven". Evil thus not only proliferates the sword, it also perverts it. But, ultimately, to no avail for, as the cross references and the Biblical passages behind the image in Book I drive home, no matter how "highly" the fallen angels rage "Against the Highest" and no matter how deafeningly they clash "on thir sounding shields the din of war" (I.668), they will eventually be silenced by those whose "impenetrable" armor is "not to have sinn'd / Not to have disobey'd" (VI.400–403). All the swords are deemed inferior to the sword of God in Book XII, thereby reassuring us of the role of God's providence in the affairs of men.

The same historical concern is seen in the visions and in the Biblical narrative reduced to its historical essentials. Most of the visions are of evil which, in a lower key, recapitulate themes recurrent throughout the epic.[38] The envy of Cain, for instance, is the human counterpart of Satan's envy of man; similarly, the sons of God lured by the daughters of Cain are the result of "Man's effeminate slackness" (XI.634) while the violent warriors who admire might alone, the "Destroyers rightlier call'd and Plagues of men" (XI.697), recall the false valor of the fallen angels in the opening books of the poem. Like his Satanic prototype, the tyrant Nimrod is also a rebel who wants to usurp authority "from God not giv'n" (XII.66). But these figures, presented here in a historic perspective, do not possess the mythic grandeur of their prototypes in the poem. They stand for the evil that is inherent in humanity.

Outweighing the allusions to evil and destruction are the examples of moral courage and freedom of choice attesting to Milton's belief in what Driver aptly calls "the Hebrew assumption of the potentiality of the new". In his concept of the future, Milton is, once more, close to the hebraic ethos: "the future ... is open in Hebraism", writes Driver, "and the moral earnestness of the prophets tended to keep it so, since it emphasized responsibility and choice".[39] This is the role of the few men of worth who stand

---

[38] A similar point has been made by Barbara Kiefer Lewalski in "Structure and the Symbolism of Vision in Michael's Prophecy, *Paradise Lost*, Books XI–XII", *PQ*, XLII (January, 1963), pp. 25–35.

[39] *The Sense of History in Greek and Shakespearean Drama*, pp. 40 and 63. On the other hand, French R. Fogle believes that the view Milton expressed in *Paradise Lost* "shows only a distant, no immediate, hope ... Within human time, at least, there was no general advance toward a discernible goal, no wave-like movement toward the redeemed society." See "Milton as Historian" in *Milton and Clarendon*, William Andrews Clark Memorial Library (Los Angeles, 1965), pp. 1–20.

out against the many visions of evil Adam is shown. Just and righteous, faithful, and devoted men like Enoch, "eminent / In wise deport" (XI.665–666), or Noah, the "Reverend Sire," who abhorred the wicked doings of his neighbors (XI.719–720), or Abraham, called "by Vision from his Father's house", "Not knowing to what Land, yet firm believes" (XII.121, 127): these are the human counterpart of angels like Abdiel. If Abdiel represents the ultimate triumph of spiritual over worldly might in Milton's Heaven, his upright Biblical characters demonstrate man's freedom within the pattern of empirical history.[40] They prove that God guides the universe but that man has a definite say in the flow of events in his own life. Like Noah and Abraham, Adam has to recognize both "hearts" – the good inclination as well as the evil one – constantly choosing between them. Through the examples he is shown, Adam learns how important it is to weigh his own deeds in terms of the present and the future.

Opinions as to the poetical and imaginative merit of the last two books are sharply divided: they range from a condemnation of their inartistic quality to the belief in the success of Milton's design both theologically and poetically and the affirmation of their structural necessity in the poem's total architecture.[41] They have two other roles. One is that by summarizing Biblical episodes which, through references and allusions, are wrought into the texture of the previous books, and by restating their principal themes, Milton's account of history confers conceptual unity upon the hebraic elements of Hell, Eden, and Heaven. The other is the summing up of one of the concepts presented in this book – namely, that when hebraic elements are thematically integrated in the poem, they keep a balance between the humanist and the Puritan elements in Milton's thought, for Milton's belief in the purpose of

[40] Professor Jason P. Rosenblatt has kindly sent me the copy of his essay now in the press, "Structural Unity and Temporal Concordance: The War in Heaven in *Paradise Lost*", in which he discusses the distinction between freedom and servitude that is made in Exodus and in Book VI of the epic.
[41] See, for example, C. S. Lewis, *A Preface to Paradise Lost*, p. 129, and Louis L. Martz, *The Paradise Within*, pp. 141–167, on the one hand, and F. T. Prince, "On the Last Two books of *Paradise Lost*", *E & S* (1958), pp. 38–52, and Helen Gardner, *A Reading of Paradise Lost*, pp. 94–98, on the other.

God's plan and his positive vision of the human predicament are both reconciled and validated in terms of Old Testament history. All that we learned about God and men hitherto fits into place now that we see it enacted in history. Through the account of history, Adam learns better to judge the past, to evaluate and recognize his own deeds in a new historic perspective. Good and evil are indeed almost inseparable, but Adam learns to distinguish between them; witnessing the moral goodness, the faith, and obedience of men like Noah and Abraham, Adam realizes that because of them and their like, the world goes on. By learning about God's dealings with his descendants, Adam achieves a state of moral and emotional readiness to face his destiny, fulfil the divine will, and become part of history.[42]

It is in this sense that Milton's historic vision agrees with Fisch's definition of hebraism which, he says, provides "an account of the relationship between Man, God and Nature in its permanent historical character. From the Hebraic point of view, Jerusalem is not a mythical ideal but rather one capable of resurrection in history through the exercise of our human faculties."[43] Therefore, the justification of God's ways to men could only be expressed in terms of human existence, by affirming God's relationship to men and the value of life itself. It is thus natural that at the end of the poem there is no moral statement of man's predicament; there is, instead, a scene "simple, sensuous and passionate" which brings us back to life, to the natural realm we know. The "brandisht Sword of God" no longer blazes before Adam and Eve, and the gate "With dreadful Faces throng'd and fiery Arms" is behind them while "The World was all before them." The tears they now drop are "natural", and they wipe them soon for the way ahead no longer seems like the way to death. It looks like a way with infinite possibilities "where to choose / Thir place of rest", including the possibility of progress to a better humanity. Adam and Eve also have a new

---

[42] This historic vision is a recurrent motif in the Old Testament which teaches that actual and personal experiences should be seen in the light of historical experience. See, for example, Exodus x. 2; Deuteronomy xxxii. 7; Judges vi. 13; Psalms xliv. 1–3; lxxviii. 2–11; Joel i. 3.

[43] *Jerusalem and Albion*, p. 14.

sense of providential care which gives them the courage to take through Eden "thir solitary way". The future is open at the end of the poem, emphasizing man's responsibility and choice. Like Abraham, whom God ordered to leave his country and his kindred to go to a newly promised land, Adam and Eve carry the faith in God's promise. After the grand procession of the fallen angels in the first books of the poem, after the formal scenes in heaven, the battle between the celestial armies, all foreshadowing the dramatic events in Eden, the last lines of the poem are, like the end of a fugue, moving in their simple presentation of the Genesis story.

APPENDIX: MILTON'S EDITORS FROM HUME TO
HUGHES

Harris Fletcher's scholarly assessments of Milton's Semitic studies and his Rabbinical readings[1] initiated a new phase in the investigation of Milton's hebraic sources. But an equally informed interest in the subject is found in Milton's first editors and commentators. In the following pages we shall review some of these earlier commentaries.

The style of *Paradise Lost* seems to have been an everlasting source of irritation to Milton's literary critics. Addison found that the English language "sunk under him [Milton]".[2] Dr. Johnson thought Milton formed "what Butler calls a *Babylonish Dialect*" and accused him of using English words with a foreign idiom.[3] The form of the argument has been modified over the centuries but, in essence, it still exists principally associated today with the names of Eliot and Leavis. This criticism seems to have sprung from a lack of understanding of the text itself and of its allusions.[4] One of the reasons for the seeming incongruity of Milton's style is his use of Biblical phrases, Hebrew words which often sound, as Johnson complained, "harsh and barbarous"[5] to the English ear.

---

[1] Harris F. Fletcher, *Milton's Semitic Studies and Some Manifestations of them in his Poetry* (Chicago, 1926); *Milton's Rabbinical Readings* (Urbana, 1930).
[2] Joseph Addison, *The Spectator* No. 297, February 9, quoted in *Milton Criticism, Selections from Four Centuries*, ed. James Thorpe, London, (1965 [1951]), p. 52.
[3] Samuel Johnson, quoted in *Milton Criticism: Selections from Four Centuries, op. cit.*, p. 86.
[4] See E. M. W. Tillyard's essay "Milton's Visual Imagination" in the *Miltonic Setting, Past and Present* (Cambridge, 1938), pp. 90–104, and also Christopher Ricks, *Milton's Grand Style* (Oxford, 1963).
[5] Samuel Johnson, *Milton*, p. 86.

While his debt to Biblical usages and metaphors seems to have been taken for granted, among his contemporary critics Milton was admired for the most part for his skillful imitation of Homer and Virgil. Although Dryden himself, for example, succeeds admirably in his Biblical allegory in the satiric mode (*Absalom and Achitophel*), he fails to understand Milton's epic usage of the Bible and thinks Milton "runs into a flat of thought, sometimes for a hundred lines, but it is when he is got into a track of Scripture".[6] Scholars seem to have been aware that Milton was also a good "Hebrician", but they did not dwell on the subject.[7]

But before the end of the seventeenth century, the first serious scholarly edition of *Paradise Lost* had appeared and solid foundations had been laid for an understanding of Milton's use of the Hebrew Bible and its Rabbinical commentaries. The editor of the 1695 edition and the author of the exhaustive annotations on the works of John Milton calls himself P.H. on the title page. He was Patrick Hume, a London schoolmaster.[8] Bishop Newton hardly conceals his contempt for Hume's work when writing in the preface to his 1749 edition that "as he [Hume] was the first, so is the most copious annotator. He laid the foundation, but he laid it among infinite heaps of rubbish."[9] Hume was certainly well acquainted with the texts of the Old and New Testament, and he constantly brings his knowledge of the Bible and the Apocrypha to bear on the text of *Paradise Lost*. He quotes extensively from the Old Testament because he believes in the superiority of "Mosaic philosophy" over the philosophy of the heathen. His annotations are thus morally biased toward the Holy Scriptures, but – as to be expected – he understands Old Testament texts in the light of New Testament doctrine. He would not, for example, question the interpretation of Genesis i. 2 as meaning God's Holy Spirit (*P.L.* I.17). In explaining the meaning of "Hosannas" (III.348) from the

[6] John Dryden, *Essay on Satire*, quoted in *Milton Criticism*, p. 338.
[7] John Toland's *Life of John Milton*, p. 343.
[8] Patrick Hume is said to have been a member of the family of Hume of Polwarth, Berwickshire. See *DNB*, ed. Sir Leslie Stephen and Sir Sidney Lee (London, 1922), vol. X, p. 231.
[9] Thomas Newton, ed. *Paradise Lost. A New Edition, with Notes of Various Authors.* 2 vols. (London, 1749). Preface (vol. I), pages not numbered.

Hebrew *yasha'*, he adds: "An exstatic confession of the Saviour of the world even by those who believed not in him." Oras rightly considers Hume to have had a wide knowledge of Biblical exegesis.[10] But the vagueness of Hume's own references, such as: "The Rabbins assure us ..." (on I.7), "the Rabbins tell us ..." (on III.359), or it is "by the Rabbis" said (on III.467) suggests a lack of close familiarity with the Biblical exegetical sources in their original. He does refer, however, to certain Rabbis by name: he very appropriately quotes Kimchi[11] on the significance of the Baalim and the Ashtarot (I.422), and on III.495, for example, he quotes Ibn Ezra (whom he calls by his Latin name Aben Ezra) in Latin, which would suggest that he did not own or have the use of a Rabbinical Bible. Hume refers to the Talmud, as when he explains the Manna (on II.113),[12] or in claiming that the Talmud derives the name *Yarden* from *Dan* and *Yarad* (on III.535) although the fact that he does not give the reference suggests that he did not consult his source directly.[13]

Hume's philological annotations are helpful and attest to his oriental scholarship. He points out, for example, that "Paradise פרדם (*pardes*) is a word of Persian Extraction, whence the Jews borrowed it, and of them the Grecians ..." (I.1), that the word *Seraph* is a derivative of שׂרף (*srf*) to burn... alluding to the brightness of those Celestial Beings ..." (I.129), that the title "*Sultan* is well applied to Satan for the word is derived from Hebrew שׁלט (*slt*) (I.348) which means to rule, and that *Baalim* and *Ashtarot* are the plural of *Baal* and *Ashtoret* (I.422). Hume was also aware of the connections of old Hebrew and Syrian traditions with Greek culture and he rightly points out that *Adonis* derives from *Adon*, Lord (I.450). He explains the names of all devils and angels: Satan (I.82), Moloch (I.392), Belial (I.490), Michael (VI.44),

---

[10] Ants Oras, *Milton's Editors and Commentators from Patrick Hume to Henry John Todd (1695–1801)* (London, 1931), p. 24.

[11] Also known as RaDaK by the initials of his name *R*abbi *D*avid *K*imchi; see Chapter II, p. 49, n. 39.

[12] The word *man* appears several times in the Talmud, but the third explanation Hume offers for the word and attributes to the Talmud appears in Exodus (xvi. 15) which he adduces for his first explanation.

[13] Berakhot, 55.a.

Gabriel (IV.549), Raphael (V.221), Uriel (III.648), Uzziel (IV.782), Ithuriel (IV.788), and Zephon (III.648). These explanations are for the most part traditional and were the accepted ones in the seventeenth century, such as: Beelzebub – Lord of Flies (I.81–82), or Eve – Mother of Mankind (I.36). At times, his etymological annotations have the characteristics of Midrash explanations or Rabbinical (and scholastic) hairsplitting as when he explains the connection between *Har ha-Mashhit* and *Har ha-Mishha* in glossing Molton's "Offensive Mountain" (I.443). However, many of his etymological explanations agree with the views of modern philologists (such as his explanation of *Jubilee* as deriving from *Yovel* (a ram) (III.348)). His explanation of *Yam Suf* as meaning the Sea of Sedge (I.306), for example, certainly contributes to the understanding of Milton's elaborate imagery in the passage.[14]

Hume may also have known some Arabic, although he writes the Arabic words in Hebrew characters without referring to his source.[15] He rightly points out that Padan "in the Arabic Language signifies a Field, a champain Country" (III.513).

Hume displays a knowledge of Hebrew not only in his etymological annotations but also through his effortless detection of hebraisms in Milton's style, such as "past through fire" (I.395), "A Man of Measure" (III.464), or "Daughter of his Voice" (IX.653).[16] His explanation of the derivation of *Hallelujas* (II.242)

---

[14] Most translations of the Bible render ים סוף as "Red Sea" (Exodus xiii. 18). Luther translated the name as "Schilfmeer". *D. Martin Luthers Werke, Die Deutsche Bibel* (Weimar, 1954), vol. VIII, p. 240.

[15] Thus Hume tries to relate this to the falling of the angels from the zenith in I.745 but there seems to be little basis for this explanation, and I have not found its source. He claims that the Arabic word נגת is a corruption of סמת zenith, and so tries to associate the two words סמת (azimuth) or סמת אלראס (zenith) and פקט (to fall) and to explain Milton's line: "Dropt from the zenith." It seems, however, that there is no relation between the two Arabic words, which are derived from different roots. Furthermore, Hume himself apparently corrupts the Arabic פקט which he renders with a ת instead of a ט.

[16] In the case of *bat qol* Hume does not refer to a specific text where this expression is used and only points out similar Biblical phrases.

One of the meanings of this felicitous expression is 'divine voice'. It does not appear in the Old Testament but we find it in the Talmud (*e.g.*, Avot 6.b, Bava Metzia 59.b, Yerushalmi, Berakhot 1.c) as well as in later writings (Maimonides, *Guide to the Perplexed* 20. 42, for example).

shows a knowledge of Hebrew grammar. Like Milton and like all his learned contemporaries, Hume was familiar with such Jewish authors as Philo (whom he mentions, *e.g.* on I.406) and Flavius Josephus (whose *Antiquities* he mentions on I.694), just as he was familiar with the Church Fathers and, specifically, with hexameral writers like Origen, Chrysostom, St. Jerome, Barcepha and many others.

A final comment: although not all Hume's annotations are useful today, they are of considerable historical value. His knowledge of Hebrew and his exegetical readings enabled him to shed light on many of the subtleties and the foreign elements of Milton's style. Perhaps Hume's greatest contribution is his insight into Milton's use of the Bible. On IX.656 he has a long note on *afki* claiming that Milton followed the Chaldee paraphrase of Genesis i. 3. He then comments: "This Heb. Particle, (af) את, plainly shews, that the short and summary account that *Moses* gives of the Serpent's Temptation, has respect to some previous Discourse, which could, in all probability, be no other than what our Poet has pitch'd upon." In other words, Hume is implying that Milton might have re-created the story that was the source of the first chapters of Genesis. This, indeed, is a fascinating hypothesis, for Milton's poetic imagination caused him to re-create, in *Paradise Lost*, many of the stories and myths behind episodes and allusions throughout the Bible.

The next edition of *Paradise Lost* was published only thirty-seven years after Hume's edition.[17] Richard Bentley's edition quickly won fame probably because of the vehement controversies it aroused at the time. It certainly deserves consideration in its own right. Its strength lies in its editor's formidable classical scholarship which he so assiduously applies to the text. But this will not be dealt with here. The main fault of this edition is, of course, its author's end – namely the emendation of the text which Bentley thought had been much corrupted by the printer. Whereas Hume's edition was almost encyclopaedic and inspired by admiration for the poetry of *Paradise Lost*, Bentley's edition,

---

[17] *Milton's Paradise Lost*, ed. Richard Bentley (London, 1732).

eccentrically strict and rigidly governed by the principle of emendation, reveals its editor's concern for Milton's language. Bentley
often misses the rhythm of Milton's lines or his puns, but his merit
is that "he may only produce a trivial piece of nagging, but has a
flair for choosing an important place to do it".[18] Bentley is also
"sharp at picking out ... implications" about the relation of
Biblical to classical myth.[19] Bentley's edition was criticized by
Pearce – although "for a serious answer he counts as on Bentley's
side"[20], attacked by Newton as a "most miserable bungling work"[21],
and ironically referred to by Todd as "a splendid edition of *Paradise
Lost*, by which he [Bentley] acquired no honour".[22]

How much Hebrew did Bentley know and how did he apply his
knowledge to the "emendation" of *Paradise Lost*? De Quincey says
that at the age of six "he read Latin, Greek and Hebrew, together
with *some* Arabic and Syriac, *some* observe, not too much, I will
answer for it."[23] However, when he was twenty and appointed
tutor to the son of Dr. Stillingfleet (then Dean of St. Paul's), he
seems to have had every opportunity to pursue his studies. De
Quincey asserts that "it is certain, that in Dean Stillingfleet's
family he had, by a most laborious process of study, made himself
an eminent master of the Hebrew, Chaldee and Syriac".[24] According to Monk, Bentley compiled a dictionary of Hebrew for his own
use "not from the late rabbins, but from the ancient versions",[25]
and Jebb quotes Bentley probably about the same dictionary:
"I wrote, before I was twenty-four years of age, a sort of *Hexapla*,
a thick volume in quarto, in the first column of which I inserted
every word of the Hebrew Bible alphabetically; and in the five
other columns, all the various interpretations of those words in the

---

[18] William Empson, *Some Versions of Pastoral* (London, 1950), p. 163.
[19] Empson, p. 172.
[20] Empson, p. 149.
[21] Preface to the 1749 edition of *Paradise Lost*, in 2 vols., volume I, Preface (pages not numbered).
[22] *The Poetical Works of John Milton*, in six volumes, ed. Henry John Todd (London, 1801), vol. I, page A3 (Preface).
[23] Thomas De Quincey, *Richard Bentley and other Writings* (Boston, 1873), p. 46.
[24] De Quincey, p. 49.
[25] James H. Monk, *Life of R. Bentley* (London, 1833), vol. I, p. 14.

Chaldee, Syriac, Vulgate."[26] Fox also mentions that in 1714 Bentley was said to be engaged in "emending a Hebrew manuscript of the Old Testament".[27] Thus, there seems no doubt that the classical scholar who graduated from Cambridge, was royal librarian at St. James and, later, Master of Trinity College and Professor of Divinity,[28] was proficient in Hebrew and could read the Old Testament in the original.

One of Bentley's emendations that may provide evidence of his knowledge of Hebrew is on I.363. The emendation of "Books of Life" to "Book of Life" is acceptable, as Lofft in his 1792 edition indicates, for "the style of the sacred Epick, and the analogy of Scripture, invincibly support" the "Book of Life".[29] Bentley is also aware of the hebraïc pronunciation of names, such as Michaël (on II.294)[30] and frequently notices Biblical echoes. Thus, he points out that lines III.153–155 relate to Genesis xviii. 25 and, similarly, that

Hither of ill-join'd Sons and Daughters born
First from the ancient World those Giants came
With many a vain exploit, . . .

III.463–465

refers to the story about the sons of God and the daughters of men in Genesis vi. 2ff.[31]

---

[26] R. C. Jebb, *Bentley* (London, 1882), pp. 7–8.
[27] Adam Fox, *John Mill and Richard Bentley, A Study of the Textual Criticism of the New Testament 1675–1729* (Oxford, 1954), p. 118.
[28] See *CBD*, ed. J. O. Thorne New Edition (New York, 1962), p. 118.
[29] Quoted by Todd on I.361. Newton, however, thinks "that Milton has written *books* in the plural, as well as *records* just before; and because the plural agrees better with the idea that he would give of the great number of the Angels" (Newton on I.363).
[30] Which Milton uses when he needs an extra syllable.
[31] On the other hand, Bentley is mistaken on VII.388. While rightly observing that *Reptile* is the latinized form for "creeping thing", he notes that creeping things were created on the sixth day and not on the fifth. Bentley further observes that the Genesis text (he quotes the Authorized Version) says, "let the waters bring forth the moving creature" and allocates *creeping* to the margin. This seems to have been written without too much care. According to the Genesis text, "the moving (or 'creeping' – margin) creature" of the waters was created on the fifth day whereas the "living creature" of the earth was created on the sixth day. Thus Milton's lines

The third important edition of *Paradise Lost* was published by Bishop Thomas Newton in 1749, seventeen years after Bentley's controversial edition.[32] If Hume's edition is that of a many-sided scholar and Bentley's that of a one-track-minded classicist, Newton's edition is that of a conservative divine more concerned with comparing the views of others than expressing his own. He also has a habit of repeating Hume verbatim without giving the author his due.[33] Because Newton draws so subtly yet so heavily on

(FOOTNOTE 31 continued)
are in full agreement with Genesis, and Bentley's remark is wrong (his error was pointed out by Pearce who is quoted by Newton [on VII.388] as well as by Todd).

With regard to the difference between *moving* and *creeping*, Bentley claims that the Hebrew word comprehends both. It is questionable what Hebrew word Bentley had in mind – *sheretz* or *remes*: verse 20 of Genesis i has the word *sheretz*, translated 'the moving creature' in the Authorized Version, whereas verse 24 has *remes*, translated 'the living creature.' *Remes* appears again in verse 25, translated 'thing that creepeth', in verse 21 *nefesh ha-hayya ha-romeset*, translated 'living creature that moveth', and in verse 26, *ha-remes ha-romes* translated 'creeping thing that creepeth'. The noun *sheretz* yields a verb, found in verses 20 and 21, where it is translated 'to bring forth abundantly'. Indeed, both verbs, *sharatz* and *ramas* mean rather to creep than to move, but, of course, creeping indicates movement as well. Ben Yehudah (*Thesaurus*, p. 7468) contends that the word *sheretz* does not indicate creeping or moving but " פריה ורביה בשפע (swarm)". Ben Yehudah seems to have accepted this from the Nachmanides' commentary on Genesis i. 20. Rashi, however, interprets both שרץ and רמש as creep, and Onkelos gives to both the same Aramaic translation – רחיש .

Bentley's remark cannot, therefore, provide a proof of his knowledge of Hebrew.
[32] The Bentley-Pearce controversy is very much alive in the annotations of the Bishop; Newton also must have found it personally distressing to be critical of Bentley, for it was through the influence of the latter (then Master of Trinity College) that he was elected Fellow of that College. *DNB*, vol. XIV, p. 403.

At times Newton is pedantic and relishes the opportunity of refuting Bentley. On VII.121 (*"nor let thine own inventions hope"*), for example, he says: "Milton seems here to allude to Eccles. VII.29. *they have sought out many inventions*; which commentators explain by reasonings. No need then for Dr. Bentley's *conceptions*. Pearce. Dr. Bentley misliking the word *inventions* changes it for *conceptions*, which, I fancy, he would not have done, had he considered the Scripture use of this term, to which, I make no doubt, Milton alluded. *Ps.* 106.29 and 38." A few lines later, however, Newton accepts Bentley's just emendations of "foul living" to "soul living" (on VII.451), and of "creeping things" to "creeping thing" (on VII.452). Upon the first emendation Newton adds that "'the living creature,' Gen. l. 24, is, in the Hebrew 'living soul,' which Milton usually follows rather than our translation".
[33] For example, on I.82: "For the word *Satan*, in Hebrew, signifies an *enemy*: He is The ENEMY by way of eminence; the chief enemy of God and man."

his predecessors, it is difficult to ascertain how much Hebrew he knew himself although, as a cleric of his time, he must have had some knowledge of the language. There is no doubt that he was well-versed in Scriptural as well as in classical lore,[34] and it is to the former that we shall now turn.

Those of Newton's glosses which would indicate a knowledge of Hebrew are not always original. Thus he repeats what Hume said on *brooding* (I.21) and adds, "As Milton studied the Scriptures in the original languages, his images and expressions are oftner copied from them than from our translation." His explanation of the name Nimrod, however, shows that he did understand Hebrew: "*And from rebellion shall derive his name* for the name Nimrod, . . . yet commonly is derived from the Hebrew word *marad* which signifies to *rebel*" (XII.24).

Regardless of whether he knew Hebrew or not, the hebraic aspect of the poem interested him. Thus on VII.261, Newton comments on another Hebrew word: "But when Milton says, that 'God made the firmament,' he explains what is meant by the firmament. The Hebrew word, which the Greeks render by ζερέωμα , and our Translators by *firmament*, signifies *expansion*: It is rendered *expansion* in the margin of our Bibles, and Milton rightly explains it by *the expanse of elemental air*." Several Biblical phrases are pointed out by Newton. On VIII.102, for example, he comments: ". . . *and his line stretch'd out so far*; A Scripture expression: 'Who hath stretched the line upon it?' *Job* 38.5. 'As if God had measured the Heavens and the earth with a line.'" And when Adam says to Raphael: "Let not my words offend thee" (VIII.379), Newton notes: "Abraham thus implores leave to speak, and makes intercession for Sodom, with the like humble deprecation . . . . *Gen*. xviii. 30". Newton comments similarly on IX.556–557: ". . . whom God, on their creation-day, / Created *mute*; this is exactly in the stile of Scripture. *Gen*. ii.4".

Newton also indicates that some short phrases in *Paradise Lost* echo the Bible, for example, "trees of God" (IX.618) reminds Newton of Psalm civ. 16; the "tree of prohibition" (IX.644) he

---

[34] *Milton's Editors and Commentators*, p. 223.

considers "An Hebraism for the prohibited or forbidden tree", and he justly observes that "Sole daughter of his voice" is "another Hebraism. *Bath Kol*, the daughter of a voice, is a noted phrase among the Jews; and they understand by it a voice from heaven. . ." (IX.653) but, like Hume whom he follows here, Newton does not point out where the phrase comes from.[35]

According to Newton's own testimony, he was (as a Bishop was expected to be) well read in Jewish sources. Thus he justifies Milton's description of a propitious fire from Heaven consuming Abel's offering: "Herein he [Milton] is justified by the authority of the best Commentators, Jewish and Christian" (XI.434). Newton also makes reference to Jewish traditions in supporting Milton's allusion to idol-worship in the days of Noah: "And from the Jewish traditions we learn further, that Terah, and Nachor his father, and Serug his grandfather, were statuaries and carvers of idols" (XII.117). That Newton, of course, was also familiar with Jewish history, through such sources as the *Antiquities* of Josephus, is evidenced by his annotation on XII.355 about Aristobulus, son of Hyrcanus, Zerubbabel, and Herod whom Milton calls the "stranger" in the same passage of Michael's prophecy.

The next variorum edition of *Paradise Lost* was published at the beginning of the nineteenth century although Todd's 1801 edition of *The Poetical Works of John Milton* virtually belongs to the eighteenth century, for it summarizes that century's critical and scholarly work on Milton.[36] Todd may have known some Hebrew but,

---

[35] See note 16 above.

[36] Although it was severely criticized, Todd's edition soon became the standard one. I do not agree with Robert Southey, who considered it "a heavy disgrace to our literature", and he is only partly right in pointing out that "of Milton's *peculiar* sources of thought and illustration – of the rabbinical readings, for example, – Todd knows absolutely nothing", Review of the Todd edition by R. Southey, *QR*, XXXVI (1827), p. 44. Another reviewer has been more just to Todd: "Greatest of all [commentators] *in bulk* arose Todd, who with a shark's maw devoured all that came into his way, and, notwithstanding the many hard things said of him as an editor his labours have been the staff upon which all later commentators have been more or less glad to lean" (from an article on Keightley by H. A. Whitney, *NAR*, LXXXII (1856), p. 390). Keightley himself certainly leaned on Todd, but he was not uncritical: "He read incessantly, and whenever he met with anything resembl-

although he quotes Latin and Greek, he never quotes from a Semitic language. Oras correctly observes that there is "little that opens up new paths in his references to biblical matters", but he seems to have been familiar with "Jewish customs".[37] Yet if he does not open "new paths" in Biblical matters, the Oxford-educated priest[38] knew the Scriptures well enough to add references of his own to those of his predecessors from time to time. Thus, he is the first commentator to suggest that Milton may have used the image " '*dove-like*' knowing that the Talmudists had thus critically illustrated the original word *brooded*", that I.444 refers to Solomon whom God gave "largeness of heart", that the *dark idolatries* are an echo of Ezekiel viii. 12 (I.456), that the bounds of the deep of VII.166–167 "go back to *Jer.* v. 22 and *Ps.* civ. 9, for the *bounds of the sea* is a Scripture phrase", that the sleep that befell Adam after the "celestial colloquy" in Book VIII may have been suggested to Milton by Daniel's similar conversations with the angel (VIII.453). These are but a few examples of many similar annotations.

Moreover, Todd was familiar with the writings of the Church Fathers and was able to correct previous editors and suggest, for

---

(*FOOTNOTE 36 continued*)
ing a passage in Milton, he secured it for his Notes; but I cannot recollect an instance of his having, from his own resources, removed the difficulty from any obscure passage. I am almost certain that he had no knowledge of Hebrew, and his acquaintance with science, if any, was very slight" (*The Poems of John Milton*, ed. Thomas Keightley [1859], vol. I, p. vi). Todd incorporates the notes of his predecessors and adds few original comments but, at the same time, he is more impartial and very rarely takes sides in the controversies between them. His edition reveals his learning as well as his industry but illuminates Milton's use of Scripture or of Hebraisms less than did the editions of Hume and Newton.

[37] *Milton's Editors and Commentators*, pp. 338–339. In the same chapter on Todd (pp. 337–338), Oras says, "An interesting remark which apparently had induced Todd to undertake further investigations, is Archibishop Laurence's observation that Milton may have made use of rabbinical words. Todd's illustrations from Moses Bar Cepha may have been collected upon this suggestion, though this writer had already been drawn upon in Hume's notes." There seems to be a small error here for although Moses Bar Cepha wrote a *Commentary on Paradise* in Syriac, he was not a Rabbi but a Bishop who lived in a convent in Mesopotamia in the 9th century.

[38] For a brief account of his education and life see *DMB*, vol. XIX, pp. 908–909.

instance, that the metaphor of the thornless rose may have come to Milton from the Church Fathers (IV.256).[39]

In his *Life of Milton*,[40] Todd repeats well-known facts about Milton's knowledge of Hebrew. Thus he praises Milton's translation of the 114th and 136th Psalms, quoting Aubrey's observation that the "application of the Greek and Latin tongues" did not "impede the cultivation of the chief oriental languages, the Hebrew, Chaldee, and Syriack, so far as to go through the Pentateuch, to make a good entrance into the Targum or Chaldee paraphrase". He also mentions Milton's habit of having a chapter of the Hebrew Bible read to him each morning when he rose and, like Johnson, states that Milton's immense erudition included Hebrew "with its two dialects".[41] But Todd draws no conclusions from these facts in his Inquiry into the *Origin of Paradise Lost*[42] where he is content to sum up the opinions of Voltaire, Wharton, Hayley, Warburton, Pearce and others.

Keightley's work on Milton, published in 1855,[43] is something of an innovation, dealing as it does with the man, the poet, and the thinker. Keightley discusses Milton's life and poetry from the historical viewpoint[44] then tries to appraise Milton as a thinker

---

[39] Milton's use of metaphors like "without Thorn the Rose" (IV.256) is not hebraic or Biblical in the historic sense. Hume suggested that the source of the metaphor was Genesis iii. 18: "Thorns also and thistles shall it bring forth to thee." He thought the metaphor was based on the "Superstition that the Earth, before it was accursed for Mans Sin and Punishment, brought forth no Thorns ..." Newton, like Hume, cites Genesis iii. 18 and gives the same explanation. Bentley called the metaphor a "puerile fancy". Todd quotes Newton and Hurd, suggests that the metaphor might be derived from Tasso, but he is the first editor to add that Milton "appears to have consulted the Fathers", and he brings as evidence St. Basil's opinion as well as Herrick's *Noble Numbers* mentioning St. Ambrose. Todd's correction is undoubtedly right. Although thorns and thistles are mentioned in connection with man's sin in Genesis, Milton is here in harmony with Christian exegetical tradition. See also George W. Whiting, *RES*, *NS*, vol. X (1959), pp. 60–62.

[40] Todd, vol. I, pp. i–cix.

[41] Todd, vol. I, pp. vii, xxxviii, cxliv, cxlv.

[42] Todd, vol. I, pp. 248–303.

[43] *The Poems of John Milton*, ed. Thomas Keightley (London, 1859), 2 vols.

[44] "Coming into the world nearly two centuries later, it is neither a merit nor a boast that my scientific knowledge should be more extensive and more correct than his; my task was to go back, and try to place myself in Milton's position with respect to science." Preface, p. vi.

through his writings on religion, tolerance, philosophy, government and education. His appraisal of Milton's religious ideas, which he bases on the *Christian Doctrine*, in some ways anticipates Kelley's study.[45]

Keightley does mention Milton's knowledge of Hebrew but on this subject he has little to add to what is already known through the works of Aubrey and Phillips.[46] On the whole he underestimates Milton's Biblical scholarship.

Keightley quotes the poet's epistle to Young, and, like Todd, adduces Milton's translation of the Psalms at the age of fifteen as evidence that he had acquired a knowledge of Hebrew before he went to Cambridge.[47] In his chapter on the "Opinions of Milton on Religion", Keightley tells us what in his view are the limitations of Milton's interpretation of Scripture. The *Christian Doctrine*, observes Keightley,

> shows the force of early prejudices, and how utterly impossible it is even for the most powerful mind totally to emancipate itself from their influence; for we shall find Milton, while fancying he is following Scripture alone, maintaining opinions which were the mere inventions of the Fathers . . .
>
> It is a question if it was possible, in the time of Milton, to arrive at the knowledge of the exact sense of the language of Scripture; and we are of the opinion that it was not.[48]

Keightley then tries to establish a criterion for the perfect Biblical critic: sincere love of truth, moral courage, and a critical sense are the qualities Keightley lists, and he exaggeratingly adds:

> an extensive and accurate acquaintance with not merely the Greek and Hebrew languages, but with the Arabic and the other kindred dialects of the latter . . . a knowledge of the man-

---

[45] Maurice Kelley, *This Great Argument: A Study of Milton's "De Doctrina Christiana" as a Gloss upon "Paradise Lost"* (Princeton, 1941). Both agree about Milton's Arianism, for example.

[46] John Aubrey's source was Christopher Milton, the brother of the poet. Edward Phillips was the poet's nephew and was, with his brother John, a pupil of Milton. See the *Early Lives of Milton*, ed. Helen Darbishire (London, 1932).

[47] *Life of Milton*, pp. 6–7.

[48] *Life of Milton*, p. 154.

ners, and the modes of thought, feeling and expression of the Orientals, and of the geology, geography, natural history, etc. of the East. It is needless to say how deficient Milton's age was in all these branches of knowledge.[49]

How qualified was Keightley to recognize Scriptural echoes and to illuminate Milton's usage of Hebrew elements in *Paradise Lost*? In his *Tales and Popular Fictions*, Keightley maintains that Milton's major inspiration was the Bible: "he who will understand Milton aright, must study the sacred volume, not merely in the translation, but in the original languages."[50] And, indeed, he considered himself qualified to "understand Milton aright": "Fortunately, in my early days, I had acquired a knowledge of Hebrew, so that I have been able to read the Old Testament through in the original. I have not however thought it necessary to follow Milton into Targums and Mishnas; for I do not think he gathered any poetic fruit in these thickets."[51] Keightley's annotations as well as his exposition of Milton's discussion of the appearances of God[52] clearly show his knowledge of the Hebrew language.[53] At times he tries to find out the function of Hebrew words, or words that are translations of the Hebrew. For example, when Adam appeals to Eve not to go and work by herself in the garden, "leave not the faithful side / That gave thee being, still shades thee and protects" (IX.265–266), Keightley comments: "It is not impossible that in using the word 'shades' of the side, he may have had in mind the similarity of *essel* (אצל) side, and *ssel* (צל)shade." The validity of this note is doubtful, but the hebraic folklore metaphor expressed in Adam's words is interesting: the concept of a person being protected by the shade of someone or someone's wings is encountered frequently in the Bible.[54] We find it, for example, in Psalm xvii. 8: "Keep me as the apple of the

---

[49] *Life of Milton*, pp. 155–156.
[50] *Tales and Popular Fictions; their Resemblances and Transmissions from Country to Country* (London, 1834), p. 24.
[51] *An Account of the Life, Opinions, and Writings of John Milton*, Preface, p. vi.
[52] *An Account ...*, p. 170.
[53] For example, on I.21; I.304; I.403; II.261; III.596; V.761; VII.264; VII.321; VII.388; IX.265, etc.
[54] This Hebrew idiom occurs again in Isaiah xxx. 2–3: "That walk to go down into Egypt, and have not asked at my mouth; to strengthen themselves in the strength

eye, hide me under the shadow of thy wings." On the lines "and Dominion giv'n / Over all other Creatures that possess / Earth, Air, and Sea" (IV.430–432), he comments: "*possess*, i.e. occupy. This is the proper sense of the Hebrew verb (ירש *yarash*) which our translators render possess."

His notes on Scriptural echoes are more copious and detailed than those of all his predecessors, save Hume. And herein lies the value of Keightley's edition. Yet Keightley's references are sometimes slovenly. On I.363, for example, he writes, "*the books of life*. He must have dictated 'book', as there is but one", yet he fails to mention that Bentley was the first to suggest this emendation. On the 'darkness visible' of the furnace whose flames give no light (I.61–62), Keightley writes: "No power of the fire might give them light ... only there appeared unto them a fire kindled of itself, very dreadful. *Wisd. of Sol.* 17–5. T." But Todd does not mention the *Wisdom of Solomon*. Todd (on I.63) quotes Pearce who says that Milton meant the words to signify gloom and also quotes Newton, who indicates that there are similar expressions in Seneca, Antonio de Solis – as Voltaire pointed out – Spenser, and Milton's *Il Penseroso*.[55]

The second major nineteenth-century edition was published in London in 1874 by the Scottish David Masson.[56] But the edition of the poems would not have brought its author fame had he not written the six-volume *Life of John Milton* (1859–80) which is one of the most complete biographies ever written[57] and which, for its insight and acumen, has not even been superseded by William Riley Parker's two-volume biography[58] though the latter's monumental work brings the recent scholarship on Milton up to date.

(*FOOTNOTE 54 continued*)
of Pharaoh, and to trust in the shadow of Egypt! Therefore shall the strength of Pharaoh be your shame, and the trust in the shadow of Egypt your confusion." In Milton's line, the side both 'shades' and 'protects'.

   The same idiom is also found in Psalms xxxvi. 7; lvii. 1; lxiii. 7; xci. 4; Ruth ii. 12.
[55] There seem to be other inexactitudes of this kind, and only a careful collation of all commentators could ascertain all of them in all editors.
[56] *The Poetical Works of John Milton*, ed. David Masson (London, 1874), 3 vols.
[57] David Masson, *Life of John Milton* (London and Cambridge, 1859–94), 6 vols.
[58] William Riley Parker, *Milton* (Oxford, 1968), 2 vols.

With regard to Milton's knowledge of Hebrew, Masson did indeed follow some clues, but it remained for Harris Fletcher to follow almost all of them. Masson, however, traces Milton's study of Hebrew from St. Paul's School to Christ's College and rightly points out that Milton may have attended the lectures of Metcalfe, the Hebrew Professorship having existed for eight years.[59] Masson also conscientiously quotes references to the Mosaic law from Milton's prose works, references to study of Hebrew from Milton's tract *Of Education*,[60] the numerous Pentateuch passages in the *Tetrachordon*,[61] Milton's attack on an anonymous pamphleteer who misspells Greek and Hebrew words in *Colasterion*, and dwells at length on the poet's translation of the nine Psalms.[62]

Yet, Masson, educated at Marischal College and at the University of Edinburgh,[63] seems not to have known Hebrew.

His approach to the question of the origins of *Paradise Lost* is more scholarly than that of previous editors. He examines the suggested sources and observes:

> What is to be said of all this? For the most part it is laborious nonsense. That Milton knew most of the books mentioned, and, indeed, a great many more of the same sort, is extremely likely; ... but that in any of the books, or in all of them together, there is to be found "the origin of *Paradise Lost*," in any intelligible sense of the phrase, is utterly preposterous ... Milton, it may be said, inherited it [the subject of *Paradise Lost*] as a subject with which the imagination of Christendom had long been fascinated.[64]

Commenting on the literary references in the poem,[65] Masson emphasizes the Biblical element, "in the first place, *Paradise Lost* is permeated from beginning to end with citations from the Bible

---

[59] Masson, *Life of John Milton*, vol. I, pp. 76, 124, 267.
[60] Masson, vol. III, pp. 48, 71, 79, 241, 247.
[61] The *Tetrachordon* is a "labour of Biblical exegesis", *Life of John Milton*, vol. III, p. 302.
[62] Masson, vol. III, pp. 319, 684.
[63] *CBD*, p. 864.
[64] "Introduction to *Paradise Lost*", *The Poetical Works of John Milton* pp. 10–11.
[65] "Introduction", pp. 16–17.

... So, though in a lesser degree, with Homer, the Greek trage-
dians ... Plato, Demosthenes ... and with Lucretius, Cicero,
Virgil, Horace, Ovid, Juvenal, Persius and the other Latins. So
with the Italian writers whom he knew so well ..." And if Masson
did not know Hebrew, his comments about the nature of *Paradise
Lost* reveal his poetic insight:

> ... what compulsion of all the lusciousness of Aegean myth and
> Mediterranean legend into the service of the Hebrew theme!
> This man, who had the Bible by heart, whose verse, when he
> chose, could consist of nothing else than coagulations from the
> Bible or concurrent Biblical gleams from the first of Genesis
> to the last of the Apocalypse, had also ransacked and enjoyed
> the classics. Though his flight was above the Aonian mount, yet
> Jove and Jason, Proteus and Apollo, Pan and the Nymphs,
> the Fauns and the Graces, all came into view as they were
> wanted, captive to his heavenly muse ...[66]

Such remarks – anticipating the writings of Osgood and Bush[67] –
and the more modern and concise annotations to the poem written
in their spirit,[68] mark the beginning of new trends in Milton editions and in approaches to *Paradise Lost*.

The revival of interest in Milton in this century also brought
about the publication of many new editions. In 1910, A. W. Verity

[66] *The Life of John Milton*, vol. VI, p. 556.
[67] Charles G. Osgood, *The Classical Mythology of Milton's English Poems* (1900),
and Douglas Bush's chapter on Milton in *Mythology and the Renaissance Tradition in English Poetry* (1963 [1932]), pp. 260–297, as well as his *Paradise Lost in
Our Time* (1957 [1945]).
[68] The annotations to *Paradise Lost* are in *The Poetical Works of John Milton*, vol.
III, pp. 114–278. Masson praises previous editors, especially Hume ("No commentator on *Paradise Lost* has surpassed the first one ..." p. 104), and he mostly
follows their notes. His originality is not in the Scriptural allusions and hebraisms
he indicates but in his more modern approach to the poem and in his recognizing
that Milton not only borrows literary allusions but makes them his own. He
appropriately quotes the poet from his *Eikonoklastes*: "It is not hard for any man
who hath a Bible in his hands to borrow good words and holy sayings in abundance; but to make them his own is a work of grace only from above" ("Introduction to *Paradise Lost*", *The Poetical Works of John Milton*, p. 17).

published a new and revised edition[69] in which he made use of the editions of Newton, Todd, Keightley, and Masson as well as of Osgood's *The Classical Mythology of Milton's English Poems*. The notes to *Paradise Lost* are excellent and almost encyclopaedic in their range. In 1931 Columbia University published *The Works of John Milton* in 18 volumes. Frank Allen Patterson was the general editor. A two-volume index which is also very helpful for Biblical references was added to the edition in 1940. Harris Fletcher edited *The Complete Poetical Works of John Milton*, and his one-volume New Cambridge edition was published in 1941.[70] In 1952, Helen Darbishire's two-volume edition of *The Poetical Works of John Milton* was published with textual commentaries and appendices on the printing of *Paradise Lost* and extant copies. In 1957, Merritt Hughes published *The Complete Poems and Major Prose* of John Milton with excellent notes and introductions for the student of Milton.[71] *Paradise Lost* with notes and introductions was published separately by the same editor in 1962.[72]

Except for Helen Darbishire who concentrates on textual problems, all editors from Verity to Hughes acknowledge Scriptural references, Biblical echoes or allusions to Biblical stories, and explain the Hebrew names in *Paradise Lost*. Although these annotators are generally reliable, they do not pretend to be specialists, and they become hearsay scholars by necessity. However limited be the nature of the hebraic element in Milton's poetry, this area deserves a highly specialized approach which, in turn, could contribute to a better understanding of passages with hebraic connotations.

---

[69] Milton, *Paradise Lost*, ed. A. W. Verity (Cambridge, 1910). The two-volume edition was issued in 1929.
[70] *The Complete Poetical Works of John Milton*, ed. Harris F. Fletcher (Cambridge, Mass., 1941).
[71] John Milton, *Complete Poems and Major Prose*, ed. Merritt Y. Hughes (New York, 1957).
[72] John Milton, *Paradise Lost, A Poem in Twelve Books*, ed. Merritt Y. Hughes (New York, 1962).

SELECTED BIBLIOGRAPHY

A. EDITIONS OF MILTON

The Poetical Works of Mr. John Milton, ed. P.(atrick) H.(ume). London, 1695.

Milton's Paradise Lost, ed. Richard Bentley. London, 1732.

Paradise Lost. A New Edition with Notes of Various Authors, ed. Thomas Newton. 2 vols. London, 1749.

The Poetical Works of John Milton, ed. Henry John Todd. 6 vols. London, 1801.

The Poems of John Milton, ed. Thomas Keightley. 2 vols. London, 1859.

The Poetical Works of John Milton, ed. David Masson. 3 vols. London, 1874.

Milton. Paradise Lost, ed. A. W. Verity. 2 vols. Cambridge, 1929 (1910).

The Works of John Milton, ed. Frank Allen Patterson. 18 vols. New York, 1931–38. 2 vols. Index, 1940.

The Complete Poetical Works of John Milton, ed. Harris F. Fletcher. Cambridge, Mass., 1941.

Complete Prose Works of John Milton, eds. Don M. Wolfe, Ernest Sirluck, Merritt Y. Hughes. Vols. I–IV. New Haven, 1953–66.

John Milton. Complete Poems and Major Prose, ed. Merritt Y. Hughes. New York, 1957.

John Milton. Paradise Lost, A Poem in Twelve Books, ed. Merritt Y. Hughes. New York, 1962.

B. EDITIONS OF THE BIBLE

The Holy Bible, containing the Hebrew and Greek Scriptures, the text conformable to that of the King James Version, New York, n.d.

The Septuagint Version. Greek and English, London, n.d.

D. Martin Luthers Werke. Die Deutsche Bibel. Weimar, 1954.
Genesis. Edited by Hartom and Cassuto. Tel-Aviv, 1962. Hebrew.
The Anchor Bible. Genesis, trans. and ed. E. A. Speiser. Garden City, 1964.
The Anchor Bible. Job, trans. and ed. M. H. Pope. Garden City, 1965.
The Book of Job. A New Commentary, ed. N. H. Tur-Sinai (H. Torczyner). Jerusalem, 1957.

C. BIBLICAL COMMENTARIES, WORKS RELATED TO RELIGION, NEAR EASTERN LITERATURE AND HISTORY, AND SEVENTEENTH-CENTURY HEBREW SCHOLARSHIP

Albright, William F. "The Location of the Garden of Eden," *AJSL,* XXXIX (1922–23), 15–31.
——. *Archeology and the Religion of Israel.* Baltimore, 1942.
——. *History, Archeology and Christian Humanism.*
Brandon, S. G. F. *Man and his Destiny in the Great Religions.* Manchester, 1962.
Calvin, John. *Institutes of the Christian Religion,* trans. John Allen. 3 vols. New Haven, 1816.
Cassuto, U. *From Adam to Noah. A Commentary on Genesis I–VI.8.* Jerusalem, 1953.
Cohn, Haim. *The Trial and Death of Jesus.* New York, 1971.
Coppens, J. "Le péché du Paradis selon M. Guiton," *ETL,* XXIV (1948), 395–401.
——. *La connaissance du bien et du mal et le péché du Paradis.* Gembloux, 1948.
——. "L'interprétation sexuelle du péché du Paradis," *ETL,* XXXIII (1957), 506–508.
Eissfeldt, O. *Molk als Opferbegriff im Punischen und im Hebräischen und das Ende des Gottes Moloch.* Halle, 1935.
Flavius, Josephus. *Works,* trans. William Whiston. 2 vols. London, 1845.
Gaster, T. H. *Thespis, Ritual, Myth and Drama in the Ancient Near East.* New York, 1950.
Genesis Rabba. Hebrew.
Glatzer, Nahum N. *Franz Rosenzweig: His Life and Thought.* New York, 1953.
Gleason, Robert W. *Yahweh the God of the Old Testament.* Englewood Cliffs, N.J., 1964.
Good, Edwin M. *Irony in the Old Testament.* Philadelphia, 1965.
Haller, William. *The Rise of Puritanism.* New York, 1957 (1938).
Haller, William and Maleville. "The Puritan Art of Love," *HLQ,* V (1942), 234–272.
Harnack, Adolf. *What is Christianity?* Trans. Thomas Bailey Saunders. New York, 1957.

Hatch, Edwin, *The Influence of Greek Ideas on Christianity.* New York, 1957.

Heidel, Alexander. *The Gilgamesh Epic and Old Testament Parallels.* Chicago, 1946.

Heisig, Karl. "Woher stammt die Vorstellung vom Paradiesapfel?" *ZNWKAK*, XXIV (1952–53), 111–118.

Honeyman, A. M. "The Etymology of Mammon," *AL*, IV (1952), 60–65.

Humbert, Paul. *Etudes sur le Récit du Paradis et de la Chute dans la Genèse.* Neuchatel, 1940.

Joüon, Paul. "Notes de Lexicographie Hébraique," *Bib.*, VI (Roma, 1925), 312–314.

Kaufmann, Yehezkel. *Toldot Ha-Emuna Ha-Israelit.* Jerusalem-Tel-Aviv, 1960 (1937). Hebrew.

Kornfeld, Walter. "Der Moloch: Eine Untersuchung zur Theorie O. Eissfeldts," *WZKM*, LI (1952), 287–313.

Kramer, Samuel Noah. *History begins at Sumer.* London, 1958.

Margulies, Mordecai ed. *Midrash Haggadol on the Pentateuch,* Jerusalem 1947. Hebrew.

McKenzie, John L. "The Literary Characteristics of Genesis 2–3," *TS*, XV (1954), 549–567.

——. "Mythological Allusions in Ezek. 28 12–18," *JBL*, LXXV (1956), 322–327.

Moore, George F. *Judaism. Judaism in the First Centuries of the Christian Era. The Age of the Tannaim.* Cambridge, Mass., 1932 (1927).

Morgenstern, Julian. "The Mythological Background of Psalm 82," *HUCA*, XIV (Cincinnati, 1939), 29–126.

Newman, Louis Israel. *Jewish Influence on Christian Reform Movements.* New York, 1925.

Pope, Marvin H. *El in the Ugaritic Texts.* Leiden, 1955.

——. "A Note on Ugaritic ndd-ydd," *JCS*, I (1947), 337–341.

——. "The Word שחת in Job 9. 31," *JBL*, LXXXIII (1964), 269–278.

Renié, J. "Un Prétendu Parallèle Sumérien de la Création d'Eve," *Mélanges de Science Religieuse.* Lille, 1953.

Rosenthal, Erwin I. J. "Torah and *Nomos* in Medieval Jewish Philosophy," *Studies in Rationalism, Judaism and Universalism,* ed. Raphael Loewe. London, 1966.

Rosenzweig, Franz. *Der Stern der Erlösung,* trans. I. Amir. Jerusalem, 1970, Hebrew.

Roth, Leon. "Hebraists and Non-Hebraists of the Seventeenth Century," *JSS*, VI (Manchester, 1961), 204–221.

Scholem, Gershom G. *Major Trends in Jewish Mysticism.* New York, 1965 (1941).

Sefer Raziel. Amsterdam, 1701.

Skinner, John. *The International Critical Commentary. A Critical and Exegetical Commentary on Genesis.* Edinburgh, 1930 (1910).

Spitz, Lewis W., ed. *The Reformation*. Boston, 1962.
Willet, Andrew. *Hexapla in Genesin*. London, 1632 (1605).

D. REFERENCE WORKS

Ben Yehudah, Eliezer. *Dictionary and Thesaurus of the Hebrew Language*. New York, 1960.
Brewer, E. Cobham. *The Readers Handbook of Allusions, References, Plots and Stories*. Philadelphia, 1883.
Buxtorf, J. B. *Epitome Radicum Hebraicarum et Chaldaicarum*. Glasgow, 1824 (1607).
Davidson, G. *A Dictionary of Angels*. London–New York, 1968.
Douglas, J. D. ed. *The New Bible Dictionary*. Grand Rapids, 1962.
Fletcher, Harris F. *Contributions to a Milton Bibliography 1800–1930*. Urbana, 1931.
Frazer, Sir James George. *The Golden Bough. A Study in Magic and Religion*. Part III:*The Dying God*. New York, 1935.
Fuerst, Julius. *A Hebrew and Chaldee Lexicon to the Old Testament*, trans. Samuel Davidson. New York, 1867.
Gilbert, Allan H. *A Geographical Dictionary of Milton*. New Haven, 1919.
Ginzberg, Louis. *The Legends of the Jews*. 7 vols. Philadelphia, 1954–55.
Hanford, James Holly. *A Milton Handbook*. New York, 1954 (1926).
Haussig, Hans Wilhelm. *Wörterbuch der Mythologie*. vol. I. Stuttgart, 1965.
Huckabay, Calvin. *John Milton. A Bibliographical Supplement 1929–1957*. Pittsburgh, 1960.
The Interpreter's Dictionary of the Bible. 4 vols. New York, 1962.
The Jewish Encyclopedia, ed. Isidore Singer. 12 vols. New York and London, 1906.
Koehler, Ludwig and Walter Baumgartner, eds. *Lexicon Veteris Testamenti Libros*. Leiden, 1953.
Lehmann, Ruth P. *Nova Bibliotheca Anglo-Judaica. A Bibliographical Guide to Anglo-Jewish History 1937–1960*. London, 1961.
Loechter, Lefferts A., ed. *Twentieth Century Encyclopedia of Religious Knowledge (An Extension of the New Schaff-Herzog Encyclopedia of Religious Knowledge)*. Grand Rapids, 1955.
Roth, Cecil. *Magna Bibliotheca Anglo-Judaica. A Bibliographical Guide to Anglo-Jewish History*. London, 1937.
Schwab, M. *Vocabulaire de l'Angélologie*. Paris, 1897.
Smith, J. Payne. *A Compendious Syriac Dictionary*. Oxford, 1903.
Stephen, Sir Leslie and Sir Sidney Lee, eds. *The Dictionary of National Biography*. 22 vols. London, 1922.
Stevens, David Harrison. *Reference Guide to Milton, 1800–1930*. Chicago, 1930.

Thorne, James O., ed. *Chambers' Biographical Dictionary*. New York, 1962 (1897).

E. OTHER BOOKS AND ARTICLES CONSULTED

Adams, Robert Martin. *Ikon: John Milton and the Modern Critics*. Ithaca, 1955.
Adamson, J. H. "The War in Heaven: Milton's Version of the Merkabah," *JEGP*, LVII (1958), 690–703.
Allen, Don C. "Milton and Rabbi Eliezer," *MLN*, LXIII (1948), 262–263.
——. *The Harmonious Vision: Studies in Milton's Poetry*. Baltimore, 1954.
——. *Doubt's Boundless Sea*. Baltimore, 1964.
——. "Milton's Busiris," *MLN*, LXV (1950), 115–116.
——. "Milton and the Name of Eve," *MLN*, LXXIV (1959), 681–683.
Auerbach, Eric. *Mimesis*. New York, 1957 (1946).
Arnold, Matthew. *Culture and Anarchy*. Cambridge, 1932.
Baker, Herschel. *The Wars of Truth*. Cambridge, Mass., 1952.
Baldwin, Edward C. "Milton and Ezekiel," *MLN*, XXXIII (1918), 211–215.
——. "Milton and the Psalms," *MP*, XVII (1919), 459–463.
——. "The Authorized Version's Influence upon Milton's Diction," *MLN*, XXXVI (1921), 376–377.
Barker, Arthur E. *Milton and the Puritan Dilemma 1641–1660*. Toronto, 1942.
——. ed. *Milton. Modern Essays in Criticism*. New York, 1965.
Berenson, Bernhard. *The Italian Painters of the Renaissance*. London, 1960 (1930).
Borchardt, Frank L. "Etymology in Tradition and in the Northern Renaissance," *JHI*, XXIX (1968), 415–429.
Bowra, Cecil M. *From Virgil to Milton*. New York, 1965 (1945).
Broadbent, J. B. *Some Graver Subject*. London, 1960.
Bush, Douglas. *Mythology and the Renaissance Tradition in English Poetry*. New York, 1963 (1932).
——. *Paradise Lost in our Time*. Gloucester, Mass., 1957 (1945).
——. "Ironic and Ambiguous Allusion in *Paradise Lost*," *JEGP*, LX (1961), 631–640.
——. *English Poetry. The Main Currents from Chaucer to the Present*. New York, 1963.
Clark, Donald Lemen. *John Milton at St. Paul's School*. New York, 1948.
Cohen, Kitty. "A Note on Milton's Semitic Studies," *MQ*, IV (1970), 7–10.
——. "A Note on Milton's Azazel," *PQ*, XLIX (1970), 248–249.
Collingwood, R. G. *The Idea of History*. Oxford, 1946.

Conklin, George Newton. *Biblical Criticism and Heresy in Milton*. New York, 1949.

Cope, Jackson I. *The Metaphoric Structure of Paradise Lost*. Baltimore, 1962.

Corcoran, Sister Mary Irma. *Milton's Paradise with Reference to the Hexameral Background*. Washington, D.C., 1945.

Daiches, David. *Milton*. London, 1966 (1957).

Darbishire, Helen, ed. *Early Lives of Milton*. London, 1932.

De Quincey, Thomas. *Richard Bentley and Other Writings*. Boston, 1873.

Driver, Tom F. *The Sense of History in Greek and Shakespearean Drama*. New York, 1960.

Eliot, T. S. *On Poetry and Poets*. New York, 1961 (1943).

Empson, William. *Some Versions of Pastoral*. London, 1950 (1935).

——. *Milton's God*. London, 1965 (1961).

Evans, J. M. *Paradise Lost and the Genesis Tradition*. Oxford, 1968.

Fisch, Harold. *Jerusalem and Albion. The Hebraic Factor in Seventeenth-Century Literature*. New York, 1964.

——. "Hebraic Style and Motifs in *Paradise Lost*," *Language and Style in Milton*, eds. R. D. Emma and J. T. Shawcross. New York, 1967.

Fletcher, Harris F. *Milton's Semitic Studies and Some Manifestations of them in his Poetry*. Chicago, 1926.

——. *The Use of the Bible in Milton's Prose*. Urbana, 1929.

——. *Milton's Rabbinical Readings*. Urbana, 1930.

——. *The Intellectual Development of John Milton*. 2 vols. Urbana, 1956.

——. "Milton and Yosippon," *SP*, XXI (1924), 496–501.

Fogle, French, R. and Trevor-Roper, H. R. *Milton and Clarendon*. Los Angeles, 1965.

Fox, Adam. *John Mill and Richard Bentley: A Study of the Textual Criticism of the New Testament 1675–1729*. Oxford, 1954.

Frye, Northrop. "Literary Criticism," *The Aims and Methods of Scholarship in Modern Languages and Literatures*, ed. James Thorpe. New York, 1963.

——. *Five Essays on Milton's Epics*. London, 1966.

Frye, Roland Mushat. *God, Man and Satan*. Princeton, 1960.

Fussner, Smith F. *The Historical Revolution. English Historical Writing and Thought 1580–1640*. London, 1962.

Gardner, Helen. *A Reading of Paradise Lost*. Oxford, 1965.

Giamatti, Bartlett A. *The Earthly Paradise and the Renaissance Epic*. Princeton, 1966.

Gilbert, Allan H. *On the Composition of Paradise Lost*. Chapel Hill, 1947.

Gilmore, Myron P. *The World of Humanism 1453–1517*. New York and Evanston, 1962 (1952).

Goldman, Jack. "Insight into Milton's Abdiel," *PQ*, XLIX (1970), 249–254.

Greene, T. *The Descent from Heaven*. New Haven, 1963.

Harding, Davis P. *Milton and the Renaissance Ovid*. Urbana, 1946.

———. *The Club of Hercules*. Urbana, 1962.

Hughes, Merritt Y. *Ten Perspectives on Milton*. New Haven, 1965.

Hunter, William B., Jr. "Satan as Comet: *Paradise Lost* II.708–711," *ELN*, V (1967), 17–21.

Jebb, R. C. *Bentley*. London, 1882.

Johnson, Samuel. *Life of Milton*, ed. K. Deighton. London, 1900 (1892).

Keightley, Thomas. *Tales and Popular Fictions*. London, 1834.

———. *An Account of the Life, Opinions and Writings of John Milton*. London, 1855.

Kelley, Maurice, "*Paradise Lost* VII.8–12, and the 'Zohar,'" *MLR*, XXIX (1934), 322–324.

———. *This Great Argument: A Study of Milton's 'De Doctrina Christiana' as a Gloss upon 'Paradise Lost.'* Princeton, 1941.

———. "Milton and the Trinity," *HLQ*, XXXIII (1970), 315–320.

Kellog, Alfred L. "Some Patristic Sources for Milton's Gehenna," *N & Q*, CXCV (1950), 10–13.

Kermode, Frank, ed. *The Living Milton*. London, 1962 (1960).

Knight, Wilson G. *Chariot of Wrath*. London, 1942.

Kristeller, Paul Oskar. *Renaissance Thought*. New York, 1961.

Kurth, Burton O. *Milton and Christian Heroism*. Berkeley and Los Angeles, 1959.

Lauter, Paul. "Milton's 'Siloa's Brook'," *N & Q*, CCIII (1958), 204–205.

Lewalski, Barbara Kiefer. "Structure and the Symbolism of Vision in Michael's Prophecy, *Paradise Lost*, Books XI–XII," *PQ*, XLII (1963), 25–35.

Lewis, C. S. *A Preface to Paradise Lost*. London, 1965 (1942).

MacCaffrey, Isabel Gamble. *Paradise Lost as "Myth."* Cambridge, Mass., 1959.

Martz, Louis L. *The Paradise Within. Studies in Vaughan, Traherne, and Milton*. New Haven, 1964.

Masson, David. *The Life of John Milton*. 7 vols. and Index. Cambridge and London, 1859–94.

Monk, J. H. *The Life of R. Bentley*, 2 vols. London, 1833.

Murray, Patrick. *Milton: The Modern Phase*. London, 1967.

Nevo, Ruth. *The Dial of Virtue*. Princeton, 1963.

Nicolson, Marjorie Hope. *John Milton. A Reader's Guide to His Poetry*. New York, 1966 (1963).

Oras, Ants. *Milton's Editors and Commentators from Patrick Hume to Henry John Todd (1695–1801)*. London, 1931.

Osgood, Charles Grosvenor. *The Classical Mythology of Milton's English Poems*. New York, 1900.

Parker, William Riley. *Milton*. 2 vols. Oxford, 1968.

Parsons, Coleman O., "The Classical and Humanist Context of Paradise Lost II, 496–505," *JHI*, XXXIX (1968), 33–52.

Patrides, C. A., ed. *Milton's Lycidas: The Tradition and the Poem*. New York, 1961.

——. *The Phoenix and the Ladder*. Berkeley and Los Angeles, 1964.

——. *Milton and the Christian Tradition*. Oxford, 1966.

——. "*Paradise Lost* and the Language of Theology," *Language and Style in Milton*, eds. R. D. Emma and J. T. Shawcross (New York, 1967), 102–119.

Pécheux, Mother Mary Christopher. "Abraham, Adam, and the Theme of Exile in *Paradise Lost*," *PMLA*, LXXX (1965), 365–371.

Peter, John. *A Critique of Paradise Lost*, New York and London, 1960.

Prince, F. T. *The Italian Element in Milton's Verse*. Oxford, 1954.

——. "On the Last Two Books of 'Paradise Lost'," *E & S*, XI (1958), 38–52.

Rajan, B. *Paradise Lost and the Seventeenth-Century Reader*. London, 1947.

Raleigh, Sir Walter. *The History of the World*. London, 1614.

Ricks, Christopher. *Milton's Grand Style*. Oxford, 1963.

Rosenblatt, Jason P. "Celestial Entertainment in Eden: Book V of *Paradise Lost*," *HTR*, LXII (1969), 411–427.

——. "Structural Unity and Temporal Concordance: The War in Heaven in *Paradise Lost*," *PMLA*, LXXXVII (1972), 31–41.

Roston, Murray. *Biblical Drama in England*. London, 1968.

Ryken, Leland. "Milton and the Apocalyptic," *HLQ*, XXXI (1968), 223–238.

——. *The Apocalyptic Vision in Paradise Lost*. Ithaca and London, 1970.

Samuel, Irene. *Plato and Milton*. Ithaca, New York, 1965 (1947).

——. *Dante and Milton. The Commedia and Paradise Lost*. Ithaca, New York, 1966.

Satan (Editor not named). Based upon a volume of the series *Collection de Psychologie Religieuse. Etudes Carmelitaines*. New York, 1952.

Saurat, Denis. *Milton Man and Thinker*. New York, 1925.

——. *Milton et le matérialisme Chrétien en Angleterre*. Paris, 1928.

Shawcross, John T. "*Paradise Lost* and the Theme of Exodus," *Milton Studies* II, ed. James D. Simmonds (Pittsburgh, 1970), 3–26.

Sims, James H. *The Bible in Milton's Epics*. Gainesville, Florida, 1962.

Smith, Logan Pearsall. *Milton and his Modern Critics*. Boston, 1941.

Steadman, John "Adam and the Prophesied Redeemer," *SP*, LVI (1959), 214–225.

——. "The Devil and Pharaoh's Chivalry," *MLN*, LXXV (1960), 197–201.

——. "Tantalus and the Dead Sea Apples," *JEGP*, LXIV (1965), 35–40.

——. "Leviathan and Renaissance Etymology," *JHI*, XXVIII (1967), 575–576.

——. "'Memphian Chivalry': Milton's Busiris, Etymology and Chronography," *UR*, XXXVII (1971), 215–231.

Stein, Arnold. *Answerable Style*. Minneapolis, 1953.

Stoll, E. E. "Belial as an Example," *MLN*, XLVIII (1933), 419–427.

Summers, Joseph H. *The Muse's Method. An Introduction to Paradise Lost*. London, 1962.

Taylor, George Coffin. *Milton's Use of Du Bartas*. Cambridge, Mass., 1934.

Thorpe, James O., ed. *Milton Criticism: Selections from Four Centuries*. New York, 1950.

Tillyard, E. M. W. *The Miltonic Setting, Past and Present*. Cambridge, 1938.

——. *Milton*. London, 1949.

——. *Studies in Milton*. London, 1951.

Tuve, Rosemond. *Images and Themes in Five Poems by Milton*. Cambridge, Mass., 1962 (1957).

Waldock, A. J. A. *Paradise Lost and its Critics*. Cambridge, 1964 (1947).

Wallerstein, Ruth. *Studies in Seventeenth-Century Poetic*. Madison, 1961 (1950).

Werblowsky, Zwi R. J. *Lucifer and Prometheus. A Study of Milton's Satan*. London, 1952.

——. "Milton and the *Conjectura Cabbalistica*," *JWCI*, XVIII (1955), 90–113.

Werkmeister, William H., ed. *Facets of the Renaissance*. New York, 1963 (1959).

West, Robert H. "The Substance of Milton's Angels," *SAMLA Studies in Milton*, ed. J. Max Patrick (Gainesville, Florida, 1953), 20–53.

——. *Milton and the Angels*. Athens, Georgia, 1955.

Whaler, James. "The Miltonic Simile," *PMLA*, XLVI (1931), 1034–74.

Whiting, George, W. "Without Thorn the Rose," *RES, NS*, X (1959), 60–62.

——. *Milton's Literary Milieu*. Chapel Hill, 1939.

——. "Notes on *Milton's Rabbinical Readings*," *N & Q*, CLXII (1932).

—— and Gossman, Ann. "Siloah's Brook, the Pool of Siloam, and Milton's Muse," *SP*, LVIII (1961), 193–205.

Willey, Basil. *The Seventeenth Century Background. Studies in the Thought of the Age in Relation to Poetry and Religion*. Garden City, New York, 1953 (1934).

Williams, Arnold. "Commentaries on Genesis as Basis for Hexameral Literature," *SP*, XXXIV (1937), 191–192.

——. "Milton and the Renaissance Commentaries on Genesis," *MP*, XXXVII (1939–40), 263–278.

——. *The Common Expositor. An Account of the Commentaries on Genesis 1527–1633*. Chapel Hill, 1948.

Wimsatt, W. K. Jr. *The Verbal Icon. Studies in the Meaning of Poetry*. New York, 1962.

Wright, B. A. "Note on *Paradise Lost* IV, 310," *N & Q*, CCIII (1958), 341.

INDEX OF REFERENCES TO MILTON'S WORKS

ERRATA

p. 45, last line of footnote 32: [1957]),; read: [1957],
p. 61, line 5 of footnote 58: [Halle, 1935]; read: [Halle, 1935])
p. 95, line 2 top: the Heav'nly stranger"; read: the "Heav'nly stranger"
p. 158, line 9 top: Molton's; read: Milton's
        line 12 top: (III. 348); read: [III. 348]
p. 159, Running Head: EDITOR; read: EDITORS
p. 165, footnote 38: *DMB*; read: *DNB*
p. 174, Section C, item 3; add: London, 1964.

Index

p. 183, item 2 top, line 2: *Remonstraxnt's*; read: *Remonstrant's*
p. 184, item 3 top, line 2: 45, n.; read: 45 n.
      references to Book I (first column), line 3 top: delete 157
         „   „   „   „   „   „   , line 4 bottom: n.32; read:
      n.33
p. 185, references to Book I   „   „   , line 19 top: . . . 28; read:
      28 n.6
      references to Book I   „   „   , line 12 bottom: . . . 156;
      read: . . . 165
p. 186, references to Book III (second column), line 16 top: 459; read:
      495
p. 187, references to Book IV (first column), line 2 top: . . . 79 n.3; read:
      79 n.30
      references to Book V (first column), line 7 bottom: 92 n.64;
      read: 92 n.46
      references to Book V (second column), lines 1, 8, 10 top should
      be Book IV

p. 188, references to Book VI (first column), line 13 top: 36; read: 32
      „   „   „   „   „   „   , line 17 top: 145; read: 415
     „   „   „   „ (second column), line 5 top: 125, 125 n.42
n.42; read: 125, 126 n.42
p. 189, first column, line 8 top: Book VII; read: Book VIII
references to Book VIII (first column), line 14 top: 546 - 522;
read: 546 - 552
references to Book XI   (second column), line 2 bottom: 359;
read: 395
p. 190, references to Book XI   (first column), line 9 top: 835; should
be Book IX
references to Book XII (second column), line 1 top: 121 - 127;
read: 121, 127
references to Book XII   „   „   , line 9 top: 210 . . . 122;
read: 210 . . . 122 n.37
references to *Psalms*, line 2: 116; read: 166